THE
WISDOM BOOKS

JOB, PROVERBS, AND ECCLESIASTES

ALSO BY ROBERT ALTER

THE
WISDOM BOOKS

JOB, PROVERBS, AND ECCLESIASTES

A Translation with Commentary

ROBERT ALTER

W · W · *Norton & Company* NEW YORK LONDON

For information about permission to reproduce selections from this book,
write to Permissions, W. W. Norton & Company, Inc.,
500 Fifth Avenue, New York, NY 10110

For information about special discounts for bulk purchases, please contact
W. W. Norton Special Sales at specialsales@wwnorton.com or 800-233-4830

Manufacturing by Courier Westford
Book design by Margaret M. Wagner
Production manager: Julia Druskin

Library of Congress Cataloging-in-Publication Data

Bible. O.T. English. Alter. Selections. 2010.
The wisdom books : Job, Proverbs, and Ecclesiastes : a translation
with commentary / Robert Alter. — 1st ed.
p. cm.
Includes bibliographical references.
ISBN 978-0-393-06812-2 (hardcover)
1. Wisdom literature. 2. Bible. O.T. — Commentaries. I. Alter, Robert. II. Title.
BS1403.A48213 2010
223'.077 — dc22

2010021583

W. W. Norton & Company, Inc.
500 Fifth Avenue, New York, N.Y. 10110
www.wwnorton.com

W. W. Norton & Company Ltd.
Castle House, 75/76 Wells Street, London W1T 3QT

1 2 3 4 5 6 7 8 9 0

for

R O N H E N D E L

treasured colleague and delightful friend

CONTENTS

ACKNOWLEDGMENTS

Most of the manuscript was prepared by Janet Livingstone, who as in the past did an admirable job in bringing electronic order out of my handwritten chaos. A substantial section of Job was typed by Margarita Zaydman with scrupulous care. Yosefa Raz checked the translations against the original with a keen eye to inconsistencies and places where I had inadvertently skipped a word in the Hebrew. The entire manuscript was read by two dear friends, Michael Bernstein, who helped me to avoid doing more violence to the English language than strictly necessary, and Ron Hendel, whose knowledge of biblical scholarship and the ancient Near East saved me from a good many mistakes. The results of an undertaking of this sort are bound to be imperfect, and those who helped me of course bear no responsibility for the flaws. Research expenses for the book were covered by funds from the Class of 1937 Chair at the University of California at Berkeley.

INTRODUCTION

The Wisdom books of the Hebrew Bible are a construct through inference by scholarship and do not figure intrinsically in the constellation of the traditional canon. Though the Babylonian Talmud (Baba Batra 14B) in its ordering of the books does show a direct sequence of Job, Proverbs, and Ecclesiastes (henceforth referred to here by its Hebrew title, Qohelet) , the Septuagint, followed by the King James Bible, interposes Psalms between Job and Proverbs, while most modern Jewish editions of the Hebrew texts have Proverbs, Job, and then the Song of Songs, Ruth, and Lamentations intervening before Qohelet. There are good empirical grounds for classifying Job, Proverbs, and Qohelet as Wisdom books, but the classification should be adopted with a degree of caution. The eminent German biblical scholar Gerhard von Rad, writing in 1972, expressed serious reservations about the general rubric: "It belongs . . . to the fairly extensive number of biblical-theological terms whose validity and content are not once [sic] for all established. . . . It could even be that scholarship has gone too far in an uncritical use of this collective term; it could even be that by the use of this blanket term it is suggesting the existence of something which never existed and that it is in this way dangerously prejudicing the interpretation of varied material." Von Rad by no means sustains the sweeping skepticism of this statement, which appears in the prefatory section of a perfectly coherent and plausible book entitled *Wisdom in Israel*. Whatever the definitional problems, there are identifiable features of Wisdom literature that give it a distinctive identity within the biblical corpus.

Abundant evidence has been uncovered, in Egypt and in Mesopotamia as well, that Wisdom writing was a fairly widespread practice in the ancient Near East. The perspective of Wisdom literature is international and, in many instances, one might say, universalist. It raises questions of value and moral behavior, of the meaning of human life, and especially of the right conduct of life. The Wisdom writers of ancient Israel evince some awareness of the activity of their counterparts in the surrounding cultures. In one clear instance, Proverbs 22:17–24:22, there is extensive borrowing, possibly through the intermediary of an Aramaic translation, of a second-millennium BCE Egyptian Wisdom text. Beyond this particular case, various arguments have been made for other borrowings, though by and large it is safer to speak of analogues and generic connections than of direct adaptations or translations.

In keeping with this international background, there is little in the three biblical Wisdom books that is specifically Israelite. The praise of Solomon's legendary sagacity in 1 Kings 5:11 properly sets it in an international frame of comparison: "And Solomon's wisdom was greater than the wisdom of all the dwellers of the East and than all the wisdom of Egypt." The characters in the Book of Job, though monotheists, are themselves "dwellers of the East" and not at all Israelites. Qohelet consists of a series of reflections on the nature of reality and the human condition into which no national considerations enter. God, occasionally referred to at the margins of the book, is always *'elohim*, the generic term, and not YHWH, the Israelite proper noun for God; and, as I argue later, the term *'elohim* itself may carry a somewhat different semantic freight from the one it bears in earlier biblical texts. The orientation of the Book of Proverbs toward the meaning and uses of Wisdom is on the whole thoroughly pragmatic (apart from one somewhat enigmatic passage just before the end). The reiterated term *torah* never refers to the revealed text of the Law but simply indicates teaching or instruction; and, as is the case in Job and Qohelet, revelation, covenant, the history of Israel, and national redemption are not part of its concerns. If Job culminates in the Voice from the Whirlwind that could be construed as a kind of revelation, that vision of a teeming and contradictory nature in which beauty and violence are intertwined has very little in common with the Sinai epiphany, which conveyed ethical and cultic instruction to Israel.

Wisdom writing continued toward the end of the biblical period in some of the texts included in the Apocrypha, and signs of the Wisdom tradition are still detectable in rabbinic literature in the early centuries

of the Christian era. It should also be said that Wisdom literature sur-
faces from time to time in other books of the Bible. Several psalms in
the canonical collection have been persuasively identified as Wisdom
psalms: among the clearcut examples are Psalm 1, Psalm 19, and Psalm
119. Many scholars have contended that there are Wisdom motifs in the
Joseph story in Genesis. And, of course, the celebration of Solomon as
a great sage, at which we have already glanced, exhibits a background in
Wisdom literature.

It is only, however, in Job, Proverbs, and Qohelet that we have books
in the Hebrew canon that are Wisdom from end to end. There is no
confident way of knowing where or how they originated. One hypothesis
that has enjoyed a certain currency among scholars is that there were
Wisdom schools in which such texts were both composed and taught.
There is some evidence for the existence of Wisdom schools in the surrounding cultures but little direct proof of their existence in ancient
Israel. It is a safe assumption that there were scribal schools throughout
the region, typically associated with temples and run by priestly scribes,
for writing and literary composition are complex skills requiring instruction. Whether these schools should also be thought of as Wisdom academies is unclear.

One passing reference in Proverbs (17:16) would seem to indicate
that people paid teachers a fee for instruction in Wisdom, though it is
hard to know whether this was a general practice.

A recent study by the Dutch scholar Karel van der Toorn, *Scribal
Culture and the Making of the Hebrew Bible*, illustrates the danger of
conflating scribal schools and Wisdom academies. For van der Toorn,
virtually everything in the Hebrew Bible is the product of scribal schools.
Thus, turning a blind eye to literature, he explains the dazzling poetic
panoramas of the Book of Job as a reflection of scribal list-making, and
he sees the extraordinary lexical richness of the poetry of Job as a reflection of vocabulary exercises for the scribes. In fact, it is difficult to
imagine that a book presenting so radical a challenge to the biblical
consensus view of reward and punishment and of an anthropocentric
creation could have been produced in any school, no less a school associated with a temple. The same thing must be said, for somewhat different reasons, of Qohelet, given its unblinking perception of the futility
of human endeavor and its vision of endless cycles of repetition instead

of the dominant biblical notion, powerfully inaugurated in Genesis, of linear progression through time toward a horizon of fulfillment.

Proverbs is the only one of the three canonical Wisdom books that might conceivably reflect the activities of some sort of academy. Composed in verse from beginning to end, it often seems to utilize the mnemonic function of poetry to inscribe in memory principles of right and wrong, and one can plausibly imagine a teacher imparting instruction of this sort to his disciples. The poetry in Proverbs, however, is by no means restricted to serving as an aid to memory, and we shall have occasion to observe a variety of arresting and at times surprising purposes to which poetry is put in this book. Job, apart from the prose frame-story of the first two chapters and the last one, is composed entirely as poetry, and it often proves to be poetry of a highly innovative and sometimes deliberately disturbing kind. Qohelet uses strongly cadenced, evocative prose, perhaps qualifying as prose-poetry, which in two extended passages moves into formal verse. All three books, then, deploy manifestly literary means to shape their visions of human life.

Wisdom literature is as close as the ancient Near East came to Greek philosophy, which was nearly contemporaneous with the latest Wisdom texts of the Hebrew Bible. It shares with Greek philosophy an inquiry into values and a disposition to reflect on the human condition, but it lacks both the purely theoretical and the systematic impulses of the Greek thinkers. Ethical issues are raised, but there is no real ontology, epistemology, anthropology, or metaphysics, and much of the thrust of Near Eastern Wisdom is pragmatic and even explicitly didactic. Job, for all its profundity, is a theological rather than a philosophic text. Its author is God-obsessed and never wonders or speculates about God's existence but rather expresses his outrage at the spectacular injustice of a world governed by a purportedly just God. Qohelet, concerned as it is with the structure of reality and how ephemeral human life is locked into that structure, is close to a genuinely philosophic work, though it articulates its philosophy through incantatory language and haunting imagery rather than through systematic thought.

What is most striking about Job, Proverbs, and Qohelet is that they are drastically different not only from almost all other biblical texts but also from each other. Proverbs founds its admonitions and observations in what it conceives to be the assured wisdom of tradition and collective knowledge. Precisely that assurance is frontally challenged in Job. Qohelet does not so much challenge traditional wisdom as subvert it, sometimes in the form of sly anti-proverbs that have the ring of conventional maxims but express a bleak skepticism antithetical to what one encounters in the Book of Proverbs. These strong disparities among the three Wisdom books vividly illustrate how the Hebrew Bible, contrary to popular preconceptions, is not a book but an anthology spanning almost a millennium and incorporating widely different views of human nature, God, history, and even the natural world. This very variety is one of the principal sources of the continuing vitality of Hebrew Scripture. The three Wisdom books are, in different ways, worlds apart from Genesis, Deuteronomy, and the Prophets and also far apart from each other. They retain an ongoing relevance to the lives of modern readers, religious and secular alike—Job and Qohelet, through the very boldness of their dissenting views, but Proverbs as well, in the worldliness and the satiric shrewdness of many of its perceptions.

JOB

INTRODUCTION

The Book of Job is in several ways the most mysterious book of the Hebrew Bible. Formally, as a sustained debate in poetry, it resembles no other text in the canon. Theologically, as a radical challenge to the doctrine of reward for the righteous and punishment for the wicked, it dissents from a consensus view of biblical writers—a dissent compounded by its equally radical rejection of the anthropocentric conception of creation that is expressed in biblical texts from Genesis onward. Its astounding poetry eclipses all other biblical poetry, working in the same formal system but in a style that is often distinct both lexically and imagistically from its biblical counterparts. Despite all these anomalous traits, it was quickly embraced by the framers of biblical tradition: extensive fragments of an Aramaic translation found in the caves at Qumran suggest that by the second century BCE the Dead Sea sectarians (and no doubt others) already regarded Job as part of the incipient canon of sacred texts.

As is the case with so many other biblical books, we know nothing about the author of Job—not his class background and certainly not any of his biographical details and not even with any certainty the time when he wrote. Some scholars, perplexed by the many peculiarities of the book, and especially by the linguistic ones, have speculated that it is a translation from Aramaic, or Edomite, or even Arabic. There is virtually no evidence for such ascriptions, and they seem especially untenable in light of the greatness of the Hebrew poetry of Job, rich as it is in strong rhythmic effects, virtuosic wordplay and sound-play—qualities that a translation would be very unlikely to exhibit.

The Book of Job belongs to the international movement of ancient Near Eastern Wisdom literature in its universalist perspective—there are no Israelite characters in the text, though all the speakers are monotheists, and there is no reference to covenantal history or to the nation of Israel—and it is equally linked with Wisdom literature in its investigation of the problem of theodicy. The troubling phenomenon of the suffering of the just is addressed in roughly analogous texts both in Mesopotamia and Egypt, though any direct influence of these on the Job poet is questionable. Scholars have often assumed that there were Wisdom schools in ancient Israel and elsewhere in the region where disciples guided by teachers mastered, and in all likelihood memorized, instructional texts and imbibed the general principles for leading a just and prudent life. It is hard to imagine that the Job poet could have been part of any such institutional setting, given the radical nature of his views. One should probably think of him, then, as a writer working alone—a bold dissenting thinker and a poet of genius who produced a book of such power that Hebrew readers soon came to feel they couldn't do without it, however vehement its swerve from the views of the biblical majority.

No confident agreement among scholars on the date of the book has been reached. There are still a few stubborn adherents to the view that it was composed early in the First Temple period, though, as I shall explain, the linguistic evidence argues against that notion. The frame-story (Chapters 1 and 2, concluded in Chapter 42) is in all likelihood a folktale that had been in circulation for centuries, probably through oral transmission. In the original form of the story, with no debate involved, the three companions would not have appeared: instead, Job would have been tested through the wager between God and the Adversary, undergone his sufferings, and in the end would have had his fortunes splendidly restored. A passing mention in Ezekiel 14:14 and 19 of Job, together with Noah and Daniel (not the Daniel of the biblical book) as one of three righteous men saved from disaster, reflects the presence of a Job figure—perhaps featuring in the same plot as that of the frame-story—in earlier folk tradition. The author of the Book of Job, however, has either reworked an old text or formulated his own text on the basis of oral tradition, using archaizing language. There is an obvious effort in the frame-story to evoke the patriarchal age, though in a foreign land with non-Israelites, but the neat symmetries of formulaic numbers and the use of prose refrains resemble nothing in the Patriarchal Narrative in Genesis. The style of the frame-story gives the general impression of early First Commonwealth Hebrew prose, but here and there a trait of

Late Biblical Hebrew shows through—for example, the use of the verb *qabel* in 2:10 for "accept," a verb that occurs in late texts such as Esther and Chronicles but not in earlier biblical writing. Other late usages, such as a couple of the prepositions that follow verbs here, have been detected by Avi Hurvitz, a historian of biblical Hebrew.

The poetry incorporates a noticeably higher proportion of terms borrowed from the Aramaic than does other biblical poetry. In some cases, even Aramaic grammatical suffixes are used, something that a translator from Aramaic would probably have avoided but that would have come naturally to a writer who was hearing a good deal of Aramaic all around him and probably actively spoke it himself together with Hebrew. (To cite one recurrent example: the Aramaic *milin*, "words," which would replace Early Biblical *devarim* in later Hebrew, appears thirty-four times in Job out of a total of thirty-eight biblical occurrences, and the Aramaic plural ending -*in*, instead of the Hebrew -*im*, is used several times.) All this suggests a historical moment when Aramaic was in the process of beginning to replace Hebrew as the vernacular of the Judean population. That would place the Job poet in the fifth century or perhaps as early as the later sixth century BCE, though it is impossible to be more precise, and one cannot exclude an early fourth-century setting.

The overall structure of the book is fairly clear, though it is somewhat obscured by certain disjunctures between the frame-story and the poem, and by two major interpolations and some gaps in the received text. There is a palpable discrepancy between the simple folktale world of the frame-story and the poetic heart of the book. God's quick acquiescence in the Adversary's perverse proposal is hard to justify in terms of any serious monotheistic theology, and when the LORD speaks from the whirlwind at the end, He makes no reference whatever either to the wager with the Adversary or to any celestial meeting of "the sons of God," a notion of a council of the gods that ultimately goes back to Canaanite mythology. The old folktale, then, about the suffering of the righteous Job is merely a pretext, a narrative excuse, and a pre-text, a way of introducing the text proper, and what happens in it provides little help for thinking through the problem of theodicy. The two major interpolations are the Hymn to Wisdom (Chapter 28), a fine poem in its own right but one that expresses a pious view of wisdom as fear of the LORD that could scarcely be that of the Job poet, and the Elihu speeches

(Chapters 32–37), which could not have been part of the original book both because Elihu is never mentioned in the frame-story, either at the beginning or at the end, and because the bombastic, repetitious, and highly stereotypical poetry he speaks is vastly inferior to anything written by the Job poet.

After the opening two chapters of the frame-story, the core of the book is introduced by Job's harrowing death-wish poem (Chapter 3), to which God will offer a direct rejoinder at the beginning of the speech from the whirlwind (see the commentary on Chapter 38). There are then three rounds of debate between Job and his three reprovers, each of the three speaking in turn and he replying to each. The third round of the debate was somehow damaged in scribal transmission. Bildad is given only a truncated speech, and the third contribution of Zophar to the debate seems to have disappeared entirely. In any case, after these three rounds, Job concludes the discussion with a lengthy profession of innocence in which he also recalls his glory days before he was overwhelmed by catastrophe (Chapters 27, 29–31, with his speech interrupted by the Hymn to Wisdom of Chapter 28). At this point, in the original text, the LORD would have spoken out from the whirlwind, but a lapse in judgment by an ancient editor postponed that brilliant consummation for six chapters in which the tedious Elihu is allowed to hold forth.

The Book of Job is, of course, a theological argument, but it is a theological argument conducted in poetry, and careful attention to the role that poetry plays in the argument may put what is said in a somewhat different light from the one in which it is generally viewed. The debate between Job and his three adversarial friends and then God's climactic speech to Job exhibit three purposefully deployed levels of poetry. The bottom level is manifested in the language of reproof of the three companions. In keeping with the conventional moral views that they complacently defend, the poetry they speak abounds in familiar formulations closely analogous to what one encounters in many passages in Psalms and Proverbs. What this means is that much of their poetry verges on cliché. The Job poet, however, is too subtle an artist merely to assign bad verse to them, which would have the effect of setting them up too crudely as straw men in the debate. Thus, there are moments when their poetry catches fire, conveying to us a sense that even the spokesmen for wrongheaded ideas may exercise a certain power of vision. One might also surmise that this writer was too good a poet to be able to resist the temptation of creating for the three companions some lines and even whole passages of fine poetry.

In any case, the stubborn authenticity of Job's perception of moral reality is firmly manifested in the power of the poetry he speaks, which clearly transcends the poetry of his reprovers. The death-wish poem that initiates his discourse is a brilliantly apt prelude to all that follows. Biblical poetry in general works through a system of intensifications, heightening or focusing or concretizing the utterance of the first verset of a line in the approximate semantic parallelism of the second verset (and in triadic lines, this process of intensification often moves on from the second verset to the third). When Job takes up his complaint in poetry in Chapter 3, he exploits this inherent dynamic of biblical verse to burrow progressively deeper into the aching core of his suffering. Anguish has rarely been given more powerful expression. All this begins in the very first line he speaks, a pounding rhythm in the initial verset, *yo'vad yom 'iwaled bo*, "Annul the day that I was born," followed by the second verset, "and the night that said, 'A man is conceived.'" In the pattern of intensification evident here, Job, longing for relief from pain through non-existence, wants to wipe out not just the event of his birth, in the first verset, but going back nine months and moving from day to night, his very conception, evoked in the second verset. The mention of night then triggers a long chain of images of night and darkness, each deepening the effect of the ones that precede it.

It should be said that almost all biblical poetry, because it is formally based in part on semantic parallelism, is driven to search for synonyms. No other biblical poet, however, exhibits the virtuosity in the command of rich synonymity that is displayed by the Job poet. He compounds the primary term *hoshekh*, "darkness," with *tsalmawet*, "death's shadow," *'ananah*, "cloud-mass," the unique *kimrirey yom*, "day-gloom" (or, perhaps, "eclipse"), *'ofel*, "murk," and a series of verbs that indicate a befouling, obscuring, or shutting down of light. The extraordinary breadth of the Job poet's vocabulary is one of the traits that has led some scholars to imagine a foreign source for the poem, but this is a rather silly inference. There are poets in many literary traditions whose imagination and relation to language lead them to stretch the lexical limits of their medium—one might think of Shakespeare, Mallarmé, and Wallace

Stevens—and the writer who fashioned the poetry of Job was clearly such a poet. This is another reason for his being drawn to tap Aramaic, as a resource that enables him to extend the reach of his vocabulary (the just cited *kimrirey* is the first instance in the poem of an Aramaic root Hebraized in order to enrich the poet's lexicon).

The English reader should be warned that this dazzling lexical abundance has created problems first for the ancient scribes and then for all who have attempted to translate this book. Scribes in general are uneasy about transcribing words with which they are unfamiliar, and as a result they tend to substitute terms they know or otherwise to introduce some graphic stutter in copying the text. This is at least one principal reason that the text of Job has come down to us at many points quite garbled, making interpretation a matter of guesswork and repeatedly inviting emendation. But when a whole line or sequence of lines of poetry has been completely mangled in transmission, efforts to recover the original formulation through emendation are bound to be highly conjectural. The present translation therefore for the most part limits itself to relatively minor emendations of the received text—changes of single letters, reversals of consonants, alterations of the vowel-points that indicate the vocalization of words—and these changes are undertaken with a somewhat greater measure of confidence when they are warranted by a variant Hebrew manuscript or by one of the ancient translations. Moreover, even when the integrity of the text appears not to have been compromised, the precise meaning of a rare term can remain in doubt, as is the case for *kimrirey* in Job's initial poem. In these instances, a struggling translator can rely only on context, common sense, an awareness of analogous forms and usages in biblical Hebrew and sometimes in rabbinic Hebrew, and the background of other Semitic languages, with Aramaic obviously being by far the most relevant.

The other chief resource deployed in the poetry that Job speaks is its extraordinary metaphoric inventiveness. This strength is already observable in the death-wish poem in the exquisite expression of the desire for unending darkness, "let it [the night of Job's conception] not see the eyelids of dawn" (3:9). In a procedure that is by no means typical for biblical poetry, the Job poet ranges far and wide through unexpected semantic fields for the sources of his similes and metaphors, drawing on weaving, agronomy, labor practices, meteorology, the sundry crafts, the preparation of foods. Here, for example, is a representation of the formation of the embryo from shapeless plasma in the womb: "Why, You poured me out like milk / and like cheese You curdled me" (10:10). The chiastic pattern of this line, abb´a´, is one of which this poet is especially fond. The fecundity of metaphor, moreover, is allied with a keenly observant interest in the processes of nature that is also rather unusual for a biblical poet. If Job compares the way his friends have betrayed him to the drying up in summer of a wadi, a desert gulch that may be filled with water during the rainy season (6:15), he then proceeds for five lines to follow the seasonal cycle, the melting of snow and ice, the caravans crossing the desert desperately looking for sources of water. It seems almost as if the vehicle of the metaphor—that is, the natural panorama—interested the poet as much as the sense of betrayal he has Job express through the metaphor.

Still another source of metaphor tapped by the Job poet, beyond quotidian reality and nature, is mythology. The mythological register, too, is invoked in Job's first poem, when the amplitude of the curse he brings down on the night he was conceived is extended through these words: "Let the day-cursers hex it, / those ready to rouse Leviathan" (3:8). Leviathan, who will be mentioned quite a few times in the course of the poem, sometimes under other names, before he makes his full-scale appearance at the climax of the Voice from the Whirlwind, is the fearsome sea-monster of Canaanite mythology (in some versions, he has seven heads) who had to be subdued by the weather-god whose realm is the dry land. The day-cursers, we may infer, about whom little is known, are also mythological figures, able to exert a magical power through language—to this Job himself in this opening poem aspires—even over the dreaded beast of the sea, enemy of the ordered realm of creation. The poetry of Job, then, at least in its metaphors, reaches deep into the chaotic sea, up to the stars where celestial beings dwell, and down into the kingdom of death, that shadowy underworld bordered by a Current that can be crossed only in one direction. In this poem where intensification is the key to so much, mythology serves as the ultimate intensifier.

The third—and, ultimately, decisive—level of poetry in the book is manifested when the LORD addresses Job out of the whirlwind. Here, too, the Job poet's keen interest in nature is evident, but in an altogether spectacular way that, one might say, trumps Job in the game of vision.

The poet, having given Job such vividly powerful language for the articulation of his outrage and his anguish, now fashions still greater poetry for God. The wide-ranging panorama of creation in the Voice from the Whirlwind shows a sublimity of expression, a plasticity of description, an ability to evoke the complex and dynamic interplay of beauty and violence in the natural world, and even an originality of metaphoric inventiveness, that surpasses all the poetry, great as it is, that Job has spoken. Many readers over the centuries have felt that God's speech to Job is no real answer to the problem of undeserved suffering, and some have complained that it amounts to a kind of cosmic bullying of puny man by an overpowering deity. One must concede that it is not exactly an answer to the problem because for those who believe that life should not be arbitrary there can be no real answer concerning the good person who loses a child (not to speak of ten children) or the blameless dear one who dies in an accident or is stricken with a terrible wasting disease. But God's thundering challenge to Job is not bullying. Rather, it rousingly introduces a comprehensive overview of the nature of reality that exposes the limits of Job's human perspective, anchored as it is in the restricted compass of human knowledge and the inevitable egoism of suffering. The vehicle of that overview is an order of poetry created to match the grandeur—or perhaps the omniscience—of God. The visionary experience that this poetry enables for Job is of a vast creation shot through with unfathomable paradoxes, such as the conjoining of the nurturing instinct with cruelty, where in place of the sufferer's longing for absolute darkness the morning stars sing together and there is a rhythmic interplay between light and darkness.

Poetry of such virtuosity and power, dependent as it must be on the expressive force of the original words and their ordering, is bound to pale in translation. The English version offered here is an attempt—which, inescapably, can be no more than intermittently successful—to convey something of the concreteness, the rhythmic compactness, the metaphoric richness, and the lexical vividness of the Hebrew. Perhaps one can draw a degree of encouragement from the fact that the greatness of the Book of Job has somehow managed to shine through in a long line of variously imperfect translations. My hope is that the present translation might manage to let that poetic light show in the English at least a little more than it has in earlier renderings.

1

A man there was in the land of Uz—Job, his name. And the man was ₁
blameless and upright and feared God and shunned evil. And seven ₂
sons were born to him, and three daughters. And his flocks came to ₃
seven thousand sheep and three thousand camels and five hundred
yokes of cattle and five hundred she-asses and a great abundance of

---

1. *A man there was in the land of Uz*. These initial words signal the fable-like
character of the frame-story. The opening formula, "A man there was," *'ish
hayah*, resembles the first words of Nathan's parable of the poor man's ewe in
2 Samuel 12, "Two men there were in a single town," *shney 'anashim hayu be'ir
ahat*. The more classical formula for starting a story in Hebrew narrative is
"there was a man," *wayehi 'ish*, the order of verb and subject reversed and the
converted imperfect form of the verb used.

Uz. Many scholars have located this land in Edom, across the Jordan from
the Land of Israel. But it is really a never-never land somewhere to the east, as
befits the fable and the universalizing thrust of the whole book. In this regard,
the fact that *'uts* in Hebrew means "counsel" or "advice" invites one to construe
this as the Land of Counsel.

2. *seven sons . . . three daughters*. These make a sum of ten, and all the numbers
that follow yield multiples of ten. If the story is meant to evoke the pastoral
world of the Patriarchs, it is clearly a stylized rendering of that world, as these
formulaic numbers suggest and as the studied use of refrain-like repetitions
throughout the tale equally suggests.

3. *flocks*. The Hebrew *miqneh*, deriving from a root that means "to acquire,"
can mean either flocks or possessions. In a pastoral society, possessions would
be chiefly flocks, and what follows is, except for the reference to slaves, a catalogue of livestock. The use in verse 10 of the verb "spread" (more literally, "burst
forth") in conjunction with *miqneh* also argues for the sense of "flocks."

4 slaves. And that man was greater than all the dwellers of the East. And his sons would go and hold a feast, in each one's house on his set day,

5 and they would call to their sisters to eat and drink with them. And it happened when the days of the feast came round, that Job would send and consecrate them and rise early in the morning and offer up burnt offerings according to the number of them all. For Job thought, Perhaps my sons have offended and cursed God in their hearts. Thus would Job do at all times.

6 And one day, the sons of God came to stand in attendance before the

7 LORD, and the Adversary, too, came among them. And the LORD said to the Adversary, "From where do you come?" And the Adversary answered the LORD and said, "From roaming the earth and walking

8 about in it." And the LORD said to the Adversary, "Have you paid heed to my servant Job, for there is none like him on earth, a blameless and

9 upright man, who fears God and shuns evil?" And the Adversary

---

5. *offer up burnt offerings.* In the pastoral, pre-national, and non-Israelite setting of the story, there is neither temple nor priesthood, and Job, the pious monotheist, performs his own sacrifices.

    cursed God. The Hebrew says, euphemistically, "blessed God." Many think this is a scribal substitution to avoid a blasphemous phrase, though it is also possible that the euphemism was actually used in speech. The same usage occurs in the Adversary's words in verse 12.

6. *the sons of God.* This celestial entourage is a literary vestige of the pre-monotheistic notion of a council of the gods and is reflected in several of the canonical psalms (perhaps, most notably, in Psalm 82).

    the Adversary. The Hebrew is *hasatan,* and invariably uses the definite article because the designation indicates a function, not a proper name. The word *satan* is a person, thing, or set of circumstances that constitutes an obstacle or frustrates one's purposes. Only toward the very end of the biblical period would the term begin to drop the definite article and refer to a demonic figure. Marvin Pope imagines *hasatan* here as a kind of intelligence agent working for God, but the dialogue suggests rather an element of jealousy (when God lavishes praise on Job) and cynical mean-spiritedness.

8. *blameless . . . upright . . . who fears God and shuns evil.* The verbatim repetition by God of the narrator's characterization of Job confirms its perfect authority.

answered the Lord and said, "Does Job fear God for nothing? Have   10
You not hedged him about and his household and all that he has all
around? The work of his hands You have blessed, and his flocks have
spread over the land. And yet, reach out Your hand, pray, and strike all   11
he has. Will he not curse You to Your face?" And the Lord said to the   12
Adversary, "Look, all that he has is in your hands. Only against him do
not reach out your hand." And the Adversary went out from before the
Lord's presence.

And one day, his sons and his daughters were eating and drinking   13
wine in the house of their brother, the firstborn. And a messenger came   14
to Job and said, "The cattle were plowing and the she-asses grazing by
them, and Sabeans fell upon them and took them, and the lads they   15
struck down by the edge of the sword, and I alone escaped to tell you."
This one was still speaking when another came and said, "God's fire fell   16
from the heavens and burned among the sheep and the lads and con-
sumed them, and I alone escaped to tell you." This one was still speak-   17
ing when another came and said, "Chaldaeans set out in three bands
and pounced upon the camels and took them, and the lads they struck

---

11. *reach out Your hand, pray, and strike all he has.* The Adversary carefully
formulates this outrageous request to strip Job of possessions and offspring
with the polite particle of entreaty, "pray," *na'*.

12. *in your hands.* The Hebrew uses the singular and pointedly plays with
"reach out Your hand" both before and after this phrase. It is therefore unwise
to render the phrase as "in your trust" or "in your power," as English translators
since 1611 have done.

14–18. The tale of disasters, hewing to the general procedure of extensive repetition deployed here, alternates between attacks by marauders (verses 15 and
17) and natural catastrophes (verses 16 and 18). It also follows a common biblical pattern of three plus one—three disasters that destroy Job's property and a
fourth that kills his children.

15. *the lads.* That is, the servants.

16. *God's fire.* This is probably a reference to lightning. "God," *'eholim*, might
be merely an intensifier—that is, "awesome fire."

18 down by the edge of the sword." This one was still speaking when another came and said, "Your sons and your daughters were eating and

19 drinking wine in the house of their brother, the firstborn. And, look, a great wind came from beyond the wilderness and struck the four corners of the house, and it fell on the young people, and they died. And I alone

20 escaped to tell you." And Job rose and tore his garment and shaved his

21 head and fell to the earth and bowed down. And he said,

> "Naked I came out from my mother's womb,
>   and naked shall I return there.
> The LORD has given and the LORD has taken.
>   May the LORD's name be blessed."

22 With all this, Job did not offend, nor did he put blame on God.

---

19. *the young people*. The Hebrew *ne'arim* is the same word used for "lads" or servants, but here it refers to Job's sons and daughters and hence a gender-inclusive translation is required.

And I alone escaped to tell you. This thrice-repeated refrain is aptly picked up by Melville in the haunting conclusion of *Moby-Dick*, when everything on the *Pequod* is wiped out, only Ishmael surviving.

20. *shaved his head*. This (like the rending of the garment) is a general sign of mourning, though prohibited in Israel and thus a neat way of reminding the audience that Job is not an Israelite.

21. *Naked I came out . . . naked shall I return there*. Job's acceptance of his dire fate (which gave rise to the notion of the "patient Job") is cast as a solemn two-line poem. This first line exhibits a link of narrative development between the two versets: first birth, then death. The reference of "there" has a loose associative logic: the grave is not the womb, but it is part of mother earth from which the first man was made. There is something "existential" in this brief poetic statement: whatever a man acquires in life—even in the children he begets— are supernumerary to the fundamental condition of nakedness in which he enters and leaves life.

May the LORD's name be blessed. Here Job makes exactly the opposite declaration to the one the Adversary expected: he says "blessed" in its actual meaning, not as an antithetical euphemism.

2

And one day, the sons of God came to stand in attendance before the LORD, and the Adversary, too, came among them to stand in attendance before the LORD. And the LORD said to the Adversary, "From whence do you come?" And the Adversary answered the LORD and said, "From roaming the earth and walking about in it." And the LORD said to the Adversary, "Have you paid heed to My servant Job, for there is none like him on earth, a blameless and upright man, who fears God and shuns evil and still clings to his innocence, and you incited Me against him to destroy him for nothing." And the Adversary answered the LORD and said, "Skin for skin! A man will give all he has for his own life. Yet, reach

---

1. *And one day.* Still following the stylized folktale narrative procedure of elaborate verbatim repetition, the story now repeats all the language of 1:6–8, with only a couple of insignificant variations: here the Adversary is said "to stand in attendance," which was merely implied in 1:6; and here God asks him "From whence" (*'ey mizeh*) rather than "From where" (*me'ayin*). The first new material appears in God's accusatory words to the Adversary at the end of verse 3: "still clings to his innocence, and you incited Me against him to destroy him for nothing."

4. *Skin for skin!* In this second dialogue between God and the Adversary, the pace picks up. Instead of offering a detailed account of Job's circumstances (1:10–11), the Adversary responds brusquely and pithily. Almost all interpreters agree that "Skin for skin" is some sort of proverb, but there is no clear consensus on its meaning. In light of the second half of the verse, which is manifestly an explanation of these three words, and in light of the Adversary's next line of attack, which is to strike Job with an acutely painful skin disease, a plausible interpretation would be the following: what is most precious to a man is his own physical being; in the end, he is prepared to sacrifice everything, even the

out, pray, Your hand and strike his bone and his flesh. Will he not curse
6 You to Your face?" And the LORD said to the Adversary, "Here he is in
7 your hands. Only preserve his life." And the Adversary went out from
before the LORD's presence. And he struck Job with a grievous burning
8 rash from the soles of his feet to the crown of his head. And he took a
potsherd to scrape himself with, and he was sitting among the ashes.
9 And his wife said to him, "Do you still cling to your innocence? Curse
10 God and die." And he said to her, "You speak as one of the base women
would speak. Shall we accept good from God, too, and evil we shall not
accept?" With all this, Job did not offend with his lips.

"skin" (or lives) of his own dear ones, but hurt him badly in his own flesh and
bones, and he will abandon all his principles of integrity.

6. *Here he is in your hands.* God's acquiescence in this perverse experiment is
a puzzle for ethical monotheism, and perhaps one must say that the origins of
the folktale are from a time when there was no real ethical monotheism. In any
case, this wager or test is never addressed in the rest of the book.

7. *And the Adversary went out . . . and he struck Job.* In keeping with the accel-
eration of narrative tempo, the Adversary immediately proceeds from his
exchange with God to his mischief, with no intervening narrative material as in
1:13–14.
    burning rash. The Hebrew *shehin* derives from a root that means "hot" and
is the same term used in Exodus for the fifth plague. Attempts at a precise
medical diagnosis are pointless: the essential idea is that a burning rash covering the entire body from the soles of the feet to the head would be agonizing
(and also disfiguring, as the initial failure of the three friends to recognize Job
suggests).

9. *Do you still cling to your innocence? Curse God and die.* Again, the euphemism
of "bless" for "curse" appears. Job's wife either assumes that cursing God will
immediately lead to Job's death, which might be just as well, or that, given his
ghastly state, he will soon die anyway, so that he might as well curse the deity
who inflicted these horrors on him. In either case, her use of the repeated phrase
"still cling to your innocence" (the Hebrew equally suggests "blamelessness" or
"integrity") is sarcastic: what is the point of your innocence, she says, after all that
has happened? In the body of the poem, Job will still cling to his innocence, in
the very act of accusing God, as God recognizes at the end of the book.

And Job's three companions heard of all this harm that had come upon ₁₁
him, and they came, each from his place—Eliphaz the Temanite and
Bildad the Shuhite and Zophar the Naamathite, and they agreed to meet
to grieve with him and to comfort him. And they lifted up their eyes ₁₂
from afar and did not recognize him, and they lifted up their voices and
wept, and each tore his garment, and they tossed dust on their heads
toward the heavens. And they sat with him on the ground seven days ₁₃
and seven nights, and none spoke a word to him, for they saw that the
pain was very great.

---

10. *accept.* The Hebrew verb *qabel* is Late Biblical, so this may be a point
where the writer's own period leaked through the archaizing style he adopted
for the frame-story. A few others, including the prepositions that follow a couple of the verbs, have been identified by Avi Hurvitz, a historian of biblical
Hebrew.

11. *Job's three companions.* The precise location of their respective homelands
has been debated by scholars, though it is clear that their places of origin reflect
a spread of a few hundred miles to the east of the Jordan. One of the companions, Eliphaz, has a name associated with the descendants of Esau, or Edom.
Bildad is probably a pagan name ("son of Adad"). In any case, the geographical
background suggests that Job, "greater than all the dwellers of the East," was a
man who had international connections.
    to grieve with him. The literal sense of the Hebrew verb is to nod the head,
as a sign of mourning or sympathy.

12. *they lifted up their eyes . . . they lifted up their voices.* In the elegant repetition, one act leads to the other, from seeing Job's disfigurement to an immediate physical response of grief.
    tossed dust on their heads toward the heavens. This, like the rending of the
garments, is a gesture of mourning. The Septuagint lacks "toward the heavens,"
perhaps because the Greek translators considered it superfluous.

13. *none spoke a word to him, for they saw that the pain was very great.* In the
frame-story, the three companions seem deeply sympathetic with Job and
respectful of his suffering. This argues for a discrepancy between the frame-
story and the poem, where they are accusatory and even contemptuous of him.
One might imagine that after the seven days of mourning, they came to the
conclusion that he must have been a scoundrel to deserve all this suffering, but
that seems forced.

3

^{1,2} Afterward, Job opened his mouth and cursed his day. And Job spoke
up and he said:

³   Annul the day that I was born
                   and the night that said, "A man is conceived."

⁴   That day, let it be darkness.
             Let God above not seek it out,
                   nor brightness shine upon it.

---

3. *Annul the day that I was born.* The Job poet displays a virtuosity that transcends all other biblical poetry. Thus, the very first words of the poem begin with a strong accent for emphasis of feeling and an emphatic alliteration: **yo'vad yom** *'iwaled* **bo**. The initial verb (intransitive in the Hebrew) means to die or to be lost, and therefore "perish," used by the King James Version and several modern translations, is semantically accurate but in regard to diction is a bit fussy and lacks the directness of the Hebrew. A couple of modern translators have opted for "damn," but *yo'vad* is neither an expletive nor does it imply damnation, which is not a biblical idea. The force of what follows is that Job would like to expunge the day of his birth from the calendar, which is a contextual justification for "annul." This choice sacrifices the initial stress but does yield an iambic cadence.

and the night that said, "A man is conceived." Day and night are a formulaic word-pair in biblical poetic parallelism. But in a spectacular deployment of the pattern of intensification that generally characterizes the relationship between the first and second verset in a line of biblical poetry, Job asks not only that the day of his birth be expunged but, nine months earlier, the very act of conception that led to the birth. The phrase "the night that said" might also be construed as a third-person singular with unspecified subject standing in for a passive: "the night when it was said." From this point on, the poet proceeds to work over first the day, then the night, summing up language to expunge each in turn.

Let darkness, death's shadow, foul it,   5
        let a cloud-mass rest upon it,
            let day-gloom dismay it.
That night, let murk overtake it.   6
        Let it not join in the days of the year,
            let it not enter the number of months.
Oh, let that night be barren,   7
        let it have no song of joy.
Let the day-cursers hex it,   8
        those ready to rouse Leviathan.
Let its twilight stars go dark.   9
        Let it hope for day in vain,
            and let it not see the eyelids of dawn.

---

5. *darkness . . . cloud-mass . . . day-gloom*. In calling up different terms for the blocking out of light, the poet reflects a richness of lexical resources that makes him stand out among biblical poets. The most unusual term here is *kimrirey yom*, "day-gloom," probably derived from an Aramaic root that means "dark-ness," and perhaps referring to an eclipse, though that is not certain. The odd-ness of the English rendering here is meant to intimate the strangeness of the word in the Hebrew.

7. *let that night be barren, / let it have no song of joy*. The line moves in a met-onymic slide from the wished-for barrenness of Job's mother to the night of conception as barren and joyless.

8. *the day-cursers . . . those ready to rouse Leviathan*. As will happen again and again in the poem, the poet switches into a mythological register. Leviathan is the fearsome primordial sea-monster subdued by the god of order in Canaanite mythology. For this reason, some scholars prefer to read "Yamm-cursers" for "day-cursers," assuming the Hebrew *yam* instead of *yom*. In either case, the cursers are mythological or magical agents.

9. *Let its twilight stars go dark*. In this triadic line, we have a temporal sequence of (a) light fading in the evening, (b) a night of hoping for a daybreak that never comes, (c) a dawn that does not come.
    the eyelids of dawn. This exquisite and surprising image—another hallmark of this poet's originality—simultaneously indicates the first crack of light on the eastern horizon and the movement of the awakening person's eyes taking in the

10   For it did not shut the belly's doors
                    to hide wretchedness from my eyes.

11   Why did I not die from the womb,
                    from the belly come out, breathe my last?

12   Why did knees welcome me,
                    and why breasts, that I should suck?

13   For now I would lie and be still,
                    would sleep and know repose

14   with kings and the councilors of earth,
                    who build ruins for themselves,

15   or with princes, possessors of gold,
                    who fill their houses with silver.

16   Or like a buried stillborn I'd be,
                    like babes who never saw light.

---

first light of day. The metaphor will recur late in the poem in the most unanticipated context.

10. *the belly's doors.* The Hebrew says "my belly," an ellipsis for "my mother's belly."
    wretchedness. This recurrent term in Job, *'amal,* is here put forth as a virtual
synonym for "life" or "the world." Job's anguish could scarcely be expressed
more compactly.

12. *knees welcome me.* The simplest explanation is a reference to the mother's
knees, parted as the newborn emerges.

14. *build ruins for themselves.* In this brilliantly compact formulation of the
futility of all human endeavor, kings build great edifices for themselves that are
destined to turn to ruins. One thinks of Shelley's "Ozymandias."

16. *stillborn . . . babes who never saw light.* Here the poem refers directly back
to the idea of dying at birth in verse 11.
    buried stillborn. Many render *tamun* as "hidden," which is what the word
means in earlier biblical Hebrew, but the term in this Late Biblical text, as the
context makes clear, has traveled toward the sense of "buried" that it has in
rabbinic Hebrew.

There the wicked cease their troubling,   17
>and there the weary repose.
All together the prisoners are tranquil,   18
>they hear not the taskmaster's voice.
The small and the great are there,   19
>and the slave is free of his master.
Why give light to the wretched   20
>and life to the deeply embittered,
who wait for death in vain,   21
>dig for it more than for treasure,
who rejoice at the tomb,   22
>are glad when they find the grave?
—To a man whose way is hidden,   23
>and God has hedged him about.

---

17. *There the wicked.* The catalogue of human types (wicked, weary, prisoners, slaves, taskmaster) reveals a vision of life that involves hierarchies of domination and acts of exploitation.

20. *Why give light.* The Hebrew says, "Why should he give light," but it is not clearly the case, as many assume, that the pronoun refers to God. As elsewhere, the unspecified third-person singular may function as a passive, and thus the translation keeps the ambiguity of grammatical reference.

deeply embittered. The Hebrew *nefesh* ("life-breath," "essential self") is an intensifier, hence "deeply."

21. *treasure.* The Hebrew *matmon* ("something buried") derives from the same root as "buried" in verse 16.

22. *the tomb.* The Masoretic text reads *gil,* "joy." This translation adopts a commonly proposed emendation, *gal,* literally, "grave mound." A scribe may have been led into the error by the proximity of a verb of rejoicing.

23. *to a man.* This phrase appears to refer back to the verb at the beginning of verse 20, "Why give . . . ?"

hedged him about. In the Adversary's words in 1:10, this very verb referred to God's protection of Job. Here, it is pointedly turned around to mean that God has blocked Job on every side.

24 For before my bread my moaning comes,
      and my roar pours out like water.
25 For I feared a thing—it befell me,
      what I dreaded came upon me.
26 I was not quiet, I was not still,
      I had no repose, and trouble came.

---

26. *not quiet . . . not still . . . no repose . . . trouble came*. The poem ends climactically with a string of terms expressing constant perturbation, the very opposite of the condition of peaceful non-existence for which Job longs.

4

And Eliphaz the Temanite spoke out and he said: 1
If speech were tried against you, could you stand it?   2
      Yet who can hold back words?
Look, you reproved many,   3
      and slack hands you strengthened.
The stumbler your words lifted up,   4
      and bended knees you bolstered.
But now it comes to you and you cannot stand it,   5
      it reaches you and you are dismayed.
Is not your reverence your safety,   6
      your hope—your blameless ways?

---

2. *If speech were tried against you.* Eliphaz's opening words register an awareness that Job is likely to resist all reproof.

3. *Look, you reproved many.* The opening rhetorical strategy is to pay Job a kind of backhanded compliment: he was known as a man who gave encouragement to the failing and also did not hesitate to rebuke those guilty of misdeeds. He should, then, be prepared to accept justified reproof himself, but Eliphaz fears this is not the case ("But now it comes to you and you cannot stand it").

6. *Is not your reverence your safety.* The whole line is cast in an elegant chiasm (abb´a´): reverence-safety-hope-blameless ways. Job should have nothing to fear from warranted rebuke because his God-fearing life and his integrity have always given him security and hope. If he reaffirms these virtues, in the light of his friends' reproof, he will still be all right, despite all that has befallen him.

7   Recall, pray: what innocent man has died,
              and where were the upright demolished?
8   As I have seen, those who plow mischief,
              those who plant wretchedness, reap it.
9   Through God's breath they die,
              before his nostrils' breathing they vanish.
10   The lion's roar, the maned beast's sound—
              and the young lions' teeth are smashed.
11   The king of beasts dies with no prey,
              the whelps of the lion are scattered.
12   And to me came a word in secret,
              and my ear caught a tag-end of it,
13   in musings from nighttime's visions
              when slumber falls upon men.
14   Fear called to me, and trembling,
              and all my limbs it gripped with fear.

---

7. *Recall.* This verb is symptomatic of Eliphaz's argument. The knowledge that the innocent are never overtaken by disaster is something we have always known, and need only recall. If Job is plunged in a sea of disasters, there must be good reason for it.

8. *plow . . . plant . . . reap.* This conventional agricultural metaphor marks a strict line of causality in the moral realm: just as the planted seed will grow according to its kind, evil acts will produce a harvest of calamity for their perpetrators.

10. *The lion's roar.* The lexical wealth of the Job poet defies translation. There are five different biblical words for lion—*'aryeh, shahal, kefir, layish,* and *lavi'*—and all five of them are used in these two lines. The King James Version, in a strategy of desperation, associated different terms with lions of different ages, but no one really knows what the original differentiations were, or if there were any. (This translation, in a gesture to tradition, adopts just one of the 1611 inventions, "young lions" for *kefirim.*)
   the young lions' teeth are smashed. The force of both lines is that even such fearsomely powerful beasts can be reduced by God to impotence, their whelps scattered with no prey to nurture them.

And a spirit passed over my face,   15
      made the hair on my flesh stand on end.
It halted, its look unfamiliar,   16
      an image before my eyes,
          stillness, and a sound did I hear:
Can a mortal be cleared before God,   17
      can a man be made pure by his Maker?
Why, His servants He does not trust,   18
      His agents He charges with blame.
All the more so, the clay-house dwellers,   19
      whose foundation is in the dust,
          who are crushed more quickly than moths.
From morning to eve they are shattered,   20
      unawares they are lost forever.

---

12. *and to me came a word in secret*. Eliphaz presents his perception of man's inevitably flawed stature before God as the revelation of a scary night-vision.

15. *A spirit*. The Hebrew *ruaḥ* can also mean "breath" or "wind," but the context of nocturnal terror surely argues for a spectral apparition.

16. *its look unfamiliar*. Literally, "I did not recognize its look."

17. *Can a mortal be cleared before God*. These are the words of the spirit speaking to Eliphaz.

18. *servants . . . agents*. These are the courtiers of the celestial entourage and the divine messengers, the "angels" of traditional terminology.

19. *clay-house dwellers*. The clay house, as both ancient and modern commentators have noted, is the human body, a transient habitation with a foundation in dust, as the account of the creation of the first human being in Genesis 2 reminds us.

20. *From morning to eve*. This is a hyperbolic representation of the brevity of the human life span.

21   Should their life-thread be broken within them,
                 they die, and without any wisdom.

---

21. *their life-thread*. The Hebrew *yeter* is a cord that can be either a tent-cord (which is how some interpreters understand it here) or a bowstring. One gets the sense of some essential cord within the human body, the breaking of which immediately leads to death. The image strongly conveys the fragility of man's physical existence, which at any moment can come to an end.

they die, and without any wisdom. Eliphaz, of course, means to impart conventional wisdom to Job. But the greater part of humankind, he proposes, is cut off by sudden death before attaining true wisdom.

5

Call out, pray: will any answer you,   1
      and to whom of the angels will you turn?
For anger kills a fool,   2
      and the simple, envy slays.
I have seen a fool striking root—   3
      all at once his abode I saw cursed.
His children are distant from rescue   4
      and are crushed in the gate—none will save.
Whose harvest the hungry eat   5
      and from among thorns they take it away,
          and the thirsty pant for their wealth.
For crime does not spring from the dust,   6
      nor from the soil does wretchedness sprout.

---

3. *I have seen a fool striking root—* / *all at once his abode I saw cursed.* This line summarizes the moral calculus of mainline Wisdom literature that the three companions bring to bear against Job: the prosperity of the fool or the wrongdoer is illusory and ephemeral. The Hebrew of the second verset says literally, "all at once his abode I cursed," and this translation understands this as an ellipsis for the speaker's perception that the house has been suddenly cursed. Others emend the verb to read "is cursed," eliminating the first-person singular.

4. *crushed in the gate.* The gates of the town were the place for enacting justice. They were also where a victorious enemy entered.

5. *from among thorns.* The Hebrew is obscure, and the text looks corrupt here.

6. *For crime does not spring from the dust.* Moral mischief is perpetrated by conscious human agents; it does not just spring up spontaneously like grass or weeds.

7   But man is to wretchedness born
> like sparks flying upward.

8   Yet I search for El
> and to God I make my case,

9   Who does great things without limit
> wonders beyond all number,

10   Who brings rain down on the earth
> and sends water over the fields.

11   Who raises the lowly on high—
> the downcast are lifted in rescue.

12   Thwarts the designs of the cunning,
> and their hands do not perform wisely.

13   He entraps the wise in their cunning,
> and the crooked's counsel proves hasty.

14   By day they encounter darkness,
> as in night they go groping at noon.

---

7. *But man is to wretchedness born*. This pronouncement may have a double edge. Man's fate is misery; but, given Eliphaz's moralism, he may also be saying that wretchedness is the predictable consequence of the perversity of human nature.

like sparks flying upward. The Hebrew *beney reshef* is understood by some to be an explicitly mythological reference because Reshef is the Northwest Semitic god of pestilence and the underworld. However, with the emphasis here on man as a source of trouble, the concrete image of sparks makes better sense: just as a fire sends burning sparks swirling upward, man creates wretchedness all around him.

8. *Yet I search for El*. Eliphaz is now quick to assert his own piety, in contrast to the general rule of troublemaking humankind that he has just expressed. What follows is a celebratory catalogue of God's power and providential acts, cast, as we might expect, in rather traditional poetry—in fact, reminiscent of Psalms. The Job poet cannily devises for each of the three companions poetry that has its moments of strength but is often rather conventional, in keeping with their worldview. The startling originality of Job's poetry stands out in contrast.

14. *By day they encounter darkness, / as in night they go groping at noon*. This line is another instance of the Job poet's fondness for chiastic structures: a (day), b (encounter), c (darkness), c´ (night), b´ (go groping), a´ (noon).

He rescues the simple from the sword,   15
        and from the hand of the strong, the impoverished,
and the indigent then has hope,   16
        and wickedness clamps its mouth shut.
Why, happy the man whom God corrects.   17
        Shaddai's reproof do not spurn!
For He causes pain and binds the wound,   18
        He deals blows but His hands will heal.
In six straits He will save you,   19
        and in seven harm will not touch you.
In famine He redeems you from death,   20
        and in battle from the sword.
From the scourge of the tongue you are hidden,   21
        and you shall fear not assault when it comes.

---

15. *the simple from the sword.* The Masoretic text appears to say "from the sword from their mouth." The only way to save this reading would be to drop the second "from" as a dittography, thus yielding "from the sword of their mouth," which is a possible biblical metaphor. This translation follows Pope, who emends *mipihem*, "from their mouth," to *peta'im*, "the simple." Perhaps "mouth" at the end of the next line influenced the copyist to make a mistake here.

18. *He causes pain and binds the wound.* This whole line is particularly addressed to Job's present predicament of terrible suffering. Job is encouraged to imagine that his agony is "reproof" from God, Who will heal him when he mends his sinful ways.

19. *In six straits He will save you.* This celebration of God's providential care for the just, which continues to the end of verse 26, is again reminiscent of Psalms. Compare, for example, Psalm 91.

21. *From the scourge of the tongue.* It is also possible to construe this phrase, as many interpreters have done, to mean: "When the tongue [that is, of slander] goes wandering."
    assault. The primary sense of the Hebrew *shod* is "plunder," but in the present context, the element of violence implied by the term is salient.

22   At assault and starvation you laugh,
         and the beast of the earth you fear not.

23   With the stones of the field is your pact,
         the beasts of the field leagued with you.

24   And you shall know that your tent is peaceful,
         probe your home and find nothing amiss.

25   And you shall know that your seed is abundant,
         your offspring like the grass of the earth.

26   You shall come to the grave in vigor,
         as grain-shocks mount in their season.

27   Look, this we have searched, it is so.
         Hear it, and you—you should know.

---

24. *find nothing amiss*. The verb *teheta'* commonly means "to offend" (King James Version, "sin"), but its original sense, derived from archery, is "to miss the mark." The likely idea here is that when the just man looks into his house, everything is in order.

26. *in vigor*. The meaning of the Hebrew *kelah* has long been disputed. The only other time it appears in the Bible is also in Job (30:2), where it is matched in the poetic parallelism with "strength," and hence the inference about what it means. If that inference is correct, then Eliphaz is saying that the just man remains hale and hearty until his death, which is simply a natural process of coming to an end, like the harvest invoked in the second verset.

27. *we have searched*. This first-person plural epitomizes Eliphaz's stance: he speaks with the assurance of collective wisdom.
    and you—you should know. The second-person pronoun, generally omitted before a conjugated verb, is emphatic, *we'atah da'-lakh*, pointing the finger at Job: as for you, you should certainly know this home truth.

6

And Job spoke out and he said: 1
Could my anguish but be weighed,   2
      and my disaster on the scales be borne,
they would be heavier now than the sand of the sea.   3
      Thus my words are choked back.
For Shaddai's arrows are in me—   4
      their venom my spirit drinks.
          The terrors of God beset me.
Does the wild ass bray over his grass,   5
      the ox bellow over his feed?
Is tasteless food eaten unsalted,   6
      does the oozing of mallows have savor?
My throat refuses to touch them.   7
      They resemble my sickening flesh.

---

3. *are choked back*. The unusual verb *la'u* appears to derive from *lo'a*, gullet. Others understand it to mean "spewed out."

4. *venom*. God, violating the ancient equivalent of a Geneva Convention, uses poisoned arrows.

5. *the wild ass bray . . . the ox bellow*. The answer to these rhetorical questions is of course "no": an animal has no need to make noise when it is given food. This phenomenon of natural eating in the animal realm is then antithetically complemented by the idea in the next line that flavorless food is inedible for humans.

7. *My throat refuses to touch them*. For Job in his suffering, all food has become nauseating.
   They resemble my sickening flesh. The translation is an educated guess. The

8   If only my wish were fulfilled,
                and my hope God might grant.
9   If God would deign to crush me,
                loose His hand and tear me apart.
10   And this still would be my comfort,
                I shrink back in pangs—He spares not.
                    Yet I withhold not the Holy One's words.
11   What is my strength, that I should hope,
                and what my end that I should endure?
12   Is my strength the strength of stones,
                is my flesh made of bronze?
13   Indeed, there is no help within me,
                and prudence is driven from me.

---

syntax of the Hebrew is crabbed, and the last word of the line, *laḥmi*, could mean either "flesh" or "bread."

9. *If God would deign to crush me.* The violence of this whole shocking line is probably an expression of the extremity of Job's suffering: given all he has undergone, he wishes that God would get done with the business and utterly destroy him.

10. *I shrink back in pangs—He spares not.* The translation reproduces the enigmatic character of the Hebrew. Many interpreters seek to save coherence by construing this as "unsparing pangs," but the word for "pangs" is feminine, *ḥilah* (singular in the Hebrew), whereas the verb "spare" is conjugated in the masculine.

Yet I withhold not the Holy One's words. Most commentators understand this as Job's words against God, but "words" and "the Holy One" are tied together in the construct state (the Hebrew equivalent of a genitive). Job may be saying that even in his acute anguish he never suppressed the words of God's ethical injunctions, knowing that he lived by them, whatever God had done to him.

11. *endure.* The literal sense is "make my life-breath long." Since elsewhere, shortness of life-breath means impatience, this is probably an antonym, "patience."

The blighted man's friend owes him kindness,   14
     though the fear of Shaddai he forsake.
My brothers betrayed like a wadi,   15
     like the channel of brooks that run dry.
They are dark from the ice,   16
     snow heaped on them.
When they warm, they are gone,   17
     in the heat they melt from their place.
The paths that they go on are winding,   18
     they mount in the void and are lost.
The caravans of Tema looked out,   19
     the convoys of Sheba awaited.
Disappointed in what they had trusted,   20
     they reached it and their hopes were dashed.

---

14. *The blighted man's.* The Hebrew *mas* is obscure and hence the translation conjectural, following a proposal by Pope.

15. *My brothers betrayed like a wadi.* The wadi is a desert ravine. In the rainy season it fills with water and gives the appearance of a flowing stream, but in the summer, when no rain falls in this region, it turns into a dry channel.

16. *They are dark from the ice.* The Job poet is distinctive among biblical poets in his searching interest in natural phenomena. Having introduced the striking image of the wadi that goes dry in the summer as a representation of betrayal, he goes on with it for the next five lines, keenly attending to different manifestations of the annual cycle. The water in the wadi here—the landscape might be northern Israel bordering on the mountains of Lebanon, or perhaps the high country of Iran—is darkened by the ice on its surface.

17. *in the heat they melt.* Evidently, the melting of the ice and the heaped-up snow is telescoped with the evaporation of water that follows.

19. *Tema . . . Sheba.* Sheba is in the southwest end of the Arabian Peninsula, Tema in the north, and in fact caravans went from one to the other on a trade route. The geography is nicely appropriate for Job as "a dweller of the East."

    looked out . . . awaited. Apparently, they are looking for a water-source in the desert as they travel, so the wadi image is continued.

21   For now you are His.
          You see panic and you fear.

22   Did I say, Give for me,
          and with your wealth pay a ransom for me,

23   and free me from the hands of the foe,
          from the oppressors' hands redeem me?

24   Instruct me—as for me, I'll keep silent,
          and let me know where I went wrong.

25   How forceful are honest words.
          Yet what rebuke is the rebuke by you?

26   Do you mean to rebuke with words,
          treat the speech of the desperate as wind?

27   Even for the orphan you cast lots,
          and haggle for your companion.

28   And now, deign to turn toward me.
          To your face I will surely not lie.

29   Relent, pray, let there be no injustice.
          Relent. I am yet in the right.

30   Is there injustice on my tongue?
          Does my palate not taste disasters?

---

21. *You are His.* The Masoretic text reads "You are no," which makes no sense as a biblical usage. For *lo'*, "no," this translation reads *lo*, "to Him" or "His." The idea, then, would be that Job's friends have gone over to God's side.

You see panic and you fear. You see the devastation I have suffered, and afraid that it might befall you as well, you hasten to become advocates for the punitive God.

30. *Does my palate not taste disasters?* The literal sense of the Hebrew verb is "understand."

7

Does not man have fixed service on earth,   1
      and like a hired worker's his days?
Like a slave he pants for shade,   2
      like a hired worker he waits for his pay.
Thus I was heir to futile moons,   3
      and wretched nights were allotted to me.
Lying down, I thought, When shall I rise?—   4
      Each evening, I was sated with tossing till dawn.
My flesh was clothed with worms and earth-clods,   5
      my skin rippled with running sores.
My days are swifter than the weaver's shuttle.   6
      They snap off without any hope.

---

1. *fixed service.* The more common meaning of the Hebrew *tsava'* is "army." By extension, the word also refers to any set term of service.

2. *shade . . . pay.* These terms are coordinated. The slave or the hired hand works in the hot sun all day, longing for the relief of shade, which he is likely to get only at evening, when he completes his work in the field. At the end of the day's work, he would also receive his pay.

3. *futile moons . . . wretched nights.* These words anticipate the account of tormented insomnia in verse 4 and of nightmares in verse 14.

5. *flesh . . . skin.* The language here clearly picks up the affliction with a terrible skin disease from the frame-story in Chapter 2.

6. *My days are swifter than the weaver's shuttle. / They snap off without any hope.* The shuttle moves back and forth rapidly, and the image illustrates the Job

7   Recall that my life is a breath.

            Not again will my eyes see good.

8   The eye of who sees me will not make me out.

            Your eyes are on me—I am gone.

9   A cloud vanishes and goes off.

            Thus, who goes down to Sheol will not come up.

10   He will not return to his home.

            His place will not know him again.

11   As for me, I will not restrain my mouth.

            I would lament with my spirit in straits

                I would speak when my being is bitter.

12   Am I Yamm or am I the Sea Beast,

            that You should put a watch upon me?

13   When I thought my couch would console me,

            that my bed would bear my lament,

14   You panicked me in dreams

            and in visions You struck me with terror.

---

poet's remarkable resourcefulness in drawing figurative language from unexpected semantic fields, including technology. His virtuosity is also evident in an untranslatable pun: the word for "hope," *tiqwah*, also means "thread." Awareness of the pun dictates the choice of the verb "snap off" in the translation. The brevity of human life and the irreversibility of death are a constant theme in Job's argument with God. Death as the inexorable end is central in verses 7–10.

12. *Am I Yamm or am I the Sea Beast?* Yamm is the sea-god of Canaanite mythology. Figured as a sea-monster, he is also called Tanin (as in the second name here), Rahab, and Leviathan. In some versions, the monster has seven heads. Yamm is subdued by Baal, the weather-god, and imprisoned so that he cannot rise up to overwhelm the land. Thus Job, acutely aware of the brevity of his life as mortal man, rhetorically asks the deity whether he is to be thought of as an undying monstrous god to be kept imprisoned under eternal guard. Variations of this potent myth will continue to crop up in the poem.

14. *You panicked me in dreams.* Job's troubled restless nights, entirely understandable given all he has suffered, are here attributed to God as still another form of torture. In the ancient Near East, dreams were generally thought to come from the gods.

And my throat would have chosen choking,   15
    my bones—death.
I am sickened—I won't live forever.   16
    Let me be, for my days are mere breath.
What is man that You make him great   17
    and that You pay heed to him?
You single him out every morning,   18
    every moment examine him.
How long till You turn away from me?   19
    You don't let me go while I swallow my spit.
What is my offense that I have done to You,   20
    O Watcher of man?
Why did You make me Your target,
    and I became a burden to You?

---

15. *my throat would have chosen choking.* Because the multivalent *nafshi* is bracketed with "choking," and parallel to "my bones," its use as a term for throat seems likely here, though it could also mean "my being."

16. *mere breath.* Here the term *hevel* favored by Qohelet is used.

17. *What is man that You make him great.* This whole line looks like a sardonic citation—and reversal—of Psalm 8:5–6: "What is man that You should remember him / and the son of man that You pay him heed. // And you make him little less than the gods, / with glory and grandeur You cloak him?" Instead of the psalmist's marveling over man's pre-eminence in creation, Job goes on to say, bitterly, that since man is such an inconsequential creature, it makes no sense for God to single him out—for such scathing, unblinking scrutiny.

19. *while I swallow my spit.* This startling phrase is another instance of the powerful physiological concreteness of Job's poetry.

20. *I became a burden to You.* The Masoretic text reads "to myself," but this is a famous case of a *tiqun sofrim*, a euphemistic scribal correction. That is, the scribes did not want to write the virtually blasphemous phrase that Job had become a burden to God, so they substituted the first-person pronoun for the second person.

21   And why do You not pardon my crime
                and let my sin pass away?
      For soon I shall lie in the dust.
                You will seek me, and I shall be gone.

---

21. *For soon I shall lie in the dust. / You will seek me, and I shall be gone.* Job invokes the previously expressed idea of the brevity of human life as grounds for asking God to relent from persecuting him: against the background of eternity, Job's life will be over in but a moment, so why should God persist in making that ephemeral moment such a miserable one?

8

And Bildad the Shuhite spoke out and he said,   1
How long will you jabber such things?—   2
     the words of your mouth, one huge wind.
Would God pervert justice,   3
     would Shaddai pervert what is right?
If your children offended Him,   4
     He dispatched them because of their crime.
If you yourself sought out El,   5
     and pleaded to Shaddai,
if you were honest and pure,   6
     by now He would rouse Himself for you,
          and would make your righteous home whole.
Then your beginning would seem a trifle   7
     and your latter day very grand.

---

3. *Would God pervert justice, / would Shaddai pervert what is right?* Bildad's complacent confidence in the traditional moral calculus is epitomized here not only in the substance of the statement but in the mechanically formulaic nature of the language. Throughout the speeches of Job's three critics, the poet performs a delicate balancing act in assigning them boilerplate poetry that reflects their conventional mind-set (see the comment on verse 8) and giving them some striking lines in which his own extraordinary poetic powers are manifest. As instances of this second category, one might consider "we are but yesterday" in verse 9 or the elaboration of the image of the spider's web in verses 14 and 15.

4. *He dispatched them because of their crime.* Eliphaz, the first of the three friends to speak, began with a diplomatic gesture toward Job. Now Bildad brutally tells a just bereaved father that his children all were killed by God because they must have committed some great offense.

8   For ask, pray, generations of old,
             take in what their fathers found out.

9   For we are but yesterday, unknowing,
             for our days are a shadow on earth.

10   Will they not teach you and say to you,
             and from their heart bring out words?

11   Will papyrus sprout with no marsh,
             reeds grow grand without water?

12   Still in its blossom, not yet plucked,
             before any grass it will wither.

13   Thus is the end of all who forget God,
             and the hope of the tainted is lost.

14   Whose faith is mere cobweb,
             a spider's house his trust.

15   He leans on his house and it will not stand,
             he grasps it and it does not endure.

---

8. *For ask, pray, generations of old.* The formulaic language of this entire verse is reminiscent of these lines from the Song of Moses: "Remember the days of old, / give thought to the years of times past. // Ask your father, that he may tell you, / your elders, that they may say to you. (Deuteronomy 32:7).

9. *For we are but yesterday, unknowing.* Because our lives are a fleeting moment, we can have no real knowledge, for which we must turn to the age-old wisdom of our forebears.
    for our days are a shadow on earth. This lovely phrase also happens to be formulaic, occurring in Psalms and elsewhere.

11. *Will papyrus sprout with no marsh.* There is an iron law in the moral realm as in nature. Just as the plant needs water to grow, a man cannot survive unless he is rooted in virtue. Only the righteous man is "like a tree planted by streams of water" (Psalm 1).
    grow grand. Pointedly, the poet uses the same verb, *yisgeh*, that is attached at the end of verse 7 to the prospect of Job's flourishing if he mends his ways.

13. *the end.* The Masoretic text here reads *'orhot*, "the paths," but the reading of the Septuagint *'aharit* (the same consonants with the order of the *r* and *h* reversed) makes more sense. *'Aharit* means "end" and, by extension, "destiny."

—He is moist in the sun,   16
    and his tendrils push out in his garden.
Round a knoll his roots twist,   17
    on a stone house they take hold.
If his place should uproot him   18
    and deny him—"I never saw you,"
why, this is his joyous way,   19
    from another soil he will spring.
Look, God will not spurn the blameless,   20
    nor hold the hand of evildoers.
He will yet fill your mouth with laughter   21
    and your lips with a shout of joy.
Your foes will be clothed in disgrace,   22
    and the tent of the wicked gone.

---

16. *—He is moist in the sun.* The subject here seems to switch from those who forget God to the virtuous man (hence the introduction of the dash in the translation). Perhaps, if one recalls the antithesis between the righteous and the wicked in Psalm 1, a phrase of transition, such as "Not so the righteous," was lost in transcription. In any case, the phrase "moist in the sun" means that he remains moist even in the blazing sun.

17. *Round a knoll his roots twist, / on a stone house they take hold.* This line, developing the pushing out of the tendrils from the previous line, is another instance of the Job poet's keen eye on the processes of nature as he elaborates his images.

19. *this is his joyous way, / from another soil he will spring.* The resilience—even in the face of disaster—of the righteous man goes beyond the laws of nature: uprooted, he will somehow find other soil from which to grow.

20. *God will not spurn the blameless, / nor hold the hand of evildoers.* At the end of his speech, Bildad again invokes stereotypical language, reminiscent of many psalms and of the Book of Proverbs.

22. *the tent of the wicked gone.* This concluding verset, formulaic in itself, picks up the image of the wicked man's flimsy habitation of cobweb from verses 14 and 15.

9

1	And Job spoke out and he said:
2	Of course, I knew it was so:
	how can man be right before God?
3	Should a person bring grievance against Him,
	He will not answer one of a thousand.
4	Wise in mind, staunch in strength,
	who can argue with Him and come out whole?
5	He uproots mountains and they know not,
	overturns them in His wrath.
6	He makes earth shake in its setting,
	and its pillars shudder.

---

2. *be right before God.* "Right" (Hebrew verbal root *ts-d-q*) here and elsewhere means being vindicated in a court of law. Thus the opening line announces the metaphor of legal disputation that dominates this whole chapter and recurs later in Job's argument. His sense of justice leads him to the legal metaphor, but he bitterly recognizes that he will never have his day in court because the two parties involved are absolutely unequal. God the accuser will always overwhelm him with His superior power and hold him guilty, whatever the facts of the case. One detects a fundamental idea that will lead to Kafka's *The Trial*.

5. *He uproots mountains.* These lines, down to the end of verse 10, invoke traditional poetic language generally used to celebrate God's power, as in many of the psalms and in Eliphaz's words (5:9–16), one line of which (5:9) is actually reproduced here (verse 10). But Job turns around the meaning of the traditional celebration of God: the divine power is deployed to dismay man and to take unfair advantage of him.

He bids the sun not to rise,   7
        and the stars He seals up tight.
He stretches the heavens alone   8
        and tramples the crests of the sea.
He makes the Bear and Orion,   9
        the Pleiades and the South Wind's chambers.
He performs great things without limit   10
        and wonders without number.
Look, He passes over me and I do not see,   11
        slips by me and I cannot grasp Him.
Look, He seizes—who can resist Him?   12
        Who can tell him, "What do You do?"
God will not relent His fury.   13
        Beneath Him Rahab's minions stoop.
And yet, as for me, I would answer Him,   14
        would choose my words with Him.
Though in the right, I can't make my plea.   15
        I would have to entreat my own judge.
Should I call out and He answer me,   16
        I would not trust Him to heed my voice.

---

7. *bids the sun.* The catalogue of God's sundry powers moves up vertically from earth to sky.

    and the stars He seals up tight. If the darkening of the sun in the first verset could refer to an eclipse, a natural phenomenon, this intensification in the second verset is altogether apocalyptic.

9. *the South Wind's chambers.* After the constellations, these may be mythological.

13. *Rahab's minions.* Rahab is another name for the primordial sea-monster, and so the minions (literally, "helpers") are his mythological henchmen. The subduing of Rahab's minions, like the trampling on the crests of the sea in verse 8, has its background in the conquest of the sea-god by the weather-god in Canaanite mythology.

17   Who for a hair would crush me
            and make my wounds many for naught.

18   He does not allow me to catch my breath
            as He sates me with bitterness.

19   If it's strength—He is staunch,
            and if it's justice—who can arraign Him?

20   Though in the right, my mouth will convict me,
            I am blameless, yet He makes me crooked.

21   I am blameless—I know not myself,
            I loathe my life.

22   It's all the same, and so I thought:
            the blameless and the wicked He destroys.

23   If a scourge causes death in an instant,
            He mocks the innocent's plight.

---

17. *for a hair.* The Hebrew *bise'arah* has a homonym and so could be construed, as many interpreters do, to mean "in a storm." (That is the word used for "whirlwind" or "storm" at the beginning of God's speech in 38:1.) But the poetic parallelism with "for naught" in the second verset argues for the sense of "for a hair"—that is, a mere trifle.

19. *If it's strength—He is staunch.* This line repeats the terms bracketed together in verse 4. As elsewhere, the Job poet has a keen eye for verbal and imagistic continuities in his poem.

22. *the blameless and the wicked he destroys.* This single verset compactly summarizes Job's argument against the mainline biblical notion of God's justice. Observing the reality of human events, including, of course, the disasters that have beset him, he sees no neat system of reward for the virtuous and punishment for the transgressor: the purported system of divine justice is essentially arbitrary.

23. *He mocks the innocent's plight.* The Hebrew uses a plural noun, which is represented as a singular here to accord with the singular "wicked man" in the next line. God's mockery of the innocent makes him not just arbitrary but sadistic.

The earth is given in the wicked man's hand,   24
        the face of its judges He veils.
                If not He—then who else?
And my days are swifter than a courier.   25
        They have fled and have never seen good,
slipped away like reed ships,   26
        like an eagle swooping on prey.
If I said, I would forget my lament.   27
        I would leave my grim mood and be gladdened,
I was in terror of all my suffering.   28
        I knew You would not acquit me.
I will be guilty.   29
        Why should I toil in vain?
Should I bathe in snow,   30
        make my palms pure with lye,

---

24. *The earth is given in the wicked man's hand.* Job now steps up his argument: God is not merely arbitrary; he actually tilts the conduct of the world to favor the wicked and prevents earthly judges (second verset) from seeing wrongdoing.

25. *my days are swifter than a courier.* In the two lines that begin here, the poet adopts an alternate strategy to the one of elaborating a single image through several lines that we observed in the previous chapter. Instead, he gives us three different images for swiftness in quick succession: from earth (the courier) to water (the reed ships) to sky (the eagle), with the last metaphor expressing the most violently rapid motion, and one that is not connected with human beings as are the two preceding ones.

27. *be gladdened.* The verb *'avligah* appears only in Job and hence its meaning is uncertain. A different understanding, "restrain myself," has become the general sense of the verb in modern Hebrew.

30. *in snow.* The translation follows the consonantal text (*ketiv*), which reads *bemo sheleg*. The marginal correction (*qeri*) reads *bemey sheleg*, "in snow waters."
    make my palms pure with lye. This is an especially violent instance of the pattern of intensification in second versets. Snow (or, snow water) would be pure, but the extreme cleansing measure of lye could do terrible damage to the palms.

31   You would yet plunge me into a pit,
            and my robes would defile me.

32   For He is not a man like me that I might answer Him,
            that we might come together in court.

33   Would there were an arbiter between us,
            who could lay his hand on us both,

34   who could take from me His rod,
            and His terror would not confound me.

35   I would speak, and I will not fear Him,
            for that is not the way I am.

---

31. *plunge me into a pit*. The clear implication is a pit filled with foul muck.

33. *an arbiter . . . who could lay his hand on us both*. This impossible fantasy underscores the actual maddening disparity between Job and the God who is persecuting him.

35. *I would speak, and I will not fear Him, / for that is not the way I am*. The wording of the second verset here is rather obscure, and divergent interpretations (and emendations) have been proposed. The general sense of the line, though, is clear: Job will not let the terror of God confound him or silence him. He still wishes to voice his protest, not succumbing to fear. In light of this, perhaps the force of the second verset is, as this translation understands it: I am not the kind of person to be subdued by fear of God's power, and so I will speak out.

10

My whole being loathes my life.   1
       Let me give vent to my lament.
           Let me speak when my being is bitter.
I shall say to God: Do not convict me.   2
       Inform me why You accuse me.
Is it good for You to oppress,   3
       to spurn Your own palms' labor,
           and on the council of the wicked to shine?
Do You have the eyes of mortal flesh,   4
       do You see as man would see?
Are Your days like a mortal's days,   5
       Your years like the years of a man,
that You should search out my crime   6
       and inquire for my offense?
You surely know I am not guilty,   7
       but there is none who saves from Your hand.

---

1. *Let me give vent.* The Hebrew verb *'azav* usually means "to forsake," and hence the meaning here is uncertain. The translation follows a proposal of Pope, but not with great conviction.

4. *Do You have the eyes of mortal flesh.* Job's complaint against God for persecuting him has two complementary sides. On the one hand, since God enjoys the perspective of divinity, it makes no sense for Him to treat Job as though He were an ignorant and angry human being. On the other hand (verses 20–23), since Job is a mere mortal whose days are few, it is unreasonable that this brief life span should be loaded with misery.

8   Your hands fashioned me and made me,
          and then You turn round and destroy me!

9   Recall, pray, that like clay You worked me,
          and to the dust You will make me return.

10   Why, You poured me out like milk
          and like cheese You curdled me.

11   With skin and flesh You clothed me,
          with bones and sinews entwined me.

12   Life and kindness you gave me,
          and Your precept my spirit kept.

---

8. *Your hands fashioned me and made me.* Picking up the word "hand" from the end of the previous verse is a bridge to a new segment of the text—such repetition of terms to mark the transition from one textual unit to another is a characteristic compositional move in the Bible in both poetry and prose. The poet launches on one of the most remarkable evocations of the sheer creatureliness of man in biblical literature.

and then You turn round. The Masoretic text reads "together all around," *yaḥad saviv.* This translation follows the reading of the Septuagint, which has *'aḥar sabota,* a phrase that makes better sense in context.

9. *like clay You worked me.* The poet picks up the image of God's creating the first human from clay in Genesis 2 and, characteristically, gives it artisanal concreteness.

and to the dust You will make me return. This notion of man's inevitable mortality (compare 1:23) is a constant theme of Job's.

10. *poured me out like milk / and like cheese You curdled me.* In keeping with his own vivid sense of metaphor and of reality—and again in the chiastic formulation he favors—the Job poet now goes beyond the figure of God the potter taken from Genesis. The embryo begins in a conjoining of fluid and protoplasm and then begins to take on the solidity of flesh, like milk congealing into cheese.

12. *and Your precept my spirit kept.* Given the way biblical syntax functions, it is also possible to switch subject and object around here (as most interpreters do): Your precept [providence?] kept my spirit, But the formulation sounds like several lines in Psalm 119, where it is the human being, or his spirit, who keeps God's precept (*pequdah*).

Yet these did You hide in Your heart;   13
      I knew that this was with You:
If I offended, You kept watch upon me   14
      and of my crime would not acquit me.
If I was guilty, alas for me,   15
    ~ and though innocent, I could not raise my head,
           sated with shame and surfeited with disgrace.
Like a triumphant lion You hunt me,   16
      over again wondrously smite me.
You summon new witnesses against me   17
      and swell up Your anger toward me—
           vanishings and hard service are mine.
And why from the womb did You take me?   18
      I'd breathe my last, no eye would have seen me.

---

13. *Yet these did You hide in Your heart.* Despite all God's seeming benefactions in giving Job physical shape and substance and afterward support, He all along hid hostile intentions toward his lovingly fashioned creature.

15. *guilty . . . innocent.* Job bitterly complains that he is damned if he does, damned if he doesn't by this inimical God.

16. *like a triumphant lion.* The syntactically obscure Hebrew of the received text here seems to say: "He triumphs, like a lion You hunt me."
   over again wondrously smite me. The translation is an interpretive guess about the enigmatic Hebrew, which literally reads: "You came back, You do wonders against [?] me."

17. *vanishings and hard service are mine.* This entire clause is one of the notable puzzles in Job. The second of the two nouns is the same word used at the beginning of Chapter 7 (and rendered there, because of the immediate context, as "fixed service"). The first noun, *halifot,* derives from a verb that means to slip away, to vanish, or to change. What Job may be saying is that his existence has become durance vile ("hard service") in which everything he would cling to slips between his fingers ("vanishings").

18. *And why from the womb did You take me?* This verse and the next obviously pick up the theme and some of the language of the death-wish poem in Chapter 3 (in particular 3:11–13).

19   As though I had not been, I would be.
                From belly to grave I'd be carried.
20   My days are but few—let me be.
                Turn away that I may have some gladness
21   before I go, never more to return,
                to the land of dark and death's shadow,
22   the land of gloom, thickest murk,
                death's shadow and disorder,
                        where it shines thickest murk.

21–22. *dark . . . death's shadow . . . gloom . . . murk.* These lines also recall the death-wish poem of Chapter 3 in deploying a whole series of synonyms for darkness, though with a difference: in the earlier poem, darkness was wished for; here it functions as an expression of the absolute extinction of life that awaits every human being in death's realm.

thickest. The usual function of the Hebrew *kemo* is as the preposition of comparison, "like," but that would yield here "gloom like murk," which does not make much sense. *Kemo,* however, occasionally occurs in poetic texts as an intensifier rather than as a preposition, and this translation construes it that way both here and in its recurrence in the next verse.

22. *where it shines thickest murk.* This is construed by some as a second-person singular referring to God, "and You shine," though a third-person feminine singular verb (the identical conjugated form) referring to "land" at the beginning of the verse seems more likely. In any case, this concluding image is a strong oxymoron (not a characteristic figure of biblical poetry): in the grim realm of death, shining itself is darkness.

11

And Zophar the Naamathite spoke out and he said: 1
Shall a swarm of words be unanswered,   2
            and should a smooth talker be in the right?
Your lies may silence folk,   3
            you mock and no one protests.
And you say: my teaching is spotless,   4
            and I am pure in your eyes.
Yet, if only God would speak,   5
            and He would open His lips against you,
would tell you wisdom's secrets,   6
            for prudence is double-edged.
                        And know, God leaves some of your crime
                        forgotten.

---

2. *Shall a swarm of words be unanswered.* The third of the friends immediately strikes an impatient note, beginning with a frontal attack on Job and making no diplomatic gesture toward him.
    smooth talker. Literally, "a man of lips."

5. *open His lips.* This idiom is probably chosen to jibe with the mocking reference to Job as a "man of lips" in verse 2.

6. *prudence is double-edged.* The application of "double-edged" (or perhaps simply "double"), *kiflayim*, is not entirely clear. Some would emend it to *pla'im*, yielding "prudence is wondrous."
    God leaves some of your crime forgotten. Zophar blithely assumes that Job is guilty of some crime so great that, even with all he has suffered for it, God has mercifully not exacted punishment for it to the full extent of the divine law.

7   Can you find what God has probed,
            can you find Shaddai's last end?
8   Higher than heaven, what can you do,
            deeper than Sheol, what can you know?
9   Longer than earth is its measure,
            and broader than the sea.
10 Should He slip away or confine or assemble,
            who can resist Him?
11 For He knows the empty folk,
            He sees wrongdoing and surely takes note.
12 And a hollow man will get a wise heart
            when a wild ass is born a man.
13 If you yourself readied your heart
            and spread out your palms to Him,
14 if there is wrongdoing in your hand, remove it,
            let no mischief dwell in your tents.

---

7. *Can you find what God has probed.* The next three verses are boilerplate language for the poetic celebration of God's world-embracing knowledge and power contrasted to man's puny grasp. When God begins to speak from the whirlwind, He will strike a similar theme, but in an entirely different poetic register and conceptual frame.

10. *Should He slip away or confine or assemble.* Interpretive attempts to find tight logical coherence in this sequence of three verbs have not been persuasive. It is best to understand them as three different instances of how God does whatever He pleases—disappears, imprisons, brings people together—without man's being able to control or affect His actions.

12. *a hollow man will get a wise heart / when a wild ass is born a man.* This pungent remark sounds, as Pope has suggested, like the invocation of a proverb.

13. *If you yourself readied your heart.* These words introduce an exhortation, which will continue to the end of Zophar's speech, for Job to turn back from his evil ways in the expectation that God will then forgive him and restore him to well-being and tranquility.

For then you will raise your face unstained,   15
   you will be steadfast and will not fear.
For you will forget wretchedness,   16
   like water gone off, recall it.
And life will rise higher than noon,   17
   you will soar, you will be like the morning.
And you will trust, for there is hope,   18
   will search, and lie secure.
You will stretch out, and none make you tremble,   19
   and many pay court to you.
And the eyes of the wicked will pine,   20
   escape will be lost to them,
     and their hope—a last gasp of breath.

---

15. *you will raise your face unstained*. The literal sense of the Hebrew is "without blemish," and Zophar may well be referring not only to the supposed moral taint in Job but to the fact that he has been hideously disfigured by his skin disease.

12

1   And Job spoke up and he said:
2   Oh yes, you are the people,
                and with you wisdom will die!
3   But I, too, have a mind like you,
                I am no less than you,
                        and who does not know such things?
4   A laughingstock to his friend I am,
                who calls to his God and is answered,
                        a laughingstock of the blameless just man.
5   The smug man's thought scorns disaster,
                readied for those who stumble.

---

2. *you are the people*. The sarcastic thrust of the line is evident: the friends have repeatedly claimed to be the voice of the wisdom of the generations and of society in general, and Job now bitterly turns this claim back against them.

3. *mind*. The Hebrew means "heart," but here its function as the organ of understanding in biblical physiology is clearly salient.
    who does not know such things? The literal sense is "who does not have such things?"

4. *who calls to his God and is answered . . . the blameless just man*. All this is, of course, a sarcastic reference to Job's three reprovers.

5. *The smug man's thought scorns disaster*. This is an interpretive guess at the Hebrew, which is extremely crabbed. The translation assumes that the obscure *'ashtut* is a shortened or defective form of *'eshtonot*, "thoughts." Something along the lines of the construction proposed here makes sense in context because the smug man scorning disaster and showing contempt for one who stumbles neatly applies to Job's friends.

The tents of despoilers are tranquil,   6
     provokers of El are secure,
         whom God has led by the hand.
Yet ask of the beasts, they will teach you,   7
     the fowl of the heavens will tell you,
or speak to the earth, it will teach you,   8
     the fish of the sea will inform you.
Who has not known in all these   9
     that the Lord's hand has done this?
In Whose hand is the breath of each living thing,   10
     and the spirit of all human flesh.
Does not the ear make out words,   11
     the palate taste food?
In the aged is wisdom,   12
     and in length of days understanding.
With Him are wisdom and strength,   13
     He possesses counsel and understanding.
Why, He destroys and there is no rebuilding,   14
     closes in on a man, leaves no opening.

---

6. *The tents of despoilers are tranquil.* Job's perception that the wicked often prosper, seemingly helped by God, is a direct rejoinder to the complacent moral calculus of the friends.

7. *Yet ask of the beasts.* It is the common knowledge of all creation, Job argues, that God's power causes everything. This sounds like a pious opening, in keeping with the view of the three companions, but he goes on to say that God's power is exercised destructively and capriciously.

10. *In Whose hand.* This entire verse is a virtual quotation of pious tradition—quoted in order to be subverted.

12. *In the aged is wisdom.* This verse and the next are a mocking imitation of the words of the three companions, and what the lines seem to say is abruptly reversed beginning in verse 14.

15   Why, He holds back the waters and they dry up,
              sends them forth and they turn the earth over.

16   With Him is power and prudence,
              His the duped and the duper.

17   He leads counselors astray
              and judges He drives to madness.

18   He undoes the sash of kings
              and binds a loincloth round their waist.

19   He leads priests astray,
              the mighty He misleads.

20   He takes away speech from the trustworthy,
              and sense from the elders He takes,

21   He pours forth scorn on princes,
              and the belt of the nobles He slackens,

22   lays bare depths from the darkness
              and brings out to light death's shadow,

23   raises nations high and destroys them,
              flattens nations and leads them away,

---

15. *the waters . . . dry up . . . they turn the earth over*. As Job sees it, God's power over creation is exerted chiefly in acts of destruction. The Voice from the Whirlwind will provide a strong rejoinder to this view.

16. *the duped and the duper*. The literal sense of the cognate Hebrew verbs is "the one who errs and the one who leads him to err."

17. *counselors . . . judges*. Those who should exercise wisdom are catastrophically deprived of it by God. In the following verses, other figures of authority—kings, elders, priests, the trustworthy—are also undone by God.

22. *lays bare depths from the darkness*. In the account of creation at the beginning of Genesis, God resoundingly calls forth light from the primordial darkness. Here He does exactly the opposite.

stuns the minds of the people's leaders,   24
        makes them wander in trackless wastes—
they grope in darkness without light,   25
        He makes them wander like drunken men.

---

24. *stuns*. Literally, "removes."

   trackless wastes. The "wastes" here, *tohu*, are the same term used for the primordial void in Genesis 1. Job continues the boldly heretical idea that God, far from being a beneficent Creator establishing order, uses His violent power perversely to mislead humankind.

25. *like drunken men*. The Hebrew uses a singular noun.

13

¹ Why, my eye has seen all,
         my ear has heard and understood.
² As you know, I, too, know.
         I am no less than you.
³ Yet I would speak to Shaddai,
         and I want to dispute with God.
⁴ And yet, you plaster lies,
         you are all quack-healers.
⁵ Would that you fell silent,
         and this would be your wisdom.
⁶ Hear, pray, my dispute,
         and to my lips' pleas listen closely.
⁷ Would you speak crookedness of God,
         and of Him would you speak false things?

---

1. *Why, my eye has seen all.* Job repeats the rhetorical move with which he began his speech (12:3), ever using one identical phrase, "I am no less than you."

3. *dispute.* The Hebrew verb, which can also mean "reprove," here has a legal connotation, and language expressing Job's desire to confront God in a court of law recurs through this chapter.

4. *plaster lies.* This idiom is also used in Psalms 119:69. It may derive from the idea of covering over the truth, as with plaster.
    quack-healers. The relevance of this epithet is that Job's companions seek to "heal" his grievous ills by telling him he has done wrong and that he will be restored to well-being if he renounces his evil ways.

Would you be partial on His behalf,   8
      would you plead the case of God?
Would it be good that He probed you,   9
      as one mocks a man would you mock Him?
He shall surely dispute with you   10
      if in secret you are partial.
Will not His majesty strike you with terror,   11
      and His fear fall upon you?
Your pronouncements are maxims of ash,   12
      your word-piles, piles of clay.
Be silent before me—I would speak,   13
      no matter what befalls me.
Why should I bear my flesh in my teeth,   14
      and my life-breath place in my palm?
Look, He slays me, I have no hope.   15
      Yet my ways I'll dispute to His face.

---

8. *Would you be partial on His behalf?* This is the crux of Job's argument against his pious reprovers. The law commands that no partiality be shown in judgment (see Leviticus 19:15), and this includes tipping the legal scales to make God seem just. To Job, this is "crookedness," "false things," and God Himself will not tolerate it. The rebuke to the three friends by God in the closing of the frame-story bears out Job in this regard.

10. *dispute.* The leading edge of the verb here is probably "reprove," but the translation preserves the continuity of terms in the Hebrew with verses 3 and 6.

12. *your word-piles, piles of clay.* All translations of the obscure Hebrew are conjectural. The construction here links *gabey* with the rabbinic *gibuv,* "heap" or "pile," and adds "word" interpretively.

14. *my life-breath place in my palm.* Elsewhere, this is an idiom for putting oneself in great danger, but the parallelism with the first verset would seem to highlight the physical concreteness of the image.

15. *Look, He slays me, I have no hope.* The intended sense of his famous line is ambiguous. This translation follows the consonantal received text (*ketiv*). The marginal correction (*qeri*) changes *lo'* (no) to *lo* (for him), yielding, "though He

16   Even that becomes my rescue,
           for no tainted man comes before Him.

17   Hear, O hear my word
           and my utterance in your ears.

18   Look, I have laid out my case,
           I know that I am in the right.

19   Who would make a plea against me?
           I would be silent then, breathe my last.

20   Just two things do not do to me,
           then would I not hide from Your presence.

21   Take Your palm away from me,
           and let Your dread not strike me with terror.

---

slay me, I will hope for Him." Others, without much warrant, understand the verb *yaḥel* as though it were a phonetically similar verb, *ḥul*, and translate "though He slay me, I will not quake."

16. *for no tainted man comes before Him.* Job, of course, is firm in his conviction that he himself is untainted, and so he is perfectly ready to stand before God. Thus, his very willingness to dispute with God is his "rescue."

19. *I would be silent then, breathe my last.* If anyone could really muster a case against Job, he would renounce his argument and be prepared to give up the ghost.

20. *Just two things do not do to me.* The Hebrew, moving from the second-person plural in earlier verses to the second-person singular, makes it clear that Job is now turning in direct address to God.

    then would I not hide from Your presence. That is, if You stopped intimidating me with Your overwhelming power (verse 21), I would be able to face You and make a case for my own defense.

21. *let Your dread not strike me with terror.* These words are only a seeming contradiction to Job's previous assertions that he is spoiling to have his day in court with God. He is in fact eager to do that, but he also feels overwhelmed by the sheer power of his divine persecutor, and so He pleads with God not to go on terrorizing him as a necessary pre-condition to his laying out his legal case.

Call and I will reply,   22
                or I will speak, and answer me.
How many crimes and offenses have I?   23
                My offense and my wrong, inform me.
Why do You hide Your face,   24
                and count me Your enemy?
Would You harry a driven leaf,   25
                and a dry straw would You chase,
that You should write bitter things against me,   26
                make me heir to the crimes of my youth?
And You put my feet in stocks,   27
                watch after all my paths,
                        on the soles of my feet make a mark.

And man wears away like rot,   28
                like a garment eaten by moths.

---

23. *My offense and my wrong.* The order of the two Hebrew nouns is reversed for the sake of the rhythm in English.

27. *stocks . . . paths . . . make a mark.* These are three discrete metaphors (if the feet are in stocks, logically there is no need to watch after the paths of the supposed miscreant), though they are all related as images of imprisonment or surveillance, and all three figures of speech are associated with feet (the middle image because in biblical idiom it is always feet that go on paths). It is likely that the marking of the soles of the feet refers to some sort of branding or tattooing that would be an indelible sign that the person is a felon.

28. *And man wears away like rot.* This entire verse actually belongs together with the first verse of the next chapter (the chapter divisions are late medieval and not intrinsic to the original biblical texts). Some scholars place this verse after 14:2. The Hebrew reads "And he wears away like rot," with the generic term *'adam,* "man," occurring at the beginning of the next line (14:1): "Man born of woman, / scant of days and sated with trouble."

14

Man born of woman,
>   scant of days and sated with trouble,

2   like a blossom he comes forth and withers,
>   and flees like a shadow—he will not stay.

3   Even on such You cast Your eye,
>   and me You bring in judgment with You?

4   [Who can make the impure pure?
>   No one.]

5   Oh, his days are decreed,
>   the number of his months are with You,
>   his limits You fixed that he cannot pass.

6   Turn away from him that he may cease,
>   until he serves out his day like a hired man.

---

3. *Even on such You cast Your eye.* Job, having evoked traditional biblical language for the brevity of human existence ("scant of days and sated with trouble, / like a blossom he comes forth and withers, / and flees like a shadow"), now asks God: how could You devote such terrible scrutiny to this ephemeral creature and how could you want to bring him to judgment? The verb rendered as "cast" is literally "open."

4. This verse has been bracketed because it looks dubious, and the second verset is too short to scan as poetry. Some have seen this as a marginal gloss that crept into the text.

6. *that he may cease.* A small emendation would convert this verb into an imperative, "cease" (that is, leave him be), which would fit better with "turn away from him."

   until he serves out his day like a hired man. Job picks up the image he used

For a tree has hope: 7
       though cut down, it can still be removed,
          and its shoots will not cease.
Though its root grow old in the ground   8
       and its stock die in the dust,
from the scent of water it flowers,   9
       and puts forth branches like a sapling.
But a strong man dies defeated,   10
       man breathes his last, and where is he?
Water runs out from a lake,   11
       and a river is parched and dries up,

---

earlier of human life as hard labor, with the worker longing for the day to come to an end.

7. *For a tree has hope.* Here the poet begins another of his fascinating forays into nature. Though he is of course aware that all things in nature eventually perish, he finds in the arboreal realm a strong image of survival that contrasts with the human condition. The cutting down of part of the trunk of a failing tree in order to allow it to regenerate appears to have been a known procedure in ancient agriculture.

9. *from the scent of water it flowers.* This quiet lyrical statement embodies a fine hyperbole: the very scent of water is enough to make the tree blossom.

10. *But a strong man dies defeated.* The noun *gever* usually indicates man in his virile strength, and is cognate with *gibor*, warrior. The adjective "strong" has been added here because there is an intended antithesis with "defeated" at the end of the verset. That verb usually means "to be weak," but in Exodus 32:18 it indicates defeat and is contrasted with "triumph" (*gevurah*, another cognate of *gever*). Since it would make little sense for the strong man to be weak after death, the probable sense is that he dies, finally defeated by death.

11. *a lake.* The Hebrew *yam* more often means "sea," but it can also mean "lake," and it makes much better sense for a lake to run dry than the sea.

12   but a man lies down and will not arise,

            till the sky is no more he will not awake

                and will not rouse from his sleep.

13   Would that You hid me in Sheol,

            concealed me till Your anger passed,

                set me a limit and recalled me.

14   If a man dies will he live?

            All my hard service days I shall hope

                until my vanishing comes.

15   Call out and I shall answer you,

            for the work of Your hand You should yearn.

16   For then You would count my steps,

            You would not keep watch over my offense.

17   My crime would be sealed in a packet,

            You would plaster over my guilt.

---

12. *till the sky is no more he will not awake.* This emphatic vision of the irrevocability of death, reiterated by Job, might conceivably be a rejoinder to a new idea of an afterlife beginning to emerge in the later biblical period, though the ephemerality of human life is a theme struck by many biblical writers, early and late.

13. *hid me in Sheol.* Job is surely not talking about survival after death, but rather, as elsewhere in biblical poetry, he invokes Sheol as a deep dark cavern below the ground where one might hide.

14. *until my vanishing comes.* Some understand *ḥalifati* as "my relief," but the primary sense of the verbal root is to be gone or slip away, with "change" as a secondary sense. Perhaps the poet is playing on both meanings of the term. See the comment on 10:17.

16. *For then You would count my steps.* Some scholars emend this clause as "For then You would not count my steps" in order to bring it into neat parallelism with the second verset. It might, however, have a positive meaning: Amos Hakham has proposed that the image is of a solicitous parent counting the steps of a toddler.

17. *sealed in a packet . . . plaster over my guilt.* The most plausible reading is that in this wished-for condition in which God would finally relent, any accusa-

And yet, a falling mountain crumbles,   18
      a rock is ripped from its place.
Water wears away stones,   19
       its surge sweeps up the dust of the earth,
         and the hope of man You destroy.
You overwhelm him forever, and he goes off,   20
       You change his face and send him away.
If his sons grow great, he will not know.   21
       And should they dwindle, he will not notice them.
But the flesh upon him will ache,   22
       his own being will mourn for him.

---

tions against Job would be sealed and covered up—in effect, expunged from the legal record.

19. *and the hope of man You destroy.* There is a pointed contrast between the solid elements of nature—mountain, rock, stones, earth—that are nevertheless overturned, and the fragility of human hope. At the same time, these metaphors suggest an analogy between the awesome forces of destruction in nature and God's implacability toward man.

20. *goes off.* Here and elsewhere, this is a euphemism for death—one that highlights the irrevocable disappearance of the man who dies.
    You change his face. Ibn Ezra plausibly understands this as a reference to the rictus of the face distorted in death.

22. *But the flesh upon him will ache.* In order to concretize the awful bleakness of death, the poet uses what may be a poetic conceit or perhaps the trace of a folk-belief: the newly dead, his flesh turned rigid and then quickly the object of decay, experiences a kind of after-image of life that is nothing but pain. In any event, the idea is clear that the dead man knows nothing of the fate of the offspring in whom he invested so many expectations but is instead locked into the anguish of his own physical extinction.

15

1   And Eliphaz the Temanite spoke up and he said:

2   Will a wise man speak up ideas of hot air
          and with the east wind fill his belly?

3   Who disputes through speech will not avail
          and from words will get no profit.

4   So you thwart reverence,
          take away prayer to God.

5   For your crime guides your mouth,
          and you choose the tongue of the cunning.

6   Your own mouth condemns you, not I,
          and your lips bear witness against you.

---

2. *hot air*. The literal sense of the Hebrew is "wind." The parallel term in the second verset, "east wind," is a hot, blighting wind that blows from the desert. It is noteworthy that in this second round of the debate, Eliphaz, whose first speech (Chapter 4) began diplomatically, launches a frontal assault against Job, denouncing him as a juggler of empty words and then an impious sinner (verses 4–6).

4. *take away*. The somewhat odd verb, which means to remove something from a whole or to subtract, is picked up in a slightly different sense in verse 8, when Job is sarcastically asked whether he has taken away wisdom from the divine council.

6. *Your own mouth condemns you*. Job's staunch defense of his own integrity as well as his challenge to God is taken by Eliphaz as clear evidence that he is an impious liar.

Are you the first man to be born,   7
> before the hills were you spawned?

Did you listen at God's high council,   8
> take away wisdom for yourself?

What do you know that we don't know,   9
> understand, that is not with us?

The gray-haired and the aged are with us,   10
> far older than your father.

Are God's consolations too little for you,   11
> and the word that He whispered to you?

How your heart has taken you off,   12
> how your eyes have prompted you,

that you should turn your hot air against God   13
> and let out words from your mouth!

What is man that he should merit   14
> and that he born of woman should be in the right?

Why, His holy ones He does not trust,   15
> and the heavens are not pure in His eyes.

All the more, one vile and foul,   16
> man who drinks mischief like water.

---

7. *Are you the first man to be born.* Again, the wisdom of the ages, and of age (compare verse 10), is invoked as an argument against what the friends construe as Job's arrogant presumption.

11. *God's consolations . . . the word that He whispered to you.* No mention of such solicitous address by God to Job has been made, but the conventionally pious Eliphaz may assume that God always whispers messages of consolation, even to egregious sinners like Job.

13. *turn your hot air against God . . . let out words.* This line is a pointed verbal echo of verses 2 and 3 and has been translated to make that clear, as it is in the Hebrew.

15. *Why, His holy ones He does not trust.* The holy ones, qedoshim, would be angelic beings, members of the celestial entourage. Perfection is God's alone, and His uncompromising gaze finds defects in all other beings, celestial and terrestrial.

17 I shall declare to you, listen to me,
            and what I saw I shall recount,
18 what the wise men have told
            and have not concealed from their fathers.
19 To them alone the land was given,
            no stranger passed in their midst.
20 All the wicked man's days he quakes,
            and few years are set aside for the tyrant.
21 The sound of fear is in his ears,
            in peacetime the despoiler overtakes him.
22 He trusts not to come back from darkness,
            and he is targeted by the sword.
23 He wanders for bread—where is it?
            He knows that the dark day awaits him.
24 Failing and foe bring him terror,
            overwhelm him like a king set for siege.
25 For he reached out his hand against God,
            and Shaddai he assaulted.

---

19. *To them alone the land was given.* The relevance of this whole verse to Eliphaz's argument is unclear. Perhaps he means to say that the sages of old, from whom he and his companions have inherited their wisdom, were free from the misleading influences of foreign presences, and hence their wisdom was irreproachable.

24. *Failing and foe.* The literal sense of the Hebrew is "foe and distress," but the two Hebrew terms are locked together in alliteration, *tsar umetsukah*, an effect the translation tries to imitate.
    set for siege. The noun *kidor* appears only here. Guesses at its meaning have been made through proposed Semitic cognates, but the sense remains uncertain.

25. *For he reached out his hand against God, / and Shaddai he assaulted.* If this general portrait of the wicked man is intended by Eliphaz to refer at least by implication to Job, the image of a martial assault on God is truly extravagant. Tur-Sinai has proposed that these lines hark back to the Canaanite creation myth, in which the assailant against El, the sky-god (that is the term for God used here), would be a mythic warrior allied with the primordial sea-monster.

He rushes against him in neck-armor,   26
    with his thickly bossed shield.
His face is covered with fat,   27
    his loins are layered with blubber.
He dwells in ruined towns,   28
    in houses where no one lives
        that are readied for rubble-heaps.
He gets no riches, his wealth will not stand,   29
    his yield does not bend to the earth.
He does not turn away from darkness,   30
    his shoots the flame withers,
        he turns away in the breath of his mouth.

---

26. *in neck-armor*. The Hebrew simply says "in neck." The translation, with an eye to the parallel phrase in the second verset, follows the proposal of Tur-Sinai and Pope that the word is an ellipsis for armor worn to protect the neck.

27. *fat . . . blubber*. The image of a fat warrior may seem incongruous, but excessive fat in Psalms is an image of wicked complacency and self-indulgence. The borderline, moreover, between being fat and robust is a little vague in the ancient Near East (one might perhaps think of the aggressive build of an NFL lineman).

28. *He dwells in ruined towns*. After the wicked man's presumption in assaulting God, he is doomed to a fate of misery, living among ruins, failing in all his endeavors (verses 29–34).

30. *he turns away in the breath of his mouth*. This translation reproduces the enigmatic character of the Hebrew, where each word is intelligible but they make little sense together. The verb "turns away," *yasur*, is identical with the verb at the beginning of the first verset, where it is used with a negative, but its meaning in this verset is unclear. The contention of many interpreters that it refers to death ("pass away") flies in the face of its use elsewhere in the Bible, where it always refers to turning away or swerving from a set trajectory or disengaging from someone or something. Perhaps, if the received text here is authentic, it might mean that the evil man through his own empty and self-deluding talk swerves from the right path.

31   Let the wayward not trust in vain things,
                for in vain will his recompense be.
32   Untimely he will wilt,
                and his boughs will not be green.
33   He will shed his unripe fruit like a vine
                and cast off his bloom like an olive tree.
34   For the crowd of the tainted is barren,
                and fire consumes bribery's tent.
35   Pregnant with wretchedness, giving birth to crime,
                their belly prepares deceit.

---

31. *recompense.* Or "transformation." The translation is somewhat conjectural.

32. *wilt.* The Masoretic text has *timalei'*, "you will fill," which makes little sense either grammatically or semantically. This translation assumes an emendation to *yimol*, "he will wilt" or "he will wither."

16

*A*nd Job spoke up and he said: 1
                 I have heard much of this sort,
                            wretched consolers are you all.
        Is there any end to words of hot air,   2
                 or what compels you to speak up?
        I, too, like you, would speak,   3
                 were you in my place
        I would din words against you,   4
                 and would wag my head over you.
        I would bolster you with my speech,   5
                 my lips' movement would hold back pain.

---

4. *din.* The root of this verb *ḥ-b-r* looks as though it were the same as the common Hebrew verb that means "to join," but, as J. J. Finklestein has shown, it actually derives from a different root (a palatal consonant *ḥet* rather than a guttural one) that indicates "noise."

wag my head over you. Here the gesture appears to indicate mockery rather than sympathy.

5. *I would bolster you with my speech.* The Hebrew says "my mouth." The switched attitude here is a little confusing. First Job said that, were his friends in his place, he would speak just as they have done, dinning accusatory words into their ears. Now he says he would comfort them. Perhaps he wants to suggest that, unlike them, he would follow accusation with genuine consolation.

hold back pain. The Hebrew says merely "hold back," but the verb in immediate context may be an ellipsis since "pain . . . held back" appears in the next line.

6   Should I speak, my pain would not be held back,
                should I desist, it would not go away from me.
7   But now He has worn me out.
                You devastate all my people.
8   And You crease my face, it becomes a witness,
                my gauntness deposes against me.
9   His wrath tore me apart, seethed against me,
                He gnashed His teeth against me,
                        my foe's eyes glare at me.
10   They gaped with their mouths against me,
                in scorn they struck my cheeks,
                        together they close ranks round me.
11   God delivers me to a wrongdoer
                lets me fall in the hands of the wicked.

---

6. *my pain would not be held back.* This is another slightly disorienting shift. Job, having taken up the fantasy that he and his three interlocutors would be in reversed positions, now drops it abruptly, for it has made him think again of his own unrelenting anguish. Now he returns to the familiar theme of his intolerable suffering: whether he speaks or is silent, it will not leave him.

7. *You devastate all my people.* The reference could well be to Job's dead children and servants. The switch from third person to second person between the two versets is fairly common in biblical usage.

8. *crease my face . . . my gauntness.* Job's ravaged body, a highly visible external sign of his suffering, has been construed as incriminating evidence that he must have done something to deserve it.

9. *tore me apart.* This violent verb is used for predatory animals rending their prey.
        my foe's eyes glare at me. The literal sense of the verb is "to hone" or "to sharpen."

10. *They gaped.* Though Job sees God as his real persecutor, here he imagines a crowd of enemies—in all likelihood, God's henchmen—who attack him and humiliate him. The three friends have, of course, arrogated to themselves the role of such henchmen.

I was tranquil—he shook me to pieces,   12
      seized my nape and broke me apart,
           set me up as a target for Him.
His archers gathered around me.   13
      He pierces my kidneys, pitiless,
           He spills my gall to the ground.
He breaches me breach upon breach,   14
      rushes at me like a warrior.
Sackcloth I sewed for my scabs,   15
      and I thrust my horn in the dust.
My face was reddened from weeping,   16
      and on my eyelids—death's shadow,
for no outrage I had done,   17
      and my prayer had been pure.
Earth, O do not cover my blood,   18
      and let there be no place for my scream.

---

12. *shook me to pieces . . . broke me apart.* In the Hebrew, the two verbs of violent assault resemble each other phonetically and morphologically: *wayefar-pereini, wayefatspetseini.*

14. *breaches me . . . rushes at me.* The two versets neatly illustrate the general pattern in biblical poetry of introducing narrative development between the first verset and the second: in the martial metaphor, first the defensive walls are breached, then the warrior rushes forward through the breach in attack.

15. *scabs.* Many interpreters, on the basis of Aramaic and Arabic cognates, understand this simply as "skin" (this is the sole occurrence of the noun *geled* in the Bible). But in rabbinic Hebrew the word means the scab over a wound, and that seems more directly relevant to Job's plight.
    my horn. As repeatedly in Psalms and elsewhere, the horn is a symbol of strength.

18. *Let there be no place.* Within the earth itself there should be no place to hide the scream or cry. The conjunction of the earth's not covering the blood and not muffling the scream is probably a reminiscence of God's words to Cain, "Your brother's blood cries out [the same verbal root as here] from the soil" (Genesis 4:10). This allusion would implicitly cast God in the role of the archetypal murderer.

19   Even now, in the heavens my witness stands,
               one who vouches for me up above.

20   My advocates, my companions!
               Before God my eye sheds tears.

21   Let a man dispute with God
               and a human with his fellow.

22   For a handful of years will come,
               and on the path of no return I shall go.

17.1   My spirit is wrecked,
               my days flicker out.
                      Graves are what I have.

---

19. *my witness stands.* The Hebrew simply uses the implied verb "to be." The witness up above is surely not God but rather the impartial mediator or judge for whom Job has already expressed a longing.

20. *My advocates, my companions!* If the received text is correct here, the only way to understand these words is as a bitingly sarcastic address to the three companions.

21. *Let a man dispute with God, / and a human with his fellow.* The Hebrew is somewhat obscure. The meaning may be: would that a man might have a confrontation in court with God just as he would with a human accuser or legal adversary.

17

1. *My spirit is wrecked.* This triadic line, though set at the beginning of the next chapter in the conventional division into chapters, clearly concludes this whole section of Job's complaint.

So help me, mockery is with me,   2
        in their galling my eye wakes through the night.
Come, stand pledge for me,   3
        who will offer his handshake for me?
Since their heart You hid from reason,   4
        and so You will not exalt them.
For profit he informs on friends,   5
        and his sons' eyes waste away.
He has made me a byword of peoples,   6
        spit in the face, I became.

---

2. *So help me*. The Hebrew *'im lo'* (ostensibly, "if not") is here the formula for beginning a solemn oath.

my eye wakes through the night. The sense of the clause is unclear. The simple meaning of the verb is "to spend the night." The phrase might suggest insomnia because of excitation.

4. *heart . . . reason*. As often elsewhere, the heart is invoked as the organ of understanding.

5. *For profit he informs on friends*. This verset is the first of several in this chapter that are not readily intelligible and probably reflect a glitch in scribal transmission. The literal sense of the three Hebrew words is "for-a-portion he-tells friends." This translation, like all others, is no more than a guess.

6. *spit in the face*. The Hebrew *tophet* is obscure. The translation, mindful of a possible Aramaic cognate, interprets it as an act of humiliation parallel to "a byword of peoples," only more extreme.

7   My eye is bleared from anguish,
        and my limbs are all like shadow.

8   The upright are outraged by this,
        and the innocent roused over the tainted.

9   The righteous will cling to his way,
        and the clean of hands augment in strength.

10   And yet, all of you, return and come,
        but I won't find a wise man among you.

11   My days have passed,
        my plans pulled apart,
           the desires of my heart.

12   Night they would turn into day,
        "Light is near"—in the face of darkness.

13   If I hope for Sheol as my home,
        that I might cushion my couch with darkness,

14   to the Pit I would say, "My father you are;
        my mother and sister, the worm,"

---

9. *The righteous will cling to his way.* Though in the previous verse Job mentions the outrage of the upright over his unwarranted suffering, this celebration of the staunchness and the augmented strength of the righteous sounds more like the three friends than like Job, and it is possible that the entire verse doesn't belong here.

12. *Night they would turn into day.* Though some critics see this verse as anomalous in context, it makes plausible sense as a withering characterization by Job of the "comfort" his three friends have been offering him. Thus, Bildad has said (8:5–7) that if Job would only seek God wholeheartedly, his latter days would be far more glorious than his beginnings. For the suffering Job, such language amounts to saying that "light is near—in the face of darkness."

13. *If I hope for Sheol as my home.* This desire for release from anguish through death is perfectly consonant with the death-wish poem (Chapter 3) with which Job began his complaint.

where then is my hope,   15
           and my good—who can glimpse it?
Will it go down to the bars of Sheol,   16
           altogether in the dust will it plunge?

---

15. *my good*. The Masoretic text has *tiqwati*, "my hope," which is the last word of the first verset and the immediately preceding word in the Hebrew text. Repetition of this sort is not common in biblical poetry, and one suspects dittography (the inadvertent scribal duplication of a word or of letters in sequence). This translation follows the Septuagint, which appears to have used a Hebrew text that read *tovati*, "my good."

16. *Will it go down to the bars of Sheol*. The Hebrew construct plural term *badey* is obscure in context. Elsewhere, *bad* is a pole, as in the poles used to carry the sanctuary, so "bars"—perhaps the bars that shut the gates of the underworld— might be appropriate here. This is also the surmise of the Revised Standard Version. The antecedent of "it" is "my hope" in the previous verse. Since the hope Job had expressed was to go down to Sheol, he may be saying, bitterly, that his hope is nowhere to be seen because it has plunged into the realm of extinction without him.

18

1   And Bildad the Shuhite spoke up and he said:
2   How long till you both put an end to words?
                    Consider, and then we may speak.
3   Why are we reckoned as beasts,
                    besotted in your eyes?
4   Who tears himself apart in his wrath—
                    for you shall the earth be forsaken
                        and the rock ripped from its place?
5   Yes, the light of the wicked will gutter,
                    and the spark of his flame will not shine.
6   Light goes dark in his tent,
                    and his lamp gutters before him.

---

2. *you both.* The Hebrew verbs in this verse and the next are plural, and the translation follows Raymond Scheindlin in assuming that Bildad is addressing Eliphaz and Zophar. He would then be expressing impatience with them: how long will you go on with your ineffectual speech, behaving as though the three of us were imbeciles, when the response to Job's outrageous stance is plain and clear, as I shall now demonstrate?

an end. The Hebrew *qintsey* is anomalous, and this rendering reflects a tradition of Hebrew commentators going back to the Middle Ages that links it with *qeits*, "end."

4. *Who tears himself apart.* As the reference switches to a single person, we realize that the guilty party is Job.

for you shall the earth be forsaken. There is, Bildad angrily contends, an established order of things that Job in his egotistical presumption seeks to overturn.

His vigorous strides are straitened,   7
> his own counsel flings him down.

For his feet are caught in a net   8
> and he treads on a tangle of lines.

The trap grips his heel,   9
> the trip-cord seizes him.

A rope is hidden for him in the ground,   10
> his snare upon the path.

All round terrors befright him,   11
> and they scatter at his feet.

His vigor turns to hunger,   12
> disaster ready at his side.

Eating his limbs and skin,   13
> Death's Firstborn eats his limbs,

tears him from his tent, his stronghold,   14
> and sends him off to the King of Terrors.

---

8. *For his feet are caught in a net.* As elsewhere in the poetry of the three friends, Bildad resorts to the boilerplate language of Psalms that describes the disaster inevitably awaiting the wicked man. At the same time, one sees here the rich resourcefulness of synonymity of the Job poet, who in three lines of verse deploys six different terms for a trap.

11. *they scatter at his feet.* The received text reads "scatter him," but "him" is not a logical object of "scatter." The Septuagint reads "they trip him up at his feet."

12. *His vigor turns to hunger.* More literally, "his vigor becomes hungry." The term *'on*, "vigor," is the same word associated with the once confident strides of the wicked man in verse 7.

13. *limbs.* This is the same doubtful term, *badim*, that appears in 17:16, so the translation is conjectural, though reference to a body part attached to skin seems probable.
    Death's Firstborn. This is clearly a mythological figure, as is the King of Terrors in the next verse. The Hebrew term for death, *mawet* (in the construct form *mot*), is identical with the name of the Canaanite god of death, Mot. The vivid cannibalistic image of Death gnawing away at the limbs of the transgressor is not conventional language.

15 He dwells in a tent not his,
            his abode is strewn with brimstone.
16 Below, his roots dry up,
            and above, his foliage withers.
17 His remembrance is lost from the earth,
            no name has he abroad.
18 They thrust him from light to darkness,
            and from the world of men drive him out.
19 No son nor grandson in his kinfolk,
            and no remnant where he sojourned.
20 At his fate, latecomers are dumbstruck
            and old-timers are seized with dread.
21 Surely these are the dwellings of evil,
            and this the place of him who knew not God.

---

15. *He dwells in a tent not his.* This could well be a continuation of the mytho-logical imagery: the wicked man is torn from his own tent, where he thought himself secure, and dragged down to the realm of the King of Terrors, where he finds himself in an abode of chaos and dissolution strewn with brimstone (an agent of destruction).

18. *They thrust him.* These anonymous plural figures are emissaries of destruc-tion, perhaps henchmen of the King of Terrors.
    the world of men. The Hebrew *tevel* indicates the inhabited world—hence "of men" in the translation.

19. *No son nor grandson.* The cutting off of a man's hereditary line is, of course, an ultimate curse in the biblical world.

20. *his fate.* The literal sense of the Hebrew is "his day."
    latecomers . . . old-timers. The terms, *'aḥaronim* and *qadmonim*, refer to latter-day or recent people and to people from earlier times or predecessors. Exegetical efforts to align these terms with west and east are unconvincing.

21. *Surely these.* The patness of Bildad's concluding formulation neatly reflects the confident complacency of his ethical outlook.

19

And Job spoke up and he said: 1
How long will you cause me grief   2
          and crush me with words?
Ten times now you have shamed me,   3
          you do not blush to spurn me.
And if in fact I have erred,   4
          with me shall my error lodge.
If in fact you vaunt over me   5
          and reprove me with my disgrace,
know, then, that God has undone me   6
          and encircled me with His net.
Look, I scream "Outrage!" and I am not answered,   7
          I shout and there is no justice.
My path He blocked and I cannot pass,   8
          and on my ways He set darkness.

---

2. *How long will you cause me grief*. Job's opening formulation is an explicit rejoinder to the beginning of Bildad's immediately preceding speech (18:2), "How long till you both put an end to words." The term "words," *milim*, also appears in Job's speech, at the end of this verse.

7. *I scream "Outrage!"* Screaming this word, *ḥamas*, would have been a desperate call for help when, say, a person was attacked by thugs. There is an implicit narrative momentum in the sequence of lines that begins here. First, Job is assailed and screams for help; then he tries to run away but his path is blocked; then he is seized, stripped, and shattered on all sides. Verse 11 summarizes this whole development, and then Job moves on from the metaphor of being mugged or attacked by brigands to a military metaphor (verse 12).

9   My glory He stripped from me,
              and took off the crown from my head.

10   He shattered me on all sides—I am gone.
              He uprooted my hope like a tree.

11   His wrath flared up against me,
              and He reckoned me one of His foes.

12   Together His troops have come,
              laid siege-works up against me
                  and encamped around my tent.

13   My brothers He distanced from me,
              and my comrades turned strangers to me.

14   My dear ones withdrew, my friends forgot me.

15   Those who dwelled in my house and my slave-girls
              reckoned me as a stranger,
                  I was an alien in their eyes.

16   To my servant I called and he did not answer,
              with my mouth I pleaded to him.

17   My breath became strange to my wife,
              I repelled my very own children.

---

13. *My brothers He distanced from me.* As elsewhere, Job's personal losses and physical affliction are painfully compounded by his becoming a social pariah, a state to which the scathing rebuke of the three companions has clearly contributed.

16. *To my servant I called and he did not answer.* Together with the estrangement from his social peers, Job has lost the authority that his wealth enabled him to enjoy: the people who had been his household staff—in all probability, "servant" implies slave status, like the feminine term in the previous verse—treat him like a stranger and ignore him. Even children (verse 18) mock him.

    with my mouth I pleaded. Though this sounds a little awkward, the obtrusion of the mouth prepares the way for Job's foul breath in the next verse.

17. *My breath . . . I repelled.* Job is probably thinking of the disgusting symptoms of his disease. It is perhaps poetic license for him to invoke his children, all of whom have been killed. "My very own children" is literally "the children of my belly."

Even little ones despised me—   18
>   when I rose, they spoke against me.
All my intimates reviled me,   19
>   those I loved have turned against me.
My bones stuck to my skin and my flesh,   20
>   and I escaped with the skin of my teeth.
Mercy, have mercy on me, my companions,   21
>   for God's hand has blighted me.
Why do you hound me like God,   22
>   and of my flesh you are not sated?
Would, then, that my words were written,   23
>   that they were inscribed in a book,
with an iron pen and lead   24
>   to be hewn in rock forever.
But I know my redeemer lives,   25
>   and in the end he will stand up on earth,

---

19. *intimates*. The literal sense of the Hebrew is "people of my council."

20. *I escaped with the skin of my teeth*. Because teeth don't have skin, some scholars have tried to emend the text. But poetry need not be bound by anatomical logic. The verse should be read as vivid hyperbole: I was so ravaged by disease and deprivation, turned into mere skin and bones, that all I came away with was the (essentially nonexistent) skin of my teeth.

22. *hound me like God*. The frequently used term for "God," *'el*, could also be understood as "a god," and this is how Scheindlin generally treats it. But the point seems to be that there is one God who is perversely persecuting Job, not that the gods in general are inimical to man.
     of my flesh you are not sated. Job represents his three reprovers as ghastly cannibals.

24. *an iron pen and lead*. The lead, initially puzzling, was explained by Rashi as the material used to darken the incised letters in order to make them more visible, and archaeology now offers some confirmation of this idea.

25. *I know my redeemer lives*. This famous line, long the subject of Christological interpretation, in fact continues the imagery of a legal trial to which Job reverts so often. The redeemer is someone, usually a family member, who will

26   and after they flay my skin,
              from my flesh I shall behold God.
27   For I myself shall behold,
              my eyes will see—no stranger's,
                    my heart is harried within me.
28   Should you say, "How more can we hound him?
              The root of the thing rests in him."
29   Fear the sword,
              for wrath is a sword-worthy crime,
                    so you may know there is judgment.

---

come forth and bear witness on his behalf, and the use of "stand up" in the second verset has precisely that courtroom connotation.

26. *and after they flay my skin, / from my flesh I shall behold God.* Amos Hakham boldly relates this strong line to Job's wish to incise his words in stone, paraphrasing it as follows: "The scars and the bruises in my flesh are the writing God inscribes in my flesh instead of the inscription I sought to make." If Hakham is right, Job would be representing himself here somewhat like the condemned man in Kafka's "In the Penal Colony" who is meant to come to an illuminating understanding of his crime through the terrible machine that inscribes his transgression on his flesh. Job, however, does not concede that he has sinned, so the idea he expresses is that through all his suffering, through the tatters of his lacerated flesh, he will in the end behold God, come face-to-face with his divine persecutor and finally vindicate himself.

27. *my heart is harried within me.* The Hebrew says literally "my kidneys come to an end [or, long] within me." This involves a prominent alliteration, *kalu kilyotay*, that the translation tries to approximate.

29. *there is judgment.* The very last word of Job's speech is problematic. The Masoretic editors were not entirely sure whether it should be pronounced *sha-dun* or *sheidin* or perhaps something in between. Consequently, interpretations have varied wildly. Some see a reference to demons, *sheidim*, or to a pagan god. This translation follows a tradition that goes back to a couple of the ancient versions and to Rashi in the Middle Ages that construes the enigmatic term as *shedin*, that there is judgment, or law.

20

Ａnd Zophar the Naamathite spoke out and he said: 1
So my thoughts give me a rejoinder,   2
       by dint of my inner sense.
I have heard the reproof to my shame,   3
       and a spirit from my mind lets me answer.
This have you known of old,   4
       from when man was set upon earth?
For the wicked men's gladness is fleeting,   5
       and the tainted man's joy but a moment.
Though his summit ascend to the heavens,   6
       and his head reach up to the clouds,
like his turd, he is lost forever,   7
       those who see him will say, "Where is he?"
Like a dream he flies off, none will find him,   8
       he will melt like a nighttime vision.

---

2. *by dint of my inner sense.* Beginning with this clause, the language of Zophar's entire speech is at many points unusually crabbed, and as a result some of the translation is conjectural. The term *ḥush* here has been construed by some to mean "hurry" or "agitation," though it seems more likely that it carries its other meaning of "sense"—Zophar confidently declaring that his own theologically correct intuition has clearly instructed him how to answer Job.

3. *a spirit from my mind.* Literally, "my understanding."

7. *like his turd, he is lost forever.* The preceding lines about the ephemerality of the wicked man's success are boilerplate Wisdom poetry. Here, however, Zophar expresses his idea with scatological pungency. "Turd" makes a vivid counterpoint to "heavens" and "clouds" in the preceding line.

9 The eye that observed him will do it no more,
nor again will his place behold him.

10 His sons will placate the poor,
and his hands will give back his wealth.

11 His bones that were full of youth
with him will lie in the dust.

12 Should evil be sweet in his mouth
and he hide it under his tongue,

13 should he cherish it, not let it go,
and hold it back on his palate,

14 his food will turn in his innards—
vipers' bile in his gut.

15 Goods he swallowed he will vomit,
from his belly God will expel them.

16 He will suck the venom of vipers,
the tongue of the asp will slay him.

17 He will see no streams of rivers
and brooks of honey and curds.

18 He will give back gain, not swallow it,
like the goods, their value, and take no pleasure.

19 For he crushed, he forsook the poor,
he stole a house that he did not build.

---

14. *his food will turn in his innards— / vipers' bile in his gut*. This constitutes a strong culminating reversal of the extended description (verses 12 and 13) of the wicked man selfishly and sensually preserving in his mouth the sweet taste of his ill-gotten bounty.

15. *from his belly God will expel them*. The literal sense of the phrase is "from his belly God will reduce him to poverty [or, take away all his gain]." The belly is featured prominently throughout this tirade as the bodily image of the wicked men's greed.

18. *like the goods, their value, and take no pleasure*. This entire verset is extremely cryptic in the Hebrew. It might possibly mean that he will have to give back (first verset) both the goods he has wrongfully seized or their full value without having had the chance to enjoy them.

For he will not know quiet in his belly,　　　　　　　　　　20
　　　　with his treasure he will not escape.
There is no remnant of his food,　　　　　　　　　　　　21
　　　　so he cannot hope to have bounty.
When his need is filled he feels distressed—　　　　　　22
　　　　every wretched man's hand comes against him.
Let him fill his belly,　　　　　　　　　　　　　　　　23
　　　　He will send against him His burning wrath
　　　　　　　　to rain down upon him as he eats.
Should he flee from the iron weapon,　　　　　　　　　24
　　　　a bow of bronze will pierce him.
Unsheathed, it comes out through his back,　　　　　　25
　　　　the blade through his gall,
　　　　　　　　casting terror upon him.
Sheer darkness lurks for his treasured larks,　　　　　26
　　　　a fire unfanned consumes him,
　　　　　　　　the remnant of his tent is smashed.

---

20. *with his treasure*. There are widely varying constructions of this phrase, but it seems likely that the *bet* before *ḥamud*, "treasure," is a *bet* of agency. The sense, then, is that his ill-gotten wealth will be of no help to him on the day of disaster.

21. *he cannot hope to have bounty*. Again, the translation is conjectural.

23. *as he eats*. The literal sense of *bileḥumo* is "in his meat" or "in his flesh." There are varying interpretations of the word here (some relate it to weaponry), but it would appear to carry forward the theme of the greedy man who stuffs his belly and then comes to grief.

24. *a bow of bronze*. This is, of course, an ellipsis for the arrow shot from the bronze bow.

25. *Unsheathed*. As the verb indicates, we have now switched to a different weapon, from bow to sword.

26. *lurks for his treasured larks*. The Hebrew uses two phonetically related terms both of which have the core sense of "hide" and the second of which often means "treasured" (that is, hidden because treasured—perhaps here the

27   The heavens will lay bare his crime
             and earth will rise up against him.

28   A torrent will take down his house,
             pouring out on the day of His wrath.

29   This is the wicked man's share from God,
             the inheritance God has willed him.

---

man's children). The two Hebrew words in immediate sequence are *tamun* (frequently associated with traps) and *tsefunaw* (singular *tsafun*).

21

And Job spoke up and he said: 1
Hear, O hear my word,   2
        and let this be your consolation.
Bear with me while I speak,   3
        and after I speak you may mock.
Is my complaint directed to man,   4
        and why should I not be impatient?
Turn to me and be appalled,   5
        put your hand over your mouth,
when I recall and am dismayed,   6
        and shuddering grips my flesh.
Why do the wicked live,   7
        grow rich and gather wealth?
Their seed is firm-founded before them,   8
        their offspring before their eyes.
Their homes are safe from fear,   9
        and God's rod is not against them.

---

2. *consolation*. Job's use of this word is probably sarcastic: the friends, having purportedly come to "console" or "comfort" Job, have vilified him; his rejoinder now will set them straight.

5. *put your hand over your mouth*. This is a sign of horror (the Hebrew says "put hand over mouth").

7. *Why do the wicked live*. The thriving of the wicked is the theme on which Job expands for the rest of this speech, in direct refutation of his three reprovers' pat notion that the wicked always get their just deserts.

10   Their bull breeds and brings no miscarriage,
          their cow calves and does not lose her young.

11   They send out their little ones like a flock,
          and their children go dancing.

12   They carry the timbrel and lyre
          and rejoice at the sound of the flute.

13   They pass their days in bounty,
          and in an instant they go down to Sheol.

14   And they say to God, "Turn away from us,
          we have no desire to know Your ways.

15   Who is Shaddai that we should serve Him,
          and what use for us to entreat Him?"

16   Look, their bounty is not in their hands—
          the counsel of the wicked is far from me!

17   How often does the lamp of the wicked gutter
          and their disaster come upon them—
             does He portion out shares in His wrath,

---

13. *They pass their days in bounty, / and in an instant they go down to Sheol.* After the elaborate picture of the wicked enjoying all the delights of worldly existence, rejoicing in their offspring (the greatest blessing in the biblical scale of values) and surrounded by material abundance, they are granted a quick and painless death.

15. *Who is Shaddai that we should serve him.* The formulation of this arrogant question may echo Pharaoh's words to Moses and Aaron, "Who is the Lord that I should heed his voice?" (Exodus 5:2).

16. *their bounty is not in their hands.* This whole verse looks like a parenthetical interjection by Job: the riches of the wicked are not their own doing, and Job himself is far from sharing their arrogant dismissal of God. Nevertheless, they prosper.

17. *portion out shares in His wrath.* The Hebrew *ḥavalim* means both "pangs" and "shares," but the verb "portion out" suggests that "shares" is the leading edge of the pun.

and are they as straw in the wind   18
     and chaff that the storm has snatched?
Does God set aside for His sons His affliction?   19
     Let Him pay him back that he may know.
Let his own eyes see his collapse,   20
     and let him drink from Shaddai's seething venom.
For what will he care for his home when he's gone,   21
     and the number of his months broken off?
Will he teach knowledge to God,   22
     and will he judge those on high?
One person dies full of innocence,   23
     completely tranquil and at peace.

---

18. *straw in the wind . . . chaff that the storm has snatched.* This image is a stock figure in Wisdom literature to represent the fate of destruction awaiting the wicked. Compare, for example, Psalm 1:4: "Not so the wicked, / but like chaff that the wind drives away." Job's argument, here and elsewhere, is that such language may sound good, but it does not jibe with the facts of experience.

19. *Let Him pay him back.* The second "him" refers to the wicked man, who, alas, is not paid back by God for his evil and hence never knows that there are consequences for wrongdoing.

20. *his collapse.* The Hebrew *kido* is anomalous, and the translation here follows an interpretive consensus that has been argued for on various grounds. One might emend the word to *be'eido, 'eid* meaning "disaster" (it occurs in verse 30) with the initial *be* used idiomatically before the object of the verb "to see."
    seething venom. The Hebrew means both "venom" and "smoldering wrath," and so the translation adds "seething" to convey the double sense of the Hebrew pun.

21. *when he's gone.* Literally, "after him."

23. *full of innocence.* Many translations render the noun *tom* as something like "vigor" on the basis of the context here, but elsewhere it always means "innocence" or "blamelessness" (as in the frame-story of Job).

24 His udders are filled with milk,
        the marrow of his bones still moist.
25 Another dies with a bitter heart,
        and he has never enjoyed good.
26 Together in the dust they lie,
        and the worm will cover them.
27 Look, I know your plans,
        and your violent schemes against me.
28 When you say, "Where is the nobleman's house,
        and where is the tent of the wicked's abode?"
29 Have you not asked the wayfarers,
        and their tokens you cannot mistake?
30 For on disaster's day harm is held back,
        on the day when wrath is unleashed.

---

24. *udders*. The Hebrew *'atinim* occurs only here in the biblical corpus. The parallelism with the second verset requires a body part, and the Targum first understood it as udders (the established meaning of the word in modern Hebrew). It may seem incongruous to attach udders to a man, but the poet is probably thinking metaphorically of the fecundity of milch-cows, and may also want to suggest a satirical image of the prospering wicked man fat from all he has eaten, with breast-like protuberances on his chest.

26. *Together in the dust they lie*. This idea is akin to a notion reiterated by Qohelet—that life portions out prosperity and misery arbitrarily, while in the end all share the fate of rotting in the grave.

28. *the nobleman's house . . . the wicked's abode*. Job was once a prospering nobleman. The fact that his house has been brought to ruin is adduced by the three reprovers as evidence that all along he has been wicked and now has gotten what he deserves.

29. *Have you not asked the wayfarers*. People who have traveled about and observed what actually happens in human affairs would be able to tell the three companions that, contrary to their complacent view, it is typically the wicked who thrive.

30. *harm is held back*. That is, the wicked are unscathed, even as disaster—storm, fire, marauders—sweeps away the innocent.

Who will tell to his face his way,   31
     and for what he did, who will pay him back?
And he is borne off to a sepulcher   32
     and on the grave-mound someone keeps watch.
The clods of the brook are sweet to him,   33
     and every man is drawn after him,
          and before him—beyond all number.
And how do you console me with mere breath,   34
     when your answers are naught but betrayal?

---

32. *a sepulcher*. The Hebrew plural *qevurot*, instead of the simple singular *qever*, "grave," suggests something grand: even in death the grandeur of the wicked is not diminished.

33. *after him . . . before him*. The image is of numberless throngs of admirers of the wicked man gathered round his burial rite.

34. *how do you console me with mere breath*. The verb "console," in an envelope structure, loops back to "your consolation" at the beginning of this poem. *Hevel*, "mere breath," is the term repeatedly insisted on by Qohelet, meaning something utterly devoid of substance.

    betrayal. This is the last, bitter word of Job's speech: what is especially galling to him is that the three figures he thought were his friends have become his harsh denouncers.

22

1 And Eliphaz the Temanite spoke up and he said:
2 Will a man avail with God,
                 will the discerning avail with Him?
3 Does Shaddai desire that you be in the right,
                 or profit if your ways are blameless?
4 Is it for your reverence that He reproves you,
                 comes to judgment against you?
5 Why, your evil is great,
                 and there is no end to your crimes.
6 For you take pawn from your brother for naught,
                 and strip the naked of their clothes.
7 No water do you give to the famished,
                 and from the hungry you hold back bread.

---

5. *Why, your evil is great, / and there is no end to your crimes.* Eliphaz's entire speech is suffused with a sense of unreflective moral certitude. Since God gets no benefit from a man's righteousness (verses 2–4), it follows "logically" that a man afflicted by God, as Job has been, is guilty of unspeakable crimes.

6. *take pawn from your brother for naught.* Eliphaz now launches on a catalogue of crimes that, like his poetry, is heavily formulaic: taking away clothes from the indigent (presumably, the clothes are the pawn—see Exodus 22:25), withholding bread and water from the hungry and thirsty, allowing the manipulation of the legal and economic system by the powerful, oppressing the widow and the orphan.

strip the naked of their clothes. This translation, like the King James Version, mirrors the wording of the Hebrew, which is, of course, a prolepsis: these victims become naked when they are stripped of their clothes.

And the strong-armed possesses the land,   8
      the privileged dwells upon it.
Widows you send off empty-handed,   9
      and the arms of the orphans are crushed.
And so there are traps all around you,   10
      sudden fear will strike you with terror,
or darkness, where you cannot see,   11
      and a spate of water will cover you.
Is not God in the height of the heavens?   12
      See the topmost stars that are lofty.
And you say, "What does God know?   13
      Through thick cloud can He judge?
Clouds are His shelter—He does not see,   14
      on the rim of the heavens He walks."
Would you keep the age-old path   15
      on which wrongdoers trod,
who are shriveled before their time,   16
      their foundation pours out like a river?
Who say to God, "Turn away from us,"   17
      and what can Shaddai do to them?
When He has filled their homes with bounty—   18
      the counsel of the wicked be far from me!

---

10. *And so.* It follows as an inevitable consequence of all these unspeakable crimes that Job is condemned to terrible torment.

12. *Is not God in the height of the heavens?* These words begin an impious speech that Eliphaz puts in Job's mouth: because God is high above, far removed from man and surrounded by thick cloud in His celestial abode, He surely cannot see what man does down below, and so a sinner like Job imagines he can act with impunity.

17. *and what can Shaddai do to them.* The first verset is the quoted speech of the wrongdoer; this second verset is essentially free indirect discourse—that is, someone's speech conveyed in the third person.

18. *the counsel of the wicked be far from me.* This clause is identical with 20:16B. It makes more sense in context here than in Job's speech, so one may suspect that it was inadvertently introduced into Chapter 20 in scribal transcription.

19   The righteous shall see and rejoice,
             and the innocent shall mock them.
20   Their substance is surely destroyed,
             and their remnant the fire consumes.
21   Be accustomed to Him, be at peace,
             and through this will your comings be blessed.
22   Take, pray, from His mouth instruction,
             and set His utterances in your heart.
23   If you come back to Shaddai, you're restored,
             if you banish evil from your tent,
24   and lay your gold down in the dust,
             on a brook-bordered rock your Ophir treasure,
25   and Shaddai will be your gold,
             heaped up silver for you.
26   For then you'll take pleasure in Shaddai,
             and lift up your face to God.

---

21. *be accustomed to Him.* This is the usual meaning of the verb *hasken.* The sense may be to enter into a habitual relationship of closeness with God.
   blessed. The literal sense of the Hebrew is "be good."

23. *restored.* Literally, "be built" (or "rebuilt").

24. *lay your gold down in the dust.* Many interpreters understand this to mean, consider your gold as dust, but the preposition *'al* ("on," or more idiomatically here in English, "in") argues for the literal sense: Job is exhorted to strip himself of all his worldly possessions and to make God alone (verse 25) his treasure. Of course, disaster has already stripped him of his wealth; so either there is a disconnect with the frame-story, or Eliphaz is assuming that such a vicious exploiter as Job would have somehow continued to hide ill-gotten gains.
   Ophir treasure. Ophir, to the south of the Land of Israel, was celebrated for its fine gold. The Hebrew says simply "Ophir."

26. *lift up your face.* Here this is a gesture of prayer.

You will entreat Him and He will hear you,   27
    and your vows you will pay.
You will decree and it will come to be,   28
    and light will gleam on your ways.
When they sink low and you say "Pride,"   29
    who casts his eyes down He rescues.
He lets the guilty escape,   30
    he escapes through your spotless palms.

---

28. *gleam.* Almost all the English versions say "shine," but the Hebrew *nagah* is a specialized poetic word for giving off light.

29. *When they sink low and you say "Pride."* Both this verse and the next are rather crabbed in the Hebrew and so the translation is conjectural. (To begin with, it is far from certain that the cryptic *gewah* means "pride" here.) The translation tentatively reconstructs the meaning as follows: The repentant Job encounters people fallen on bad times and condemns them for having been proud (as in "Pride goes before a fall," Proverbs 16:18). When these unfortunates then embrace humility ("who casts his eyes down"), God rescues them. Though they were guilty (the meaning of *'i-naqi* in the next verse has been much contested), God enables them to escape from their disaster, granting them that favor because He takes into consideration the intervention on their behalf of the now blameless Job ("he escapes through your spotless palms"). All this is no more than an educated guess about the meaning of these two stubbornly obscure lines.

23

1   And Job spoke up and he said:

2   Even now my complaint is defiant,
             His hand lies heavy as I groan.

3   Would that I knew how to find Him,
             that I might come to where He dwells.

4   I would lay out my case before Him
             and would fill my mouth with contentions.

5   I would know the words that He answered me,
             and would grasp what He said to me.

6   With great power would He debate me?
             No! He alone would pay heed to me.

7   There the upright can contend with Him,
             I would get away for all time from my Judge.

---

2. *His hand lies heavy as I groan.* This is the first of a series of obscure clauses in this speech. The literal sense is "my hand was heavy on my groan." The translation emends "my hand," *yadi*, to "His hand," *yado*, a very small difference in Hebrew script. The preposition "on" before "groan" is understood to mean something like "in the midst of"—hence, "as I groan."

4. *lay out my case.* Job again resorts to his fantasy of meeting God for a fair legal argument in court.

6. *He alone would pay heed to me.* The Hebrew says literally "pay [or "put"] in [against?] me." An ellipsis or omission is assumed here: pay heed (*sim lev*). The idea seems to be that if only Job could have his day in court with God, his divine persecutor would put aside His advantage of overwhelming power and pay attention to Job's argument in his own defense.

Look, to the east I go, and He is not there,   8
> to the west, and I do not discern Him,

To the north where He acts, and behold Him not,   9
> He veils the south, and I do not see Him.

For He knows the way with me,   10
> tests me—I come out as gold.

To His steps my foot held fast,   11
> His way I kept, and I did not swerve.

From His lips' command I did not turn,   12
> in my bosom I stored His mouth's dictates.

Yet He wants but one thing—and who can divert Him?   13
> What he desires He will do.

For He will finish out my fixed tally,   14
> and much more of the same is with Him.

---

8. *east . . . west*. These directional terms, like the ones in the next verse, can also refer to forward, backward, left, and right, and interpreters are divided as to which set of references is intended here. Since Job has spoken about searching out the place where God dwells (verse 3), the points of the compass seem more likely, and it makes more sense for God to "veil" (verse 9) the south than the right hand.

11. *To His steps my foot held fast*. It must be said that the language of this verse and the next sounds more like a conventionally pious Wisdom psalm (compare Psalm 119) than like Job. Given the relatively undistinguished poetry of this chapter and its textual difficulties, one might suspect that at least some of this text has been smuggled in from another source.

12. *in my bosom*. The translation reads *beheiqi* instead of the Masoretic *meihuqi*, "from my statute [tally?]." This reading is reflected in the Septuagint and the Vulgate. A scribal error might have been triggered by the occurrence of *huqi* in verse 14.

13. *He wants but one thing*. The literal sense is "He is in one."

14. *He will finish out my fixed tally*. The probable reference is to the tally of Job's afflictions. The same verb and object, *hishlim hoq*, occur in Exodus 5:14 in reference to the tally of bricks of the Hebrew slaves.
and much more of the same is with Him. God has an abundance of further nasty things that he can inflict on human beings.

15   So I am dismayed before Him,
           I look, am afraid of Him.
16   And God has made my heart quail,
           Shaddai has dismayed me.
17   For I am not severed from darkness,
           and my face the gloom has covered.

---

17. *my face.* The received text reads "from my face" (or "from my presence"), *mipanay*, but the suspect initial *mem* ("from") before the word for "face" is probably a dittography induced by the occurrence of *mipney* ("from" or "from before") in the first verset.

24

Why are dire times not stored by Shaddai   1
       and those who know Him behold not his days?
They set aside boundary-stones,   2
       a flock they steal and pasture it.
The orphans' donkey they drive off,   3
       they take in pawn the widow's ox.
[They steal the orphan from the breast,   9
       and the poor man's suckling they take in pawn.]
They push the paupers from the road,
       together the earth's poor go in hiding.

---

1. *Why are dire times not stored by Shaddai.* In this verse, the individual words and their syntactical connection are perfectly clear, but the meaning remains obscure. "Dire" has been added interpretively to "times," following one prevalent construction of the verse. The sense then would be, why does God fail to reserve a time of punishment for the wicked, and why does He not allow His faithful to see His days of judgment?

2. *They.* The reference switches to the wicked, the ones Shaddai should punish.

9. *They steal the orphan from the breast.* This verse, bracketed to indicate it is probably out of place, does not seem to belong between verses 8 and 10, which are part of a description of the destitute who have been forced to flee to the wilderness, but it does fit here in the report of victimizing widows and orphans.

5   Why, like wild asses in the wilderness
                they go forth on their task
    searching for food,
                the steppe offers bread to the lads.

6   In the field they harvest their fodder,
                glean leavings from the wicked's vineyard,

7   naked, pass the night with no garment
                and no clothing in the cold.

8   By the mountain stream they are soaked
                and unsheltered they hug a rock.

10   Naked, they go round with no garment,
                and hungry, they carry the sheaf.

11   In the groves they make olive oil,
                they trample the winepresses and they thirst.

12   From the town the folk groan,
                the dying breath of the fallen cries out,
                      and God finds no cause for blame.

13   They joined the rebels against the light,
                they did not know its ways,
                      and they did not dwell in its paths.

---

5. *like wild asses.* The "like" is merely implied in the Hebrew. Those who are now like these untamed beasts are the destitute who have run off to the badlands in order to escape persecution.

    the steppe offers bread to the lads. The impoverished young are driven to forage in the wilderness for whatever sustenance they can find.

6. *fodder.* The term, generally indicating animal feed, reflects the bleak circumstances to which these destitute refugees have been reduced.

10. *hungry, they carry the sheaf.* They labor for landowners, carrying sheaves of grain from which they cannot partake. The same idea is expressed in the next verse in the image of trampling grapes while going thirsty.

12. *God finds no cause for blame.* This summarizing clause succinctly states Job's indictment of divine justice: the poor go hungry and thirsty, brutally exploited by the ruthless rich; multitudes of murdered people cry out in their death-throes; yet God sees nothing awry.

By light the murderer rises,   14
          he slays the poor and the indigent,
             and at night he is like a thief.
The adulterer's eye watches for twilight,   15
          saying, "No eye will make me out."
            He puts a mask on his face.
They tunnel by dark into houses.   16
          By day they seal themselves up.
            They do not know light.
For morning to all them is death's shadow   17
          when they know the terrors of death's shadow.

---

14. *By light the murderer rises*. Some interpreters, through a rather forced invocation of a rabbinic idiom, claim that *'or* means "evening," not "light." But the plain meaning of the line, in complementary parallelism, is that the murderer gets up in broad daylight to commit his crime impudently, and then at night, in a different criminal style, sneaks around to do more of the same.

16. *By day they seal themselves up*. The reference is not entirely clear. Perhaps the clause suggests that after tunneling into the house, the thieves shut and shutter it in daylight so they can ransack its contents with impunity. This would provide a practical explanation for "They do not know the light"—both night and day they work in darkness. At the same time, these words obviously catch up the larger symbolic significance of the criminals' status as "rebels against the light."

17. *For morning to all them is death's shadow*. In the perverted world of the criminals, they fear the light that would expose them as others fear the darkness of death.

18   Let him be swiftly swept off on the waters,
           cursed be his field in the land.
                 Let him not turn on the vineyard path.
19   Parched land and heat steal away the snow;
           Sheol, those who offend.
20   Let the womb forget him.
           He is sweet to the worm.
    Let him no more be recalled,
           and let wickedness break like wood.
21   Let his mate be barren and not give birth,
           left a widow denied of good.

---

18. *Let him be swiftly swept off on the waters.* The passage that runs from here to the end of verse 24 is one of the most notoriously obscure in the Book of Job. Some scholars think it belongs in its entirety either to Chapter 25 (where a sizable section of Bildad's speech has obviously been lost) or to Chapter 26. Such radical transporting of chunks of text is based on risky conjecture, and so it seems best to leave the passage where it is, construing the verbs as curse-forms (their form in the Hebrew gives no clear indication of their mode): may all these dire things befall the wicked whose offenses have just been enumerated.

swiftly swept off. The Hebrew says only "swift."

Let him not turn on the vineyard path. The wicked man, his own field cursed, is condemned to wander in wasteland, not to enjoy a pleasant stroll through any fruitful vineyard.

19. *steal away the snow.* The Hebrew says "snow waters," telescoping the snow and its melting and evaporation, but that phrase sounds cumbersome in English.

Sheol, those who offend. That is, just as the desert heat melts the snow, the underworld takes away those who offend. But this entire line has probably been damaged because there are five accented syllables in the first verset and just two in the second verset, an extreme imbalance that is not admissible in biblical versification.

20. *womb . . . worm.* In a neat encompassing maneuver, the line moves from womb to tomb in cursing the life of the wicked man.

He who hauled bulls with his strength   22
        will stand up and not trust in his life.
Though God grant him safety on which he relies,   23
        His eyes are on their ways:
They are on top a moment and are gone.   24
        Laid low, like the weeds they shrivel,
            and like heads of grain they wither.   25
If it be not so, who will give me the lie,
        and render my word as naught?

---

22. *He who hauled bulls with his strength.* This rendering is an educated guess at the meaning of the Hebrew.

in his life. The Masoretic text reads "in life," *baḥayin* (with an unusual Aramaic ending), but some manuscripts more plausibly have *beḥayaw*, "in his life."

23. *Though God grant him safety.* The Hebrew reads merely "he," but the antecedent that makes the best sense of this sentence is God. The idea, then, would be that God may accord the wicked temporary security, but He continues to scrutinize their acts (the Hebrew swings from singular to plural as it does elsewhere in the passage), and retribution will come. It must be said that this view sounds more like one of the three friends than like anything we would expect from Job. Perhaps we can justify verses 22–24 as integral to Job's speech by seeing them as statements impelled by the momentum of the preceding series of curses against the wicked: having wished them to be swept away and driven into the grave, Job now indulges in a kind of fantasy that his wishes will really be fulfilled, that the triumphant wicked will actually get their just deserts from God.

24. *like the weeds.* The received text reads "like all," *kakol.* But the Qumran text of the Aramaic Targum shows *kayabla'*, "like the weed," which might reflect *kayablit* in the Hebrew, and that reading is followed here.

25

1   And Bildad the Shuhite spoke up and he said:
2   Dominion and fear are with Him,
             who makes peace in His heights.
3   Is there a number to His brigades,
             and on whom does His light not rise?
4   And how can man be right with God,
             how can he born of woman be clear?

Bildad's speech as we have it in the received text—only six verses—is inordinately brief, less than a third the length of the other speeches in the debate, and a section, or sections, of it almost certainly have been displaced or lost in the process of scribal copying. This translation follows a common proposal in transposing 26:5–14 to Bildad's discourse here. Those verses, which are wholly devoted to a rhapsodic celebration of God's cosmic powers, are altogether implausible as part of Job's speech, though that is how they are assigned in the received text.

2. *who makes peace in His heights.* This clause, which was later adopted in the Jewish liturgy for the conclusion of the *kadish*, may well refer, as Pope has suggested, to God's victory in a primordial battle of gods. The reference to "brigades" in the next line suggests that idea, and if in fact 26:5–14 is a direct continuation of this speech, the invocation of a triumphant warrior god there would be a further development of this mythological plot.

3. *on whom does His light not rise.* As the next two lines make clear, these words suggest that God's searching scrutiny holds all beings, terrestrial and celestial, to account.

5. *the moon itself does not give light.* In God's stern judgment, even the bright moon is considered to be dim.

Why, the moon itself does not give light,   5
      and the stars are not clear in his sight.
How much more, man the maggot,   6
      and humankind the worm.

The shades shudder down below,   **26.**5
      the waters and their denizens.
Sheol is naked before Him,   6
      and Perdition is without garb.
He stretches Zaphon over the void,   7
      hangs earth over emptiness,
bundles water in His clouds,   8
      the scud does not burst below,

---

the stars are not clear. The Hebrew uses a strategic pun because the verb *zaku* can mean both "to be pure" (or "innocent") and "to be bright."

26

5. *down below.* This adverb is moved here from the beginning of the second verset, where the Masoretic cantillation marks place it, to the end of the first verset, where it makes better sense and rhythm.

6. *Sheol is naked before him.* Even the depths of the underworld are exposed to God's searching gaze. (Compare 25:3.)

7. *Zaphon.* Zaphon is the mountain dwelling of Baal, the Syro-Canaanite weather-god. This mythological reference sets the stage for the invocation of the battle with the primordial sea-monster in verses 11–13.

8. *below.* The Hebrew says "below them," the third-person plural suffix referring back to "clouds" in the first verset.

9   covers the face of the throne,
                spreads His cloud upon it,
10   draws a circle over the water
                to the border of light and darkness.
11   The heavens' pillars quaver,
                are dumbfounded by His roar.
12   Through His power He subdued Yamm,
                and in His cunning He smashed Rahab.
13   With His wind He bagged the Waters.
                His hand cut down the elusive Serpent.
14   Why, these are but the least of His ways,
                the tag-end of the word that is heard of Him.
                        And His might's thunder who can grasp?

---

10. *draws a circle over the water / to the border of light and darkness.* The essential idea is that God circumscribes the roiling sea, preventing it from surging over the dry land. The border of light and darkness would have to be the horizon, which may not be logically correct but is poetically evocative as an image of fixing a vast boundary on the sea, from the horizon to—implicitly—the edge of the land.

12. *Yamm . . . Rahab.* These, as we have seen earlier, are different names for the menacing sea-god who is subdued by YHWH (or, in the Canaanite version, Baal), Who pushes back the forces of chaos and establishes the created order.

13. *With His wind He bagged the Waters.* The Hebrew here is somewhat obscure, but a construction that continues the picture of a primordial battle against the sea-monster seems plausible. Thus, following Tur-Sinai, the translation understands the anomalous *shifrah* to be a cognate of the Akkadian term that means "net," and instead of the Masoretic *shamayim,* "heavens," *sam mayim,* "He put the Waters [in a net, *shifrah*]," is assumed. The Water is given an upper-case *W* here because it appears to be a poetic epithet for Yamm.

26

And Job spoke up and he said:
How have you helped without power,
                    rescued by an arm without strength?

Chapter 26 and 27 sharply reflect the damaged state of the text of the whole sequence of chapters leading to Job's last confession of innocence. As noted on page 106, only the first four verses of Chapter 26 can plausibly be attributed to Job. The formula that begins Chapter 27, "And Job again took up his theme," would seem to signal the end of the debate proper and the introduction of Job's long confession of innocence that runs to the end of Chapter 31. But verses 8–23 of Chapter 27 are an emphatic declaration in the style of the three reprovers that God invariably punishes the guilty. Attempts to save these verses as Job's discourse by reading them as irony are forced and quite unconvincing. One of the three friends must be the speaker, and the most likely suspect, as many scholars have inferred, is Zophar, whose contribution to the third round of debate is missing from the received text. A bracketed formulaic sentence introducing these lines as Zophar's speech has been added in the translation before verse 8. Verses 8–23, however, could not be the entirety of Zophar's speech because the passage breaks off abruptly and is about half the length of the other speeches in the debate.

2. *helped without power.* Some understand this to mean: help someone who has no power. Given the parallelism, however, with offering counsel without wisdom in the next line, it is far more likely to refer to pretending to help when the one offering help is powerless to do so. What remains puzzling is that the second person is singular where one would expect Job to address all three friends.

3   How have you counseled without wisdom,
        and abundantly proffered advice?
4   To whom have you told words,
        and whose breath has come out of you?

2–4. These verses break off, to be followed by a new formula for introducing Job's speech. Either a long section has been lost, or these lines belong somewhere in a previous speech of Job's.

27

*A*nd Job again took up his theme and he said: 1
By God, Who denied me justice   2
      and by Shaddai Who embittered my life,
as long as my breath is within me,   3
      and God's spirit in my nostrils,
my lips will never speak evil;   4
      nor my tongue ever utter deceit.
Far be it from me to declare you right,   5
      till I breathe my last I will not renounce my virtue.
To my rightness I cling, I will not let go,   6
      my heart has not caused reproach all my days.
Let my enemy be deemed a wicked man   7
      and my adversary a wrongdoer.

[And Zophar the Naamathite spoke up and he said:]
For what hope has the tainted to profit,   8
      when God takes away his life?
Will God hear his scream   9
      when disaster befalls him?

---

2. *By God . . . by Shaddai.* Job begins his confession of innocence by pronouncing a solemn oath in the name of the very deity who has been persecuting him.

8. *For what hope has the tainted to profit.* This speech begins with a recurrent central theme of the friends' verbal assault on Job: the man who has polluted himself through evil acts will never really profit from them because God's stern retribution will overtake him (as it has overtaken Job).

10 Will he delight in Shaddai,
　　　　　will he call upon God at all times?
11 Let me teach you with God's own force,
　　　　　what is with Shaddai I will not conceal.
12 Look, all of you have beheld it,
　　　　　and why do you spew empty breath?
13 This is the wicked man's share with God,
　　　　　the portion that oppressors take from Shaddai.
14 If his sons be many, it is for the sword,
　　　　　and his offspring will go without bread.
15 His survivors will be buried in the death-plague,
　　　　　and his widows will not keen.
16 Should he heap up silver like dust
　　　　　and like mud lay up apparel,
17 he'll lay up, and the just man will wear it,
　　　　　and the silver the blameless share out.
18 He will build his house like the moth,
　　　　　like a shack that a watchman puts up.
19 Rich he lies down—it's not taken away.
　　　　　He opens up his eyes and it's gone.

---

11. *Let me teach you with God's own force.* This smug assumption that the speaker knows what God knows about good and evil, reward and punishment, is characteristic of the friends.

12. *Look, all of you have beheld it, / and why do you spew empty breath?* These impatient words make sense coming from Zophar as the last of the three reprovers to speak in the debate. He turns to his two friends and berates them for not making their case against Job more forcefully clear to him.

15. *his widows will not keen.* The plural, of course, presupposes polygamy. Presumably, the widows will not mourn because they have no use for their good-for-nothing husband.

19. *it's not taken away.* The referent of the Hebrew verb is ambiguous, but it seems likely that it refers to the rich man's wealth.

Terror will take him like water;   20
        by night the storm snatches him up.
The east wind bears him off and he's gone,   21
        it sweeps him away from his place.
It flings itself on him unsparing,   22
        from its power he strives to flee.
It claps its hands against him,   23
        and hisses at him from its place.

---

20. *like water*. Though some emend this word, thinking it an odd simile, it may simply refer to the way a flood overwhelms a person or sweeps him away—a very common image for death or disaster in Psalms. "Water" and "storm" would then be parallel terms for destruction in the two versets.

21. *the east wind*. As elsewhere (including the frame-story), the east wind, blowing from the desert, parches and blights.

23. *claps its hands . . . hisses*. Both are conventional gestures of scorn, but at the same time the sounds of clapping and hissing or whistling neatly evoke the violent motion of the storm-wind.

28

1 Yes, there's a mine for silver
and a place where gold is refined.
2 Iron from the dust is taken
and from stone the copper to smelt.

---

1. *Yes, there's a mine for silver*. This rhapsodic celebration of divine wisdom is clearly not part of the debate between Job and his three reprovers, and the strong scholarly consensus is that it is an editorial interpolation, perhaps with the aim of introducing a pious view of wisdom in this book that is such a radical challenge to the guiding assumptions of Wisdom literature. Robert Gordis, noting some affinities with the general poetic language of Job, imagines that this is an earlier composition by the Job poet, which he decided to insert here as a kind of interlude before Job's final confession of innocence. That proposal, though beguiling, is fanciful: this looks like the work of another poet with a very different worldview. As a hymn to divine wisdom, however, it does exhibit considerable poetic force.

silver . . . gold. These precious substances appear later in the poem in the list of objects of value that cannot equal the worth of wisdom. The mining of silver and gold and then the smelting of copper also introduce the notion of man's technological resourcefulness. As the lines that follow vividly declare, man searches out all the remote places of the earth, sinking mine-shafts into the depths of the ground, damming rivers, everywhere in ardent pursuit of treasure. Yet all this brilliant technology is nothing in comparison to the value of real wisdom.

a place where gold is refined. The movement from the source of silver in the first verset to the place of refining gold in the second verset participates in the general pattern of narrative development between the two halves of lines in biblical poetry.

An end has man set to darkness,   3
    and each limit he has probed,
        the stone of deep gloom and death's shadow.
He breaks under a stream without dwellers,   4
    forgotten by any foot,
        remote and devoid of men.
The earth from which bread comes forth,   5
    and beneath it a churning like fire.
The source of the sapphire, its stones,   6
    and gold dust is there.
A path that the vulture knows not   7
    nor the eye of the falcon beholds.
The proud beasts have never trod on it,   8
    nor the lion passed over it.
To the flintstone he set his hand,   9
    upended mountains from their roots.
Through the rocks he hacked out channels,   10
    and all precious things his eye has seen.
The wellsprings of rivers he blocked.   11
    What was hidden he brought out to light.

---

3. *An end has man set to darkness.* The Hebrew says merely "he has set"; the implied antecedent, "man," has been added for the sake of clarity. Given the image in the third verset of stone as the abode of darkness, what is probably suggested here is that man, tunneling into stone for precious minerals, opens it to the light, or, perhaps, brings torchlight down into the mines.

4. *breaks under a stream.* This is a poetic image of digging tunnels under rivers.

5. *beneath it a churning like fire.* Thought it is unlikely that the poet had any notion of the earth's molten core, he seems to have had a sense of what is beneath the surface of the earth as a realm of fluid unstable forces, while the surface above provides humankind its daily bread.

8. *The proud beasts have never trod on it.* The places that man the restless miner reaches in his quest for precious minerals are so remote that even wild animals do not live there. The existence of copper mines in the rocky desert region near the Gulf of Aqaba might have encouraged this image.

12 But wisdom, where is it found,
     and where is the place of insight?

13 Man does not know its worth,
     and it is not found in the land of the living.

14 The Deep has said, "It is not in me,"
     and the Sea has said, "It is not with me."

15 It cannot be got for fine gold,
     nor can silver be paid as its price.

16 It cannot be weighed in the gold of Ophir,
     in precious onyx and sapphire.

17 Gold and glass cannot equal it,
     nor its worth in golden vessels.

18 Coral and crystal—not to be mentioned,
     wisdom's value surpasses rubies.

19 Ethiopian topaz can't equal it,
     in pure gold it cannot be weighed.

20 And wisdom, from where does it come,
     and where is the place of insight?

21 It is hidden from the eye of all living,
     from the fowl of the heavens, concealed.

---

12. *But wisdom, where is it found.* All this human searching into the dark and remote places of the earth may discover treasure but not what is far more precious, wisdom.

15. *fine gold.* This is the first of four different Hebrew terms for gold that the poet deploys in the next five lines.

20. *And wisdom, from where does it come.* The use of this entire line as a refrain is in keeping with the celebratory purpose of the poem.

Perdition and Death have said,   22
    "With our own ears we heard its rumor."
God grasps its way,   23
    and He knows its place.
For He looks to the ends of the earth,   24
    beneath all the heavens He sees,
to gauge the heft of the wind,   25
    and to weigh water with a measure,
when He fixes a limit for rain   26
    and a way for the thunderhead.
Then He saw and recounted it,   27
    set it firm and probed it, too.

---

22. *Perdition and Death.* This mythological pair answers to the pair, Deep and Sea, in verse 15. The effect of both is to give a cosmic sweep to the celebration of divine wisdom: it is not to be found in the sea or the great abyss or the underworld realm of death but only with God.

25. *to gauge the heft of the wind.* The wind, of course, cannot be weighed—except by God.
    to weigh water with a measure. Several English versions render this as "mete out water with a measure." The point, however, is not that God doles out measures of water but rather that He alone, as Creator, can weigh the huge mass of the primordial waters.

27. *Then He saw and recounted it.* The past tense of the verbs indicates that this act of divine reflection comes at the end of the process of creation, a process intimated in verses 24–26. The poet may have in mind the reiterated "And He saw that it was good" in the first account of creation. The recounting, then, might be the authoritative narrative of creation in Genesis.
    set it firm. This is the verb regularly used for establishing things on a firm foundation—houses, dynasties, the world.
    and probed it, too. God not only set creation on a firm foundation but also, through His unique wisdom, searched out and understood every one of its components.

28   And He said to man:
                  Look, fear of the Master, that is wisdom,
                        and the shunning of evil is insight.

---

28. *And He said to man.* This clause (two words in the Hebrew) is an extra-metrical introduction to the concluding line of the poem. Extra-metrical elements, especially for the introduction of direct speech, are fairly common in prophetic poetry.

the Master. The Hebrew uses *'adonai* here, and only here, in the Book of Job, which has led some scholars to think it is textually suspect. Many manuscripts read YHWH, but that divine name is also not used in Job until the Voice from the Whirlwind. Since by the Late Biblical period YHWH was pronounced as though it were *'adonai*, that may have led to the switch here, though it is hard to know which term was the original one.

fear of the Master . . . the shunning of evil. The reiterated question in the refrain of where is wisdom is now given a resonant answer at the very end of the poem. But such neat confidence is alien to the Job poet, even where he evokes God's speech at the end of the book.

29

And Job again took up his theme and he said: 1
Would that I were as in moons of yore,   2
        as the days when God watched over me,
when He shined his lamp over my head,   3
        by its light I walked in darkness,
as I was in the days of my prime—   4
        God an intimate of my tent,
when Shaddai still was with me,   5
        all around me my lads;

---

1. *And Job again took up his theme.* With the repetition of this formula from
27:1, we are back on track with Job's concluding confession of innocence.

3. *when He shined his lamp over my head.* The concrete image is of God "watching over" Job solicitously, holding a lit oil lamp (which would have been a wick
in oil in a shallow concave ceramic dish) above him so that he can walk safely
through the dark.

4. *God an intimate of my tent.* Literally, "When God's council [that is, His
exclusive intimate company] was at my tent."

5. *my lads.* Though the Hebrew *ne'arim* could refer either to Job's seven dead
sons or to his retainers, the latter meaning is more likely because the context
here is Job's recollection of the imposing standing in society he enjoyed before
all the disasters befell him.

6   when my feet bathed in curds
           and the rock poured out streams of oil,

7   when I went out to the city's gate,
           in the square I secured my seat.

8   Lads saw me and took cover,
           the aged arose, stood up.

9   Noblemen held back their words,
           their palm they put to their mouth.

10   The voice of the princes was muffled,
           their tongue to their palate stuck.

11   When the ear heard, it affirmed me,
           and the eye saw and acclaimed me.

12   For I would free the poor who cried out,
           the orphan with no one to help him.

13   The perishing man's blessing would reach me,
           and the widow's heart I made sing.

14   Righteousness I donned and it clothed me,
           like a cloak and a headdress, my justice.

15   Eyes I became for the blind,
           and legs for the lame I was.

16   A father I was for the impoverished,
           a stranger's cause I took up.

17   And I cracked the wrongdoer's jaws,
           from his teeth I would wrench the prey.

---

6. *curds . . . oil.* These are, of course, hyperbolic expressions of affluence. Compare Deuteronomy 32:13: "He suckled him honey from the crag / and oil from the flinty stone."

7. *the city's gate . . . the square.* The square before the city's gate was the place where justice was deliberated, and Job, as the leading notable of the community—compare verses 8–11—would have had a regular place there.

11. *affirmed me.* The verb '*asher* literally means to say '*ashrey,* "happy is he."

12. *I would free the poor.* Exercising his role in administering justice, Job acted on behalf of the helpless—the poor, the orphan, the widow, the man about to perish, the handicapped, the victim of wrongdoing (verses 12–17).

And I thought: In my nest I shall breathe my last,   18
    and my days will abound like the sand.
My root will be open to water,   19
    and dew in my branches abide,
my glory renewed within me,   20
    and my bow ever fresh in my hand.
To me they would listen awaiting   21
    and fall silent at my advice.
At my speech they would say nothing further,   22
    and upon them my word would drop.
They waited for me as for rain,   23
    and gaped open their mouths as for showers.
I laughed to them—they scarcely trusted—
    but my face's light they did not dim.
I chose their way and sat as chief,

---

18. *In my nest I shall breathe my last.* As a consequence of a life dedicated to virtuous acts, Job thought he had every reason to expect he would die a tranquil death in the bosom of his family.

my days will abound like the sand. The Hebrew word for "sand," *hol,* has a homonym that means "phoenix," and many interpreters have been attracted to that meaning because the phoenix is eternal, reborn out of its own ashes. However, Job is not imagining eternal life, only a very long life, and the equation between (grains of) sand and things so abounding, or so many (the verbal stem *r-b-h,* as here) that they are innumerable, is a common biblical idiom.

20. *within me.* The literal sense of the Hebrew preposition is "with me" or "alongside me."

my bow ever fresh in my hand. The poet probably has in mind that after very extended usage, the bowstring begins to go slack and the wood of the bow loses its spring, but this bow—a metaphor for Job's strength—is constantly renewed.

22. *At my speech they would say nothing further.* This verse and the previous one pick up the theme of verses 9 and 10. Some critics have proposed moving these lines to earlier in the poem for the sake of seamless continuity, but such wholesale rearrangement of the text seems neither necessary nor warranted.

my word would drop. The "dropping" is of a liquid, and is close to "drip," an image of blessed fructification in a semi-arid region that was reflected in verse 19 and is vividly developed in verse 23.

24   I laughed to them—they scarcely trusted—
               but my face's light they did not dim.
25   I chose their way and sat as chief,
               I dwelled like a king in his brigade
                       when he comforts the mourning.

---

24. *I laughed to them—they scarcely trusted.* This whole verse is the one obscure juncture in an otherwise transparent chapter. The interpretation assumed in this translation is that Job, expatiating to his listeners, expresses a joyfulness that they in their plight can hardly trust, yet they do not presume to object to his buoyant mood. The verb understood here as "dim" has given rise to widely divergent constructions and hence to very different readings of the line.

25. *when he comforts the mourning.* Some critics, puzzled by this clause, have drastically emended the Hebrew, but it seems reasonably intelligible as it stands in the received text: Job, like a king in the midst of his royal brigade, offers comfort to those of his men who have suffered losses—metaphorically, the loss of comrades fallen in battle—as in general he has rescued victims, fought on behalf of orphans and widows, and so forth.

30

A nd now mere striplings laugh at me   1
        whose fathers I spurned
                to put with the dogs of my flock.
The strength of their hands—what use to me?   2
        From them the vigor has gone:
In want and starvation bereft   3
        they flee to desert land,
                the darkness of desolate dunes,
plucking saltwort from the bush,   4
        the roots of broomwood their bread.

---

1. *mere striplings.* The Hebrew says "ones younger than I" or, more literally, "lesser than I in days."

whose fathers I spurned. The society in which Job was once one of the greatest of those who dwell in the East is hierarchical in regard both to social-economic standing and to age. Even the fathers of Job's mockers would have been beneath his notice, unfit to run with his sheep dogs, and how much more so their half-baked sons.

2. *the strength of their hands—what use to me?* Job's mockers assail him in the ostensible vigor of their youth, but he imagines that it will vanish in a moment, and he proceeds to elaborate a fantasy of the striplings turned into miserable pariahs banished to the wilderness (verses 3–8).

3. *the darkness of desolate dunes.* The Hebrew shows prominent alliteration and wordplay: *'emesh sho'ah umesho'ah.* The last two words would literally mean something like "desolation and desolateness."

5   From within they are banished—
          people shout over them as at thieves.
6   In river ravines they encamp,
          holes in the dust and crags.
7   Among bushes they bray,
          beneath thornplants they huddle.
8   Vile creatures and nameless, too,
          they are struck from the land.
9   And now I become their taunt,
          I become their mocking word.
10   They despised me, were distant to me,
          and from my face they did not spare their spit.
11   For my bowstring they loosed and abused me,
          cast off restraint toward me.
12   On the right, raw youths stand up,
          they make me run off
             and pave against me their roadways of ruin.
13   They shatter my path,
          my disaster devise,
             and none helps me against them.

---

5. *from within*. The Hebrew *min-gew* is the first of a whole series of obscure places in this chapter. Some interpreters, arguing from a proposed Northwest Semitic cognate, understand it to mean "from the community." In rabbinic Hebrew, *gew* or *go* can mean "inside," and that linguistic connection seems less of a stretch than the purported Semitic cognate. "Within" then would refer to home, companionship, the boundaries of civilized habitation.

7. *they bray*. The Hebrew verb *yinhaqu*, generally used for donkeys, nicely conveys the reduction of the banished men to brutishness.

9. *And now I become their taunt*. Job, having vividly conjured up the wretched fate deserved by, or about to overtake, his young mockers, now bitterly turns to the unrestrained derision to which they are subjecting him.

11. *my bowspring they loosed*. The slackening of the bowspring is an image of deprivation of power, of unmanning.

12. *they make me run off*. Literally, "they send off my feet."

Like a wide water-burst they come,   14
   in the shape of a tempest they tumble.
Terror rolls over me,   15
   pursues my path like the wind,
     and my rescue like a cloud passes on.
And now my life spills out,   16
   days of affliction seize me.
At night my limbs are pierced,   17
   and my sinews know no rest.
With great power He seizes my garment,   18
   grabs hold of me at the collar.
He hurls me into the muck,   19
   and I become like dust and ashes.
I scream to You and You do not answer,   20
   I stand still and You do not observe me.
You become a cruel one toward me,   21
   with the might of Your hand You hound me.

---

15. *my path.* The translation reads *netivati,* "my path," with several manuscripts and the Syriac version, instead of the Masoretic *nedivati* ("my nobility"?).

my rescue like a cloud passes on. There is no need to see, as many interpreters have done, an exotic meaning in *yeshu'ati,* which everywhere else means "rescue." Job, cast into deepest desperation, sees a fleeting vision of his hoped-for rescue sailing off from him like a cloud.

17. *my limbs are pierced.* One might also understand this as "He pierces my limbs," the antecedent being God.

18. *With great power He seizes my garment.* The wording of this entire verse is obscure, and hence any translation is conjectural.

20. *You do not observe me.* The received text reads "You observe me," but various manuscripts as well as the Vulgate show the negative.

22 You bear me up, on the wind make me straddle,
    break me apart in a storm.

23 For I know You'll return me to death,
    the meetinghouse of all living things.

24 But one would not reach out against the afflicted
    if in his disaster he screamed.

25 Have I not wept for the bleak-fated man,
    sorrowed for the impoverished?

26 For I hoped for good and evil came.
    I expected light and darkness fell.

27 My innards seethed and would not be still,
    days of affliction greeted me.

28 In gloom did I walk, with no sun,
    I rose in assembly and I screamed.

29 Brother I was to the jackals,
    companion to ostriches.

30 My skin turned black upon me,
    my limbs were scorched by drought.

31 And my lyre has turned into mourning,
    my flute, a keening sound.

---

22. *storm.* The marginal gloss (*qeri*) instructs us to read the word in the Hebrew consonantal text, *tushiwah*, as *tushiah*, "wisdom" or "prudence," but it is more likely a variant spelling of *teshu'ah*, "uproar" or "storm."

24. *the afflicted . . . he screamed.* The verse as it stands in the received text is opaque. The translation reads *'ani*, "the afflicted," for the Masoretic *'i*, "heap of ruins," and *shiwea'*, "he screamed," for *shua'*, "nobleman." If all this is correct, the idea would be that no one would abuse a helpless suffering person—so why does God persecute me in this way?

25. *bleak-fated.* Literally, "hard of day."

29. *Brother I was to the jackals.* In a painful reversal, the fate of brutalization and banishment from society that Job conjured up for his mockers has befallen him instead.

31

A pact I sealed with my eyes—
    I will not gaze on a virgin.   1
And what is the share from God above,   2
    the portion from Shaddai in the heights?
Is there not ruin for the wrongdoer,   3
    and estrangement for those who do evil?
Does He not see my way,   4
    and all my steps count?
Have I walked in a lie,   5
    has my foot hurried to deceit?
Let Him weigh me on fair scales,   6
    that God know my blamelessness.
If my stride has strayed from the way,   7
    and my heart gone after my eyes,
        or the least thing stuck to my palms,

---

1. *A pact I sealed with my eyes.* After the catalogue of woes in the previous section of this final speech, Job begins a series of affirmations of the scrupulously virtuous life he led. Not only did he avoid promiscuity (verse 9), but he even strictly refrained from gazing with lust at nubile women. This profession of innocence is interrupted in verses 2–4 by a declaration—not exactly in keeping with what Job says elsewhere—that God watches wrongdoers from above and punishes them. Some scholars have proposed moving around various verses in this chapter in order to produce better continuities, but all such surgical procedures on the text are necessarily conjectural.

5. *Have I walked.* This line initiates a whole series that employs the Hebrew form that indicates swearing an oath.

8   let me sow and another shall eat,
    my offspring torn up by the roots.

9   If my heart was seduced by a woman,
    and at the door of my friend I lurked,

10   let my wife grind for another
    and upon her let others crouch.

11   For that is lewdness,
    and that is a grave crime.

12   For it is fire that consumes to Perdition,
    and in all my yield eats the roots.

13   If I spurned the case of my slave
    or my slave-girl, in their brief against me,

14   what would I do when God stands up,
    and when He assays it, what would I answer?

15   Why, my Maker made him in the belly,
    and formed him in the selfsame womb.

16   Did I hold back the poor from their desire
    or make the eyes of the widow pine?

17   Did I eat my bread alone,
    and an orphan not eat from it?

---

8. *sow . . . eat . . . torn up by the roots.* In an agricultural society, these images are standard metaphors for all forms of endeavor.

10. *let my wife grind for another.* The verb here is a kind of violent pun. Grinding in a small stone hand mill is a domestic activity regularly performed by the woman in preparing food for her husband and family. But the crouching of other men over her in the second verset turns the grinding into a representation of the sexual act.

13. *If I spurned the case of my slave.* Job moves on from sexual morality to social justice. Even a slave has legal rights and may bring a suit against his master, and Job says that in the days of his prosperity he always honored those rights.

15. *the selfsame womb.* Job, of course, does not mean that he and the slave had the same mother but rather that they share the same human condition, each having been formed in the womb. Hence, despite the economic disparity, an existential parity obtains between them.

For from my youth like a father I raised him,   18
       and from my mother's womb I led him.
If I saw a man failing, ungarbed,   19
       and no garment for the impoverished,
did his loins not then bless me,   20
       and from my sheep's shearing was he not warmed?
If I raised my hand against an orphan,   21
       when I saw my advantage in the gate,
let my shoulder fall out of its socket   22
       and my arm break off from its shaft.
For ruin from God is my fear,   23
       and His presence I cannot withstand.
If I made gold my bulwark,   24
       and fine gold I called my trust,
if I rejoiced that my wealth was great   25
       and that abundance my hand had found,
if I saw light when it gleamed   26
       and the moon gliding grand,

---

18. *from my mother's womb I led him.* The received text says "led her," a difference of one syllable in a suffix, which some then understand to refer to the slave-girl in the second half of verse 13. Such a distant antecedent seems unlikely, and it is more plausible to emend the suffix. The "mother's womb" is obviously a hyperbole, Job declaring that from his earliest days he looked after the poor.

20. *did his loins not then bless me.* The loins, now comfortably wrapped in the garment Job provides, are the poetic enunciator of the blessing.

21. *my advantage in the gate.* The gate is where courts of justice were conducted. The term rendered here as "advantage" is in most other contexts "rescue," the idea being that you come out on top.

22. *let my shoulder fall out of its socket.* This would be measure-for-measure justice, a retaliation for raising one's hand against the orphan.

26. *light when it gleamed . . . the moon gliding grand.* As the erotic language of the next line makes clear, this would be an ecstatic response to the moon, perhaps as manifestation of a deity.

27   and my heart was seduced in secret,
            and my hand caressed my mouth,

28   this, too, would be a grave crime,
            for I would have denied God above.

29   If I rejoiced at my foe's disaster,
            and exulted when harm found him out—

30   yet I did not let my mouth offend
            to seek out his life in an oath.

31   Did the men of my tent ever say,
            "Would that we were never sated of his flesh."

32   The sojourner did not sleep outside.
            My doors to the wayfarer I opened.

33   Did I hide like Adam my wrongdoings,
            to bury within me my crime,

34   that I should fear the teeming crowd,
            and the scorn of clans terrify me,
                fall silent and keep within doors?

---

27. *my hand caressed my mouth.* The gesture is both sensual and cultic. We should keep in mind that Job, for all his quarrel with God, remains a staunch monotheist.

28. *this, too, would be a grave crime.* It is fitting that the same term of condemnation used for adultery in verse 11 is presented here in connection with succumbing to the pagan-erotic seduction of the moon.

29. *If I rejoiced at my foe's disaster.* Job's profession of innocence here goes beyond the norm of biblical morality, which often (as in Psalms) is happy to express exultation when disaster overtakes an enemy.

31. *"Would that we were never sated of his flesh."* The victim of this metaphoric cannibalism would have to be the helpless and the unhoused—perhaps explicitly the sojourner and the wayfarer of the next line.

33. *Did I hide like Adam my wrongdoings.* This would be the first human after eating the forbidden fruit and trying to hide from God.

Would that I had someone to hear me out.   35
     Here's my mark—let Shaddai answer me,
        and let my accuser indict his writ.
I would bear it upon my shoulder,   36
     bind it as a crown upon me.
The number of my steps I would tell Him,   37
     like a prince I would approach him.
If my soil has cried out against me,   38
     and together its furrows wept,
if I ate its yield without payment,   39
     and drove its owners to despair,

---

35. *Would that I had someone to hear me out.* Job reverts to the idea of having his day in court with God that he repeatedly favored earlier.

Here's my mark. The mark is probably the mark with a personal seal by which a person would authenticate a legal document.

36. *I would bear it upon my shoulder.* So confident is Job that the accusations against him are baseless that he would proudly wear the writ of indictment as an ornament.

37. *The number of my steps I would tell Him.* Job would readily report everything he has done because he is confident, as he said in verses 5 and 6, that he never walked in a lie or allowed his stride to stray.

like a prince. The Hebrew *nagid* puns on *agidenu,* "I would tell him," the two words sharing the same root.

39. *drove its owners to despair.* Some would like to understand this as "its tenants" because Job has just referred to the soil as his, but the Hebrew *be'alim* means "owners." Perhaps the possessive attached to "soil" refers to renting soil (note the reference to payment). It is conceivable that a wealthy man like Job, besides the plots he owned outright, might have rented additional fields in order to grow crops for profit.

40   instead of wheat let nettles grow,
            and instead of barley, stinkweed.

Here end the words of Job.

---

40. *stinkweed*. It is notable that the last angry word of Job's argument in his own defense is "stinkweed," *bo'shah*.

   Here end the words of Job. This is a formal marker of closure and may well be original in the text. At this point, one might expect God's response to Job. Instead, as we shall now see, someone else intervenes.

32

And these three men left off answering Job because he was right in his 1
own eyes. And Elihu the son of Barachel the Buzite from the clan of Ram 2
flared up in anger, against Job his anger flared, for his claiming to be in
the right more than God. And against his three companions his anger 3
flared because they had not found an answer that showed Job guilty. And
Elihu waited out Job's words, for they were his elders. And Elihu saw 4,5
that the three men could utter no answer, and his anger flared.

---

2. *Elihu*. Though some scholars have tried to save the Elihu speeches as an
integral part of the book, the plausible consensus is that it is an interpolation,
the work of another poet. No hint of Elihu's presence is made in the frame-
story at the beginning, and he is equally absent from the closing of the frame
in Chapter 42. The poetry he speaks is by and large not up to the level of the
poetry in the debate between Job and his three reprovers, and there is a whole
series of Hebrew terms that appear only in the Elihu speeches. His name,
though feasible in biblical usage, appears to be satirically devised as an intima-
tion of his impatiently presumptuous character. The literal meaning of Elihu
the son of Barachel the Buzite from the clan of Ram is "He-is-my-God the son
of God-has-blessed the Scornful One from the High Clan."

4. *waited out Job's words*. The implication is that he waited out both Job's words
and those of the three companions, but it is Job's argument that he wants to
refute.

5. *could utter no answer*. Literally, "there was no answer in the mouth."

6 And Elihu the son of Barachel spoke up and he said:

> I am young in years,
>> and you are aged.
> Therefore was I awed and feared
>> to speak my mind with you.

7 I thought, Let years speak,
>> and let great age make wisdom known.

8 Yet it is a spirit in man,
>> and Shaddai's breath that grants insight.

9 It is not the elders who are wise
>> nor the aged who understand judgment.

10 Therefore do I say, O listen to me,
>> I, too, will speak my mind.

11 Look, I have waited for your speech,
>> hearkened to your understandings,
>>> while you tested words.

12 And I attended to you,
>> and, look, Job has no refuter,
>>> none to answer his talk among you.

13 Should you say, "We have found wisdom—
>> God will confound him, not man,"

---

6. *I am young in years, / and you are aged.* This invocation of relative ages lines up with the traditional notion, repeatedly mentioned by the three companions, that wisdom lies with the elders.

8. *Yet it is a spirit in man.* Elihu, having listened impatiently to the ineffectual arguments of his three elders, now rejects the idea that wisdom resides with the aged and instead contends that it derives from God's gift of the spirit in a person, without regard to age.

13. *God will confound him, not man.* The literal sense of the verb represented as "confound" is "push back," "drive away." In attributing this statement to the three reprovers, Elihu shows them admitting the failure of their own arguments.

he has not made his brief to me,   14
      and with your words I would not answer him.
—they take fright, they no longer respond,   15
      words leave them in the lurch—
I waited, for they did not speak,   16
      for they stood and no longer responded.
I, too, will speak out my part,   17
      I will speak my mind, I, too.
For I am full up with words,   18
      the wind in my belly constrains me.
Look, my belly is like unopened wine,   19
      like new wineskins it bursts.

---

14. *he has not made his brief to me.* If he had done so, Elihu contends, I would have answered him in words quite different from yours. A small emendation of the initial Hebrew word here, "not," yields a subjunctive statement: "had he made his brief to me."

15. *they take fright.* This entire verse is set out here between dashes because it is a narrative statement about the three friends and not part of Elihu's direct address to them. Whether it is a glossing interpolation or part of the poet's expository strategy is unclear. If the latter, we might read it as a kind of aside to the audience by Elihu.

17. *I, too, will speak out my part, / I will speak my mind, I, too.* Such repetitiousness is characteristic of Elihu's speeches and of a piece with his bombastic character.

18. *the wind in my belly constrains me.* This metaphoric representation of the impatient urge to speak as an explosive condition of flatulence is surely satiric, at least in effect and perhaps in intent. It is extended in the image of bursting wineskins in the next line.

19. *new wineskins.* The wine, still fermenting in the new skins, which are not yet supple with use, threatens to burst them.

20   Let me speak that I may be eased,
             let me open my lips and speak out.

21   I will show favor to no man,
             nor flatter any person.

22   For if I knew how to flatter,
             my Maker would soon take me away.

---

20. *Let me speak that I may be eased*. This verset continues the idea of speech as release from painful flatulence.

21. *I will show favor to no man*. As Elihu, concluding his rebuke to the three friends, prepares to launch his frontal assault on Job, he intimates that they have been too kind to this reprobate, something that he, representing himself as a perfectly objective person, will not do.

22. *my Maker would soon take me away*. The Hebrew verb at the end puns on "show favor," *lasei't panim* (very literally, "to bear a face"), because "take away" (or "bear off") is also *lasei't*.

But hear, Job, my speech,   1
   and hearken to all my words.
Look, I've opened my mouth,   2
   my tongue speaks on my palate.
My heart's truth—what I say,   3
   and my lips utter lucid knowledge.
God's spirit has made me,   4
   and Shaddai's breath has quickened me.
If you can answer me,   5
   lay it out before me, take your stance.
Why, I am like you to God,   6
   from clay I, too, was pinched.
Look, fear of me does not dismay you,   7
   my urging does not weigh upon you.

---

1. *But hear, Job, my speech.* Elihu now turns from the three friends to the man he considers to be the malefactor. Much of this speech is formulaic, and rather repetitious, and the poetry is undistinguished, lending plausibility to the surmise that this is not the work of the Job poet.

4. *God's spirit.* Elihu appears to refer not merely to his own creaturely condition but to the fact (see 32:8) that God has inspired him with insight.

7. *Look.* It is almost a verbal tic that Elihu begins so many sentences with the ostensive particle (*hineh* or *hen*), which in his case expresses an impatient sense that he knows it all.
 fear of me does not dismay you. The self-assured Elihu is indignant that Job shows no signs of quailing before the reproof that Elihu administers, certain of its rightness.

8   Why, you said in my ears,
              and the sound of words I heard:
9   "Pure I am with no wrong,
              guiltless, I am free of crime.
10   Look, He finds pretexts against me,
              He counts me His enemy.
11   He puts my feet in stocks,
              He watches all my ways."
12   Look, where you fail to be right I will answer you,
              for God is greater than man.
13   Why do you contend with Him,
              if He answers not all of man's words?
14   For God speaks in one way
              or in two, and no one perceives Him:
15   In a dream, a night's vision,
              when slumber falls upon men,
                    in sleep upon their couch.
16   Then He lays bare the ear of men,
              and terrifies them with reproof,

---

9. *Pure I am with no wrong.* The speech attributed to Job, which continues to the end of verse 11, is in fact a paraphrase of several declarations of innocence and complaints about God's relentlessness that Job made in the course of the debate with the three friends.

13. *all of man's words.* The Hebrew says merely "all of his words," but the likely antecedent of "his" is "man" at the end of verse 12, so that word has been added for clarity.

14. *For God speaks in one way.* The fact of the matter, Elihu argues, is that God really answers man in more than one way, but unwitting humans don't realize they are being addressed. The particular mode of divine communication then stipulated is dream visions.

16. *terrifies them with reproof.* The Hebrew here is obscure. Instead of the Masoretic *yaḥtom* ("He seals"?), this translation reads, with the Septuagint, *yeḥitem,* "terrifies them."

to make humankind swerve from its acts   17
        to put down pride in a man,
that he save himself from the Pit   18
        and his life from the Current.
And he is chastened with pain on his couch—   19
        shuddering in his bones unrelenting.
His life-breath despises bread,   20
        his gullet, desirable food.
His flesh wastes away before one's eyes,   21
        and his bones, once unseen, are laid bare.
And his being draws near to the Pit,   22
        his life-breath to the Killers.
If he had an advocate,   23
        one spokesman out of a thousand,
            to declare for man his uprightness,
he could pity him and say, "Redeem him   24
        from going down to the Pit. I found ransom."

---

17. *its acts.* The Hebrew uses a singular noun. A long exegetical tradition, beginning in Late Antiquity, assumes that what is implied is evil acts.

18. *the Current.* The translation concurs with one line of interpreters who conclude that the Hebrew *shelaḥ*, which can mean "weapon" as well as "stream," is a parallel to the Pit and refers to a mythological river, such as the one known in Mesopotamian mythology that marks the boundary of the realm of death.

21. *before one's eyes.* The literal sense of the Hebrew is "from sight."

22. *the Killers.* If the received text is accurate, this would refer to angels of destruction in Sheol.

24. *Redeem him / from going down to the Pit.* This whole line is also awkward in the Hebrew and doesn't scan as poetry. This is the least of the textual difficulties in this chapter.

25   His flesh would become sleeker than in youth,
    he'd return to the days of his prime.

26   He entreats God, Who grants him favor,
    and he sees His face with a joyous cry
     and He restores to man his right standing.

27   He sings out to men and says,
    "I offended, perverted what's straight,
     and it was not worth it for me."

28   He redeemed his being from crossing to the Pit,
    and his life-breath enjoys the light.

29   Look, all this God performs
    twice or thrice with a man,

30   to bring back his being from the Pit,
    to glow in the light of life.

31   Attend, Job, listen to me,
    be still and I will speak.

32   If there are words, answer me.
    Speak, for I would find you in the right.

33   If not—you, listen to me,
    be still, and I will teach you wisdom.

---

25. *become sleeker.* The Hebrew verb is anomalous and may reflect a corrupted text, so the translation is conjectural.

27. *sings out.* The form of the verb is peculiar and its meaning somewhat uncertain.

31. *Attend, Job, listen to me.* Characteristically, this speech of Elihu's ends not with poetic imagery or genuine argumentation but with emphatic exhortation, in a repetitive series of declarations that Job should be silent and listen to the wisdom that Elihu is about to impart to him.

34

And Elihu spoke up and he said: 1
Listen, you sages, to my words,   2
      and you who know, O hearken to me.
For the ear probes words   3
      as the palate tastes in eating.
Let us take us a case to court,   4
      let us know what is good between us.
For Job has said, "I'm in the right,   5
      and God has diverted my case.
He lies about my case,   6
      I'm sore-wounded from His shaft for no crime."

---

2. *Listen, you sages.* True to character, Elihu lines himself up with the sages but also suggests that he knows even better than they.

4. *Let us take us a case to court.* Elihu's desire to argue his case against Job in quasi-legal terms borrows from the metaphor of legal disputation that Job has frequently used and anticipates the polemic quotation of Job's legal imagery in verses 5 and 6.

6. *He lies about my case.* The Masoretic text reads "I lie," but the *yod* signaling the third person may have been dropped by a scribe because the previous word ends with a *yod* (haplography).
    sore-wounded from His shaft. The Hebrew is syntactically cramped and cryptic, literally reading "sore-wounded my shaft." Presumably the shaft, shot by God, is "mine" because it has pierced Job's body.

7   Who is a man like Job,
                lapping up scorn like water?

8   He consorts with wrongdoers
                and walks with wicked men.

9   For he has said, "What use to a man
                to find favor with God?"

10   Therefore, discerning men, hear me:
                far be from God any wickedness,
                    from Shaddai any wrong.

11   For a man's acts He pays him back,
                and by a person's path He provides him.

12   Surely God does not act wickedly,
                and Shaddai does not pervert justice.

13   Who assigned the earth to Him,
                and placed the whole world with Him?

14   Should He set His mind on man,
                his living breath He would gather to Him.

15   All flesh would expire together,
                man to the dust would return.

16   If you understand, then listen to this,
                hearken to the sound of my words.

17   Would one who hates justice hold sway,
                would you call the great Righteous One wicked?

---

9. *what use to a man / to find favor with God*. These words are in fact a succinct summary of Job's argument about the arbitrariness of God's justice.

13. *who assigned the earth to Him*. That is, God alone, having no superiors, is responsible for ruling the earth, and thus one can expect that He will do so justly.

17. *the great Righteous One*. The translation follows the lead of most interpreters, who understand this as a designation of God, though the Hebrew phrase *tsadiq kabir* sounds a little odd in biblical usage as a divine epithet.

Does one say of a king "scoundrel,"   18
      "wicked" of the nobles?
Who did not show favor to princes   19
      nor was partial to rich over poor,
           for they all are the work of His hands.
In a moment they die, at midnight,   20
      a people's upturned, passes on,
           the mighty swept off, by no hand.
For His eyes are on a man's ways,   21
      and all his steps He does see.
There is no dark and no death's shadow   22
      where wrongdoers can hide.
For He sets no fixed time for man   23
      to come in judgment with God.
He smashes the unlimited mighty   24
      and puts others in their place.
Therefore He knows their deeds,   25
      overturns them, in a night they are crushed.

---

18. *Does one say of a king "scoundrel."* Elihu's theological conservatism is reinforced by his social and political conservatism: whoever rules is right.

20. *In a moment they die, at midnight.* God as the world's impartial judge works in unanticipated ways. The wicked may prosper, but then they are swept off to destruction in the blink of an eye, in the middle of the night. This assertion jibes with a view often reiterated in Psalms.

23. *He sets no fixed time.* The received text appears to say "He does not set still" (or "yet"). But the puzzling "still," *'od*, is probably a haplography obscuring *mo'ed*, "fixed time," since the preceding word, "sets," *yasim*, ends with a *mem*. The *'ayin* and the *waw* of *mo'ed* would then have been scribally reversed to produce an erroneous *'od*.

26   For their wickedness He strikes them
                in a place where all can see,
27   because they turned away from Him,
                and all His ways they did not grasp,
28   bringing the poor man's scream before Him,
                and the scream of the lowly He heard.
29   Should He be silent, who could condemn Him?
                Should He hide His face, who could glimpse Him,
                        whether a nation or a man?
30   —rather than a tainted man ruling,
                than snares for the people.
31   Did he ever say to God,
                "I shall bear my punishment and not sin,
32   I did not see—You must instruct me,
                if I have done wrong, I won't do it again"?

---

26. *For their wickedness.* Textual difficulties proliferate from here through verse 31. Instead of the Masoretic *resha'im*, "the wicked," this translation reads *rish'am*, "their wickedness."
        in a place where all can see. The literal sense is "in a place of seers."

29. *Should He be silent.* If the translation mirrors the meaning of the Hebrew, which is not entirely certain, the sense is: even if God chooses to be silent and hide His presence, His justice is never in question.

30. *—rather than a tainted man ruling.* This entire verse remains obscure.

31. *bear my punishment.* "Punishment," perhaps the most likely object of the verb, is merely implied.

Should He by your dictates mete out justice,   33
　　　　for it is you who reject or choose, not I?
　　　　　　And what do you know?—speak.
Discerning men will say to me   34
　　　　and a wise man listening to me:
"Job speaks without knowledge,   35
　　　　and his words are without any sense."
Would that Job might be tested forever   36
　　　　for responding like villainous men.
For he adds to his offense,   37
　　　　　makes crime abound among us,
　　　　　　　and compounds his talk against God.

---

33. *who reject or choose, not I.* Again, the Hebrew wording is rather crabbed and the meaning far from certain. The evident sense is a sarcastic challenge to Job: is it you who makes the decisions about the implementation of justice in the world and not God? The sudden switch from third-person reference to God to the first person ("not I") is a little disorienting but an allowable procedure in biblical usage.

34. *Discerning men.* Elihu concludes this speech as he began it by invoking the support of the wise for his argument.

36. *like villainous men.* The received text reads "in" (or "against") "villainous men," but the Septuagint and some Hebrew manuscripts show "like."

35

1 And Elihu spoke up and he said:
2 Is this what you count as justice,
       you say, "I am more right than God"?
3 That you should say, What use is it to you,
       what shall I gain from my offense?
4 I will answer you in words,
       and your companions with you.
5 Look to the heavens and see,
       and the sky that is high above you.
6 If you offended, how do you affect Him,
       if your crimes be many, what do you do to Him?
7 If you're in the right, what do you give Him,
       or what could He take from your hand?
8 On a man like yourself your wickedness acts,
       and on a human being your righteousness.

---

3. *What use is it to you, / what shall I gain from my offense?* The line shifts from second-person reference to Job in the first verset to first-person citation of Job in the second verset, a switch permissible in biblical usage though disconcerting to the English reader. Job's gaining from his offense is a little cryptic, but the evident sense is that he feels it makes no difference whether he is virtuous or sinning, and he has no special motive to offend because he gets nothing from it.

5. *Look to the heavens and see.* The invocation of the vastness of the heavens prepares the ground for the contention (verses 6–8) that man's actions have no effect on God high above.

8. *acts.* A verb to this effect is merely implied in the Hebrew.

From much oppression they cry out,   9
    call for help from the arm of the powerful.
And none says, "Where is God my Maker,   10
    Who gives us melodies in the night,
instructs us more than the beasts of the earth,   11
    makes us wiser than the birds of the heavens?"
Then they cried out—and He did not answer—   12
    from evil men's haughtiness.
But to falseness God will not listen,   13
    and Shaddai will not behold it.
How much more, when you say, you don't behold Him,   14
    the case is before Him and you await it,
and now, His wrath requites nothing,   15
    and He knows nothing of any crime.

---

9. *From much oppression they cry out.* This sudden switch to the suffering multitudes is intended to make the argument that many undergo terrible affliction but only Job accuses God for his suffering.

10. *Who gives us melodies in the night.* Many modern interpreters prefer to understand the noun *zemirot* as deriving from a (rare) homonymous root *z-m-r* that means "strength." There is nothing, however, in the immediate context to indicate that "strength" is the more likely meaning. By opting for the meaning "melodies," one accords the poet of the Elihu passages his first line of haunting poetry in an otherwise lackluster performance.

13. *But to falseness God will not listen.* Job has been objecting that God refuses to listen to his complaint. Elihu's rejoinder is that when a complaint is entirely baseless, God will of course refuse to listen.

15. *and now, His wrath requites nothing.* This entire line is completely opaque in the Hebrew. A very literal translation of this first verset is "And now that there is nothing, His wrath requites [or singles out]."
    and He knows nothing of any crime. The word represented as "crime," *pash,* is unintelligible, and the translation assumes, with many critics, that it was originally *pesha'*, "crime," the last consonant having been somehow dropped in scribal transcription. Even so, the clause sounds garbled and scarcely in keeping with biblical idiomatic usage. A literal rendering: "And he knows nothing in [of?] crime very much." In any case, this line is meant to be a summary of Job's impious words.

16   And Job—with mere breath he opens his mouth.
          Devoid of knowledge, he heaps up words.

---

16. *And Job.* The switch from second person to third person at the end of this speech has a certain rhetorical logic: Elihu, having rebuked Job in direct address, now refers to him, contemptuously, in these summarizing words in the third person.

36

And Elihu went on to say: 1
Wait for me a bit while I tell you   2
    that there are still words on God's behalf.
I shall speak my mind far and wide,   3
    and show that the right's with my Maker.
For, indeed, my words are no lie,   4
    one perfect in knowledge is with you.
Look, God is great, He does not despise us,   5
    great in power and understanding.
He will not let the wicked live,   6
    and He grants justice to the afflicted.
He does not take His eye off the righteous   7
    nor off kings for the throne,
        whom He seats on high forever.
And if captives are in fetters   8
    ensnared in the bonds of affliction,

---

4. *one perfect in knowledge is with you.* Elihu is referring to himself, with characteristic lack of modesty. Ever bombastic, he begins this fourth discourse with a three-line windup (verses 2–4) entirely devoted to announcing his own wisdom.

5. *despise us.* The object of the verb is merely implied in the Hebrew.
    power and understanding. The Hebrew says literally "power of heart," but the heart is clearly referred to here as the organ of understanding.

9   He tells them their acts,
           and their crimes, which grow great.

10   And He lays bare their ear to reproof,
           and says they must turn from wrongdoing.

11   If they obey and serve,
           they will finish their days in bounty
              and their years in pleasantness.

12   And if they obey not, they will cross the Current,
           and expire unawares.

13   And the tainted in heart keep up anger,
           they do not cry out when He binds them.

14   They die in youth,
           perish among catamites.

15   He frees the afflicted through their affliction
           and through oppression He lays bare their ear.

16   He even drew you away from the straits,
           a broad place unconfined beneath you,
              your table heaped with rich fare.

---

9. *their crimes.* It is Elihu's complacent assumption that if someone is subjected to captivity or some other terrible misfortune (verse 8), it must be because he is being punished for some crime that he has committed.

12. *the Current.* As in 33:18, the probable reference of the Hebrew *shelaḥ* is to a mythological river marking the border of the realm of death.

14. *catamites.* The Hebrew *qedeishim* is in dispute. Though it has often been understood as a term for homosexual cult-prostitutes, some scholars deny there was any practice of cultic prostitution, male or female, in the ancient Near East. The parallelism with "youth" here is obscure. If the term does refer to male prostitutes, perhaps Elihu assumes that they would have been cut off at an early age because of their promiscuity.

15. *frees the afflicted through their affliction.* The evident idea is that the experience of suffering leads to a new and liberating insight in the sufferers—into what they have done and how they must change.

And you were filled with the case of the wicked,   17
    the case and the ruling on which they depend.
For look out, lest he lure you with riches,   18
    lest great bribery lead you astray.
Will your wealth matter to Him in straits   19
    and all the efforts of power?
Do not pant for the night,   20
    for peoples to vanish from where they are.
Watch out, do not turn to wrongdoing,   21
    which you chose instead of affliction.
Why, God looms on high in His power.   22
    Who is like Him as a teacher?
Who has assigned Him His way,   23
    and who has said, "You have done wrong?"
Recall that you exalt His deeds   24
    which men have espied.
All humankind has beheld Him,   25
    man looks from afar.
Why, exalted is God, and we know not,   26
    the number of His years is unfathomed.

---

17. *you were filled with the case of the wicked*. The Hebrew wording, reflected in this translation, is somewhat obscure. Textual difficulties become more and more dense as the chapter goes on.

18. *For look out*. With many scholars, this translation reads *hameh* (an Aramaicism for "look") instead of the Masoretic *heimah*, "anger."
    lest he lure you. The "he" would be one of the wicked.

19. *Will your wealth matter to Him in straits*. The translation supposes *lo* (to Him) instead of the Masoretic *lo'* ("not"). In any case, the meaning of the whole is uncertain.

20. *for peoples to vanish*. Literally, "for peoples to go up." The possible sense of all this is, don't count on a sudden upheaval in the middle of the night, when whole peoples are suddenly destroyed, and your own fortune changed.

21. *instead of affliction*. Affliction, one recalls, is, in Elihu's view (verse 15), an agency of moral correction.

27   For He draws down drops of water,
                they are distilled in the rain of His wetness,
28   as the skies drip moisture,
                shower on abounding humankind.
29   Can one grasp the spread of cloud,
                the roars from His pavilion?
30   Why, He spreads over it His lightning,
                and the roots of the sea it covers.
31   For with them He exacts justice from peoples,
                gives food in great abundance.

---

27. *For He draws down drops of water.* A prime instance of God's greatness, beheld by humankind (verse 25), is His bringing the rains to sustain life.

wetness. The term *'eid* occurs only here and in the second creation story, Genesis 2:6, where it refers to the moisture rising from the primeval earth.

29. *the roars from His pavilion.* The pavilion, *sukah*, is the heavenly abode of the deity in Canaanite mythology, and the roars from it are the sound of thunder.

30. *His lightning.* The usual sense of the Hebrew *'or* is "light," but the Elihu poet, both here and in verse 32, uses this instead of the common word *baraq*.

the roots of the sea it covers. The verb here is a little odd, but the idea seems to be that God's lightning penetrates even to the roots of the sea.

31. *For with them He exacts justice from peoples.* "Them" refers to the just mentioned thunder and lightning, which are the traditional weapons of the sky-god in pre-Israelite mythology.

gives food in great abundance. The two versets of this line express respectively the acts of the God of judgment and of the God of mercy. He brings down a thundering assault of punishment on wayward nations but provides sustenance to humankind at large. The opposing acts are associated because the lightning occurs in rainstorms, and the gentler rains (see verses 27 and 28) water the earth to make it fruitful.

Lightning covers His palms,   32
    and He commands it to hit the mark.
His roaring tells about Him,   33
    His zealous wrath over evil acts.

---

32. *Lightning covers His palms.* The lightning bolts rest on God's palms before He hurls them at their target.

33. *His roaring tells about Him.* The translation of this cryptic verset is an educated guess, based on the surmise that this line is a continuation of the thunder imagery and that the rumbling of the thunder is heard as a manifestation of God's awesome power. The second verset in the original sounds altogether like gibberish, an effect mirrored—inadvertently?—in the King James Version for the entire line: "The noise thereof showeth concerning it, the cattle also concerning the vapour." This translation tries to rescue the verset from pure gibberish by emending *miqneh*, "cattle," to *meqanei'*, "to be zealous," and revocalizing *'oleh* ("going up"?) as *'awlah*, "wrongdoing" or "evil act."

37

1   For this, too, my heart trembles,
           and it leaps from its place.

2   Hear, O hear His voice raging
           and the murmur that comes from His mouth.

3   Beneath all the heavens He lets it loose—
           His lightning to the corners of earth.

4   After it roars a voice,
           He thunders in the voice of His grandeur,
               and He does not hold them back as His voice
               is heard.

---

1. *For this, too, my heart trembles.* This chapter is the completion of Elihu's fourth speech. The prominence of thunder and lightning as manifestations of God's awesome power is a direct continuation of the lightning theme that is at the center of 36:29–32. In evoking God's power in the natural world, the Elihu section moves beyond hectoring exhortation and almost rises to the level of poetry, though the language in biblical terms is still relatively routine for this subject, with many parallels to Psalms. The editor of the book may have been drawn to insert the Elihu passages precisely here because this concluding section of the fourth speech is a kind of prelude to the Voice from the Whirlwind, resembling it thematically though scarcely its equal in poetic power.

2. *His voice raging.* As in Canaanite poetry, often mirrored in Psalms, the rumbling of thunder is understood as the voice of the deity.

4. *hold them back.* This translation understands the unusual verb 'aqev as the equivalent of the rabbinic 'akev, "to hold back" or "restrain." The pronoun "them" then refers to the bolts of lightning.

God thunders wondrously with His voice, 5
    doing great things that we cannot know.
For to the snow He says: "Be on earth," 6
    and rain in torrents, the rain of His mighty torrents.
Every man He shuts in, 7
    that all men know His deeds.
And the beast comes into its lair, 8
    and in its den it dwells.
From the sky-chamber comes the tempest, 9
    and from the winds' dispersal the cold.
From God's breath the ice is made, 10
    and wide waters turn solid.
With heavy moisture He loads the cloud, 11
    the thunderhead scatters His lightning,
and round about it spins in its designs 12
    to perform all that He charges them
        on the face of inhabited earth,
whether for a scourge to His earth, 13
    whether for mercy, He makes it happen.
Hearken to this, O Job, 14
    stand, and take in the wonders of God.
Do you know when God directs them, 15
    and His thunderhead's lightning shines?
Do you know of the spread of cloud, 16
    the wonders of the Perfect in Knowledge,
when your garments feel warm
    as the earth is becalmed from the south? 17

---

7. *Every man He shuts in.* The torrential rains compel every man to take shelter.

10. *From God's breath.* In the vivid anthropomorphism of the imagery, God's cooling breath, passing over the water, turns it to ice.

15. *Do you know.* This repeated question anticipates the challenge to Job's limited human knowledge in the Voice from the Whirlwind.

18   Will you pound out the skies with Him,
        which are strong as a metal mirror?

19   Let us know what to say to Him!
        We can lay out no case in our darkness.

20   Will it be told Him if I speak,
        will a man say if he is devoured?

21   And now, they have not seen the light,
        bright though it be in the skies,
            as a wind passes, making them clear.

22   From the north gold comes;
        over God—awesome glory.

---

18. *Will you pound out the skies with Him.* The prevalent notion in the ancient Near East was that the sky was a great slab (*raqiaʿ*, the "vault" of Genesis 1, a noun derived from the Hebrew verb that means to pound out). Since that verb appears only here in this particular conjugation, some interpreters understand it as "soar to the skies" (the sense that this conjugation of the root has in modern Hebrew). However, the reference to the solidity of the skies in the second verset makes the sense of pounding out a metallic slab more likely.

    a metal mirror. Mirrors were made not from glass but from polished bronze.

19. *in our darkness.* The Hebrew says, somewhat cryptically, "from darkness," and "our" has been added interpretively. The sense seems to be that we humans in our ignorance are unable to articulate a legal argument against God, and you, Job, will surely not be able to tell us how to do it.

20. *will a man say if he is devoured.* Paltry man, standing before the all-powerful deity, has nothing to say in the face of the prospect of being overwhelmed and destroyed by God.

21. *they have not seen the light.* "They" refers to people in general. Even under clear skies, their limited human perception prevents them from seeing the bright light of the sun.

22. *From the north gold comes.* The claim of many interpreters that this refers to "the golden rays of the sun," in the New Jewish Publication Society (JPS) translation, is unconvincing both because the Hebrew sounds very much like a literal reference to gold and because the north is definitely not the direction from which the sun comes. Pope has proposed that behind this verset is the

Shaddai, whom we find not, is lofty in power,   23
             in judgment and great justice—He will not oppress.
Therefore men do fear Him.   24
             He does not regard all the wise of heart.

---

image of Baal's palace on Mount Zaphon (that is, North Mountain), a structure made out of gold, silver, and lapis lazuli. The verset would then be an apt parallel to the invocation of the glorious nimbus around God in the second verset.

23. *He will not oppress.* Some interpreters revocalize the Hebrew verb to yield "He will not answer." That is, though God is just, we cannot expect Him to address mere mortals. This reading would be in keeping with man's inability to gain access ("find out") to the lofty deity. But the emphasis on divine justice in this verset argues for the sense of "will not oppress."

24. *Therefore men do fear Him.* They fear Him (the Hebrew verb means both "to fear" and "to revere") because He is at once lofty in power and just.
He does not regard all the wise of heart. As the Hymn to Wisdom concluded in Job 28:28, "fear of the Master, that is wisdom," and God has no special regard for those who imagine they have attained understanding independently through the exercise of intellect. This final line would be a last rebuke to Job, who has had the presumption to think he knows how the system of divine justice should work and hence has dared to challenge God.

38

1   And the LORD answered Job from the whirlwind and He said:
2   Who is this who darkens counsel
                    in words without knowledge?
3   Gird your loins like a man,
                    that I may ask you, and you can inform Me.
4   Where were you when I founded earth?
                    Tell, if you know understanding.

---

1. *the whirlwind*. Though the Hebrew *se'arah* probably means simply "storm," this translation choice, and the consequent phrase, the Voice from the Whirlwind, have been so deeply embedded in the imagination of speakers of English after the King James Version that it seems wise not to tamper with it.

2. *Who is this who darkens counsel*. With God's speech as the climax of the book, the Job poet takes a risk that only a supreme artist confident in his genius could do. He had already created for Job the most extraordinarily powerful poetry to express Job's intolerable anguish and his anger against God. Now, when God finally speaks, the poet fashions for Him still greater poetry, which thus becomes a poetic manifestation of God's transcendent power and also an image-for-image response to the death-wish poem that frames Job's entire argument. The unusual phrase "darkens counsel" is not merely an indication of speaking ignorantly (as the parallel in the second verset spells out) but a rejoinder to the spate of images of darkness blotting out light in the death-wish poem of Chapter 3. In pointed contrast to that poem, the opening section of the Voice from the Whirlwind introduces images of light and then traces a dynamic interplay between light and darkness.

4. *Where were you when I founded earth*. God's speech moves in a narrative progression from cosmogony (38:4–21) to meteorology (38:22–38)—which is to

Who fixed its measures, do you know,   5
    or who stretched a line upon it?
In what were its sockets sunk,   6
    or who laid its cornerstone,
when the morning stars sang together,   7
    and all the sons of God shouted for joy?
Who hedged the sea with double doors,   8
    when it gushed forth from the womb.
when I made cloud its clothing,   9
    and thick mist its swaddling bands?

---

say, the play of natural forces across the created world invoked in the cosmo-gonic section—to zoology (38:39–39:40)—which is to say, the panorama of living creatures thriving in the play of the natural forces of creation—to zoology with a mythic heightening (40:15–41:26).

5. *a line*. This is the builder's line, used to construct straight angles.

7. *when the morning stars sang together*. The verb for singing, *ron*, is from the same root as *renanah* "glad song," which Job (3:7) wished to expunge from the night he was conceived. The morning stars are also a counterpoint to the stars of dawn on the night of conception that Job wished never to appear. This splendid vision of the celestial beings joining in joyous song in celebration of creation is not intimated in other biblical accounts of how God created the world.

8. *hedged the sea*. The idea of blocking, or imprisoning, the fiercely raging sea, which continues in some of the subsequent lines, shows the trace of the Canaanite creation myth. But the verb chosen here is the same one Job used (3:23) in his complaint that God had closed off all routes to him.
    the womb. This metaphor for the sea as the matrix of creation is the first of a whole series of birth images that answer to the language of the death-wish poem, in which Job expresses the desire never to have been born, for the womb to have been his tomb. Here, by contrast, an awesome surge of energy comes forth from the womb of creation.

9. *swaddling bands*. This utterly original metaphor depicts the sheets or strips of white mist hovering over the primordial sea, and because swaddling bands are used for infants, it extends the imagery of birth.

10   I made breakers upon it My limit,
          and set a bolt with double doors.

11   And I said, "Thus far come, no farther,
          here halt the surge of your waves."

12   Have you ever commanded the morning,
          appointed the dawn to its place,

13   to seize the earth's corners,
          that the wicked be shaken from it?

14   It turns like sealing clay,
          takes color like a garment,

15   and their light is withdrawn from the wicked,
          and the upraised arm is broken.

16   Have you come into the springs of the sea,
          in the bottommost deep walked about?

17   Have the gates of death been laid bare to you,
          and the gates of death's shadow have you seen?

18   Did you take in the breadth of the earth?
          Tell, if you know it all.

19   Where is the way that light dwells,
          and darkness, where is its place,

---

12. *morning . . . dawn.* Looking beyond the primordial sea to the earth, the poet begins, strategically, with images of light—again, precisely what Job wanted to extinguish forever.

13. *to seize the earth's corners.* Evidently, it is light that takes hold of the far corners of the earth, "shaking out," or exposing, the wicked who hide in night's darkness.

14. *It turns like sealing clay.* The antecedent of "it" is the earth: just as the unshaped matter of sealing clay becomes a distinct form when the seal is stamped on it, the earth, shapeless in darkness, assumes distinct form as the light of day spreads over it.
    takes color. The Masoretic *yityatsvu*, "take a stand," makes no sense, and it is emended here to *titstaba'*.

19. *Where is the way that light dwells, / and darkness, where is its place.* The poet naturally begins with light, but in the complementary parallelism of the line,

that you might take it to its home   20
      and understand the paths to its house?
You know, for were you born then,   21
      and the number of your days is great!
Have you come into the storehouse of snow,   22
      the storehouse of hail have you seen,
which I keep for a time of strife,   23
      for a day of battle and war?
By what way does the west wind fan out,   24
      the east wind whip over the earth?
Who split a channel for the torrent,   25
      and a way for the thunderstorm,
to rain on a land without man,   26
      wilderness bare of humankind,

---

darkness also has its place. Creation, like the diurnal cycle, is a pulsing rhythm of light and darkness, whereas Job, in the egoism of his suffering, exercised an imagination only of darkness.

21. *You know, for you were born then.* This whole line is of course a sarcastic address to Job, whose minuscule life span could not measure up to the vastness of timeless creation. It also echoes back ironically against Job's wish never to have been born.

23. *which I keep for a time of strife.* The storehouses of snow and hail are manifestly mythological locations where God stockpiles these elements as weapons for future combat against some unspecified cosmic foe.

24. *the west wind fan out.* The noun *'or* usually means "light," but that sense is hard to reconcile with the verb, which may have a military connotation, as in Genesis 14:15, where it means to fan out or deploy. Some construe it as "lightning," though that use of the term is restricted to the Elihu speeches and accords neither with the verb nor with the poetic parallelism. This translation deems likely the scholarly proposal that in this instance *'or* reflects the Aramaic *'oriya,* "west wind."

26. *to rain on a land without man.* It is one of the many enigmas of God's creation that rain pours down on places utterly devoid of human habitation. This idea is in keeping with the radical rejection of anthropocentrism, elsewhere assumed in biblical thought, that informs God's poem.

27   to sate the desolate dunes
            and make the grass sprout there?

28   Does the rain have a father,
            or who begot the drops of dew?

29   From whose belly did the ice come forth,
            to the frost of the heavens who gave birth?

30   Water congeals like stone,
            and the face of the deep locks hard.

31   Can you tie the bands of the Pleiades,
            or loose Orion's reins?

32   Can you bring constellations out in their season,
            lead the Great Bear and her cubs?

33   Do you know the laws of the heavens,
            can you fix their rule on earth?

34   Can you lift your voice to the cloud,
            that the water-spate cover you?

35   Can you send lightning bolts on their way,
            and they will say to you, "Here we are!"?

---

27. *desolate dunes*. See the comment on the identical phrase in 30:3, page 123.

28. *a father . . . begot*. Again, the poet invokes imagery of conception and birth in answer to Job's expressed desire to expunge them.

29. *whose belly . . . who gave birth*. The birth imagery now moves from father to mother. In keeping with the boldness of the poet, it is a daring move because it evokes a virtually oxymoronic picture of hard cold ice coming out of a womb.

32. *constellations*. Many interpreters, going back to the King James Version and before it, construe the Hebrew *mazarot* as the name of an unidentified constellation, but it seems more likely that it is a dialectic variant of *mazalot*, which simply means "constellations."

33. *their rule*. The Hebrew suffix indicates "his" or "its," which has led some to identify God as the antecedent. But the plausible antecedent is the stars, thought to govern or predict the affairs of men. This could be a small scribal error, though fluid switching between singular and plural is rather common in biblical usage.

Who placed in the hidden parts wisdom,   36
        or who gave the mind understanding?
Who counted the skies in wisdom,   37
        and the jars of the heavens who tilted,
when the dust melts to a mass,   38
        and the clods cling fast together?
Can you hunt prey for the lion,   39
        fill the king of beast's appetite,
when it crouches in its den,   40
        lies in ambush in the covert?
Who readies the raven's prey   41
        when its young cry out to God
            and stray deprived of food?

---

36. *the hidden parts . . . the mind.* The meaning of the two nouns here, *tuḥot* and *sekhwi*, have long been disputed. Some think they refer to birds, the ibis and the rooster, or even to mythological figures.

37. *Who counted the skies.* What is probably assumed is a multiplicity of heavens (in the Pseudepigrapha and in some rabbinic legends they are seven in number).
    the jars of the heavens who tilted. This is an original image of the source of rain. Elsewhere, as in the Flood story, there are casements in the vault of the heavens that are opened to let down the rain.

38. *the clods cling fast together.* This image of rain-soaked clods of earth turned into an amalgam of mud completes the meteorological section of the poem. After rain, snow, hail, ice, wind, and the patterns of the stars, the poet is ready to turn to the animal kingdom.

39. *the lion . . . the king of beast's appetite.* The Hebrew actually switches from the singular in the first verset to a plural in the second verset (see the comment on verse 33) and then continues in the plural in the next line. The translation keeps all these references in the singular in order to avoid confusion for the English reader. Many modern translations show "lioness," presumably because it is the lioness who does the hunting, but the Hebrew nouns in both halves of the verse are masculine.

39

D o you know the mountain goats' birth time,
         do you mark the calving of the gazelles?

2   Do you number the months till they come to term
         and know their birthing time?

3   They crouch, burst forth with their babes,
         their young they push out to the world.

4   Their offspring batten, grow big in the wild,
         they go out and do not return.

5   Who set the wild ass free,
         and the onager's reins who loosed,

6   whose home I made in the steppes,
         his dwelling-place flats of salt?

7   He scoffs at the bustling city,
         the driver's shouts he does not hear.

8   He roams mountains for his forage,
         and every green thing he seeks.

---

1. *the mountain goats' birth time*. Continuing the images of a creation teeming with births that is a thematic rejoinder to Job's language longing for death, the poet offers a vivid vignette of the birthing of mountain goat and gazelle.

3. *burst forth*. The literal meaning of the Hebrew verb is "split open," a word choice that strikingly conveys the poet's sense that the procreative drive in nature (and the nurturing one as well) cannot be separated from violence.

4. *they go out and do not return*. The separation of the young from their mothers, a biological imperative, prepares the way for the subsequent images of feral freedom in the wild, beyond the realm of human control.

Will the wild ox want to serve you,   9
    pass the night at your feeding trough?
Bind the wild ox with cord for the furrow,   10
    will he harrow the valleys behind you?
Can you rely on him with his great power   11
    and leave your labor to him?
Can you trust him to bring back your seed,   12
    gather grain on your threshing floor?
The ostrich's wing joyously beats.   13
    Is the pinion, the plume, like the stork's?
For she leaves her eggs on the ground,   14
    and in the dust she lets them warm.
And she forgets that a foot can crush them,   15
    and a beast of the field stomp on them—
harsh, abandons her young to a stranger,   16
    in vain her labor, without fear.

---

13. *the ostrich's wing joyously beats.* This entire verse is notoriously obscure. Modern scholars are generally agreed that the bird in question is an ostrich, though the term used here is not the usual *bat-ya'anah* but rather a kind of poetic epithet, "wing of song," or perhaps, better, "screech-wing," a designation alluding to the loud sounds the ostrich makes. The somewhat enigmatic verb *ne'elasah* appears to derive from a root associated with joy, or perhaps joyful movement (in Proverbs 7:18 it appears in a verb for sex).

Is the pinion, the plume, like the stork's? Although each Hebrew word of this verset is understandable, they make little sense together and hence any translation is no more than a guess. A very literal rendering of the Hebrew would sound like this: "is a pinion a stork and plume."

14. *For she leaves her eggs on the ground.* This notion that the ostrich abandons all the eggs she lays and does not stay to hatch them is no more than ancient folk zoology.

16. *harsh, abandons her young to a stranger.* The translation is an interpretive surmise. The literal, cryptic sense of the Hebrew is "She hardened [the verb is in the wrong grammatical gender] her young to [someone?] not hers."

in vain her labor, without fear. This reproduces the Hebrew literally. The labor in vain would refer to her going to the trouble of laying these neglected eggs. Perhaps the cryptic "without fear" might mean that she exhibits no fear, though she should, about what might happen to her offspring.

17   For God made her forgetful of wisdom,
                and He did not allot her insight.
18   Now on the height she races,
                she scoffs at the horse and its rider.
19   Do you give might to the horse,
                do you clothe his neck with a mane?
20   Do you make his roar like locusts—
                his splendid snort is terror.
21   He churns up the valley exulting,
                in power goes out to the clash of arms.
22   He scoffs at fear and is undaunted,
                turns not back before the sword.
23   Over him rattles the quiver,
                the blade, the javelin, and the spear.
24   With clamor and clatter he swallows the ground,
                and ignores the trumpet's sound.
25   At the trumpet he says, "Aha,"
                and from afar he scents the fray,
                        the thunder of captains, the shouts.

---

17. *God made her forgetful of wisdom.* The ostrich, abandoning her young, is one of the enigmas of nature, suggesting that there is no readily discernible moral pattern in the order of creation. Other creatures, as the poem has already shown and will show again, lavish care on their offspring.

18. *she races.* The verb *hamri'* occurs only here. The Aramaic translations understood it to mean "soar" (and in modern Hebrew it is used for a plane's taking off from the ground), but ostriches don't fly. The translation is a guess based on context.

20. *roar like locusts.* The poet seems to be thinking of the great clamorous sound—a frightening sound—made by a vast swarm of locusts.

24. *With clamor and clatter.* The translation emulates the strong alliteration of the Hebrew, *berá'ash werógez*, though the second Hebrew term is closer to "rage" or a state of disturbance.

Does the hawk soar by your wisdom,   26
      spread his wings to fly away south?
By your word does the eagle mount   27
      and set his nest on high?
On the crag he dwells and beds down,   28
      on the crest of the crag his stronghold.
From there he seeks out food,   29
      from afar his eyes look down.
His chicks lap up blood,   30
      where the slain are, there he is.

---

26. *soar*. The unusual Hebrew verb is cognate with *'evrah*, "pinion," a poetic term for "wing," so it is conceivable that it refers not to the act of flight but, like the second verset, to spreading wings.

28. *the crag*. This remote, inaccessible habitat of the bird of prey complements the uninhabited steppes where the wild ass lives.

30. *His chicks lap up blood*. One of the remarkable aspects of the Job poet's vision of nature is that it so completely unsentimental. The creatures of the wild (with the exception of the peculiar ostrich) are endowed with an instinct to nurture their young. For carnivores, however, that nurture involves violence—destroying living creatures in order to sustain life in the offspring. The concluding image, then, of God's first speech is of the fledgling eagles in the nest, their little beaks open to gulp down the bloody scraps of flesh that their parent has brought them. The moral calculus of nature clearly does not jibe with the simple set of equations and consequences laid out in Proverbs and in Psalms.

40

1   And the LORD answered Job and He said:

2   Will he who disputes with Shaddai be reproved?

       Who argues with God, let him answer!

3   And Job answered the LORD and he said:

4   Look, I am worthless. What can I say back to You?

       My hand I put over my mouth.

5   Once have I spoken and I will not answer,

       twice, and will not go on.

6   And the LORD answered Job from the whirlwind and He said:

7   Gird your loins like a man.

       Let me ask you, and you will inform Me.

8   Will you indeed thwart My case,

       hold Me guilty, so you can be right?

9   If you have an arm like God's,

       and with a voice like His you can thunder,

---

1. *And the* LORD *answered Job and He said*. After completing the poetic sweep of the great panorama of creation from the beginning of things to the world of living creatures, God turns in direct confrontation to Job, who now (verses 4 and 5) is abashed and renounces his challenge to God.

7. *Gird your loins like a man*. As the LORD launches on His second speech, He repeats verbatim the opening formula of the first speech. He then proceeds to turn around Job's language of a legal dispute (verse 8) and to ask Job sarcastically whether he is capable of exercising God's power (verses 9–14).

put on pride and preeminence,   10
        and grandeur and glory don.
Let loose your utmost wrath,   11
        see every proud man, bring him low.
See every proud man, make him kneel,   12
        tramp on the wicked where they are.
Bury them in the dust together,   13
        shut them up in the grave.
And I on my part shall acclaim you,   14
        for your right hand triumphs for you.

Look, pray: Behemoth, whom I made with you,   15
        grass like cattle he eats.

---

10. *pride and preeminence . . . grandeur and glory.* The translation follows the double alliteration of the Hebrew: **ga'on** we**gov**ah . . . we**hod** we**ha**da*r.*

11. *your utmost wrath.* The Hebrew says literally "the wraths of your fury," but, as elsewhere, the locking together of synonymous nouns in the construct state is an intensifier.

13. *the grave.* The Hebrew *tamun* means literally "the hidden [place?]," but this is evidently an epithet for the grave (or, perhaps, the underworld), especially since the verbal stem *t-m-n*, also used at the beginning of the line, means both to hide and to bury.

15. *Behemoth.* The Hebrew word means "beast." It is in plural form, possibly a plural of intensification or majesty, but the noun is treated as singular and masculine (indeed, spectacularly masculine) throughout. Behemoth clearly takes off from the Egyptian hippopotamus, but in his daunting proportions, his fierce virility, and his absolute impregnability, he represents a mythological heightening of the actual beast, just as Leviathan is even more patently a mythological heightening of the Egyptian crocodile. The fact that the poet probably never laid eyes on these fabled beasts but knew of them through travelers' yarns no doubt facilitated this transition from zoology to myth. Whether there is some counterpart to Behemoth in Canaanite or Sumerian myth, as some have claimed, is a matter of dispute.

16   Look, pray: the power in his loins,
           the virile strength in his belly's muscles.
17   He makes his tail stand like a cedar,
           his balls' sinews twine together.
18   His bones are bars of bronze,
           his limbs like iron rods.
19   He is the first of the ways of God.
           Let his Maker draw near him with His sword!
20   For the mountains offer their yield to him,
           every beast of the field plays there.
21   Underneath the lotus he lies,
           in the covert of reeds and marsh.
22   The lotus hedges him, shades him,
           the brook willows stand around him.
23   Look, he swallows a river at his ease,
           untroubled while Jordan pours into his mouth.

---

16. *loins . . . virile strength.* Both terms point to sexuality—the loins by metonymy and "virile strength" because the Hebrew term *'on* is characteristically used for sexual potency.

17. *makes his tail stand like a cedar.* The exiguous tale of the hippopotamus scarcely fills this bill, but in all likelihood "tail" is a euphemism for a different part of the male animal's anatomy.
     balls. The rare *peḥadim* has long been understood—and was so understood by the King James translators, who rendered it as "stones"—as an Aramaicism reflecting *paḥda'*, testicle.

19. *Let his Maker draw near him with His sword.* More literally, "bring His sword near to him." The verset is a little enigmatic, but it is usually understood to mean that only Behemoth's Maker would dare to approach him with a sword.

21. *the lotus . . . the covert of reeds and marsh.* This native habitat of the hippopotamus is distinctly Egyptian.

23. *swallows.* The verb usually means "to oppress." The hyperbolic sense here may be that Behemoth demolishes a whole river in one long, easy gulp.
     untroubled. Literally, "he is secure."
     Jordan. In biblical poetry, which constantly needs synonyms because of its dependence on semantic parallelism, both Jordan and the Nile (*ye'or*) are used as terms for "river."

Could one take him with one's eyes,   24
      with barbs pierce his nose?

Could you draw Leviathan with a hook,   25
      and with a cord press down his tongue?
Could you put a lead line in his nose,   26
      and with a fishhook pierce his cheek?
Would he urgently entreat you,   27
      would he speak to you gentle words?
Would he seal a pact with you,   28
      that you take him as lifelong slave?
Could you play with him like a bird,   29
      and leash him for your young women?
Could hucksters haggle over him,   30
      divide him among the traders?
Could you fill his skin with darts,   31
      and a fisherman's net with his head?
Just put your hand upon him—   32
      you will no more recall how to battle.

---

25. *Leviathan.* Though associated with the crocodile of the Nile, Leviathan (Ugaritic *lotan*, Hebrew *liwyatan*) is a prime actor in Canaanite mythology as a sea-monster, and in keeping with his role here in the climactic passage of the poem, he is more prominently mythological than Behemoth. There is no formal introduction or indication of transition for the Leviathan section, but the "barbs" of the last Behemoth line and the hook of the first Leviathan line create a linkage.

26. *lead line.* The Hebrew *'agmon* usually means "reed," so this rendering is a guess based on context.

31. *Could you fill his skin with darts.* This notion of the absolute invulnerability of Leviathan to all human weapons—which caught Melville's attention in *Moby-Dick*—is elaborated in 41:19–21.
    and a fisherman's net with his head. The translation follows the Hebrew, which in the first verset has Leviathan's skin as the object of the verb "fill" and here has, as the object of the same verb, a fisherman's net, into which Leviathan's head would be put.

32. *you will no more recall how to battle.* The Hebrew syntax is somewhat cryptic, though the general sense seems clear. Very literally, it reads, "Recall battle, you will do no more."

41

1   Look, all hope of him is dashed,
            at his mere sight one is cast down.
2   No fierce one could arouse him,
            and who before Me could stand up?
3   Who could go before Me in this I'd reward,
            under all the heavens he would be mine.
4   I would not keep silent about him,
            about his heroic acts and surpassing grace.

---

1. *all hope of him is dashed.* That is, any hope to vanquish Leviathan will be frustrated.

one is cast down. The translation is an interpretive inference from a single word in the Hebrew, *yutal,* "will be cast."

2. *arouse him.* The same verb is used with Leviathan as its object in 3:8, "ready to rouse Leviathan." One suspects it was part of the mythological scenario.

3. *Who could go before Me in this I'd reward.* The Hebrew is cryptic. The possible meaning is that God alone has the power to subdue Leviathan, but if a mortal man could really do it, God would abundantly reward him.

4. *I would not keep silent about him.* These words would seem to refer to the hypothetical hero who would vanquish Leviathan, though they are ambiguous enough that they might refer to Leviathan himself. In that case, instead of the conditional "I would not keep silent," the translation would require a simple indicative, "I will not keep silent." "Heroic acts," however, sounds more appropriate for a human.

Who can uncover his outer garb,   5
        come into his double mail?
Who can pry open the doors of his face?   6
        All around his teeth is terror.
His back is rows of shields,   7
        closed with the tightest seal.
Each touches against the next,   8
        no breath can come between them.
Each sticks fast to the next,   9
        locked together, they will not part.
His sneezes shoot out light,   10
        and his eyes are like the eyelids of dawn.
Firebrands leap from his mouth,   11
        sparks of fire fly into the air.

---

5. *outer garb . . . double mail.* The description of the fabled beast begins with physical features of the crocodile—here, its plated armor. The second noun in the received text is *risno,* "his reins," but the Septuagint reading, *siryono,* "his armor," is more plausible.

6. *the doors of his face.* These are, of course, his powerful jaws.

7. *back.* The received text reads *ga'awah,* which means "pride," but both the Septuagint and the Vulgate used a Hebrew text that must have read, more plausibly, *gewah,* "back."

10. *His sneezes shoot out light.* At this point, the poet clearly moves from the Egyptian crocodile to a mythological fire-breathing dragon.
    and his eyes are like the eyelids of dawn. This verset is one of the most arresting—and daring—moves of the Job poet. He had used this altogether striking image at the beginning of the book, in Job's death-wish poem (3:9, and see the comment on that verse). Now he brings it back, not hesitating to locate an image of exquisite beauty at the heart of terror. It is precisely this paradox that epitomizes his vision of Leviathan—a frightening and alien creature—yet, in God's creation, also a thing of beauty.

11. *fly into the air.* More literally, "escape."

12   From his nostrils smoke comes out,
            like a boiling vat on brushwood.
13   His breath kindles coals,
            and flame comes out of his mouth.
14   Strength abides in his neck,
            and before him power dances.
15   The folds of his flesh cling together;
            hard-cast, he will not totter.
16   His heart is cast hard as stone,
            cast hard as a nether millstone.
17   When he rears up, the gods are frightened,
            when he crashes down, they cringe.
18   Who overtakes him with sword, it will not avail,
            nor spear nor dart nor lance.
19   Iron he deems as straw,
            and bronze as rotten wood.
20   No arrow can make him flee,
            slingstones for him turn to straw.

---

14. *power dances.* The precise meaning of the noun *de'avah* is a little in doubt. Some construe it as "violence" or "terror." The verb *taduts* usually means "to exult." Some ancient versions show *taruts* (a small orthographic difference), "runs."

16. *nether millstone.* In the biblical-poetic pattern of intensification from first verset to second, the beast's heart is at first hard as stone, then hard as a nether millstone, which would have to be especially hard and heavy in order to bear the pressure of grinding.

17. *rears up . . . crashes down.* Both words in the Hebrew are semantically ambiguous, and so this interpretation is conjectural.

18. *sword.* This paradigmatic weapon then triggers a whole catalogue of weapons that would be useless against Leviathan.

20. *arrow.* The Hebrew uses a poetic epithet, "son of the bow."

Missiles are deemed as straw,   21
      and he mocks the javelin's clatter.
Beneath him, jagged shards,   22
      he draws a harrow over the mud.
He makes the deep boil like a pot,   23
      turns sea to an ointment pan.
Behind him glistens a wake,   24
      he makes the deep seem hoary.
He has no match on earth,   25
      made as he is without fear.
All that is lofty he can see.   26
      He is king over all proud beasts.

---

21. *Missiles.* The mysterious *totaḥ* appears only here, and all that is known about it is that it must be some sort of weapon. Modern Hebrew has adopted it for "cannon."

24. *Behind him glistens a wake.* The last visual sighting of Leviathan is of his wake as he churns through the water and out of the field of human vision. It is notable that this whole poem, which began with the light of the morning stars and a question about where light dwells, concludes with a wake shining on the surface of the abyss.

26. *He is king over all proud beasts.* The same phrase, *beney shaḥats,* "proud beasts," occurs in 28:8, in the Hymn to Wisdom. Since there it refers to beasts, it is reasonable to assume that the meaning here is the same. What is remarkable about this whole powerfully vivid evocation of Leviathan is that the monotheistic poet has taken a figure from mythology, traditionally seen as the cosmic enemy of the god of order, and transformed it into this daunting creature that is preeminent in, but also very much a part of, God's teeming creation.

42

1   And Job answered the Lord and he said:
2   I know You can do anything,
                 and no devising is beyond You.
3   "Who is this obscuring counsel without knowledge?"
                 Therefore I told but did not understand,
                         wonders beyond me that I did not know.
4   "Hear, pray, and I will speak.
                 Let me ask you, that you may inform me."

---

2. *I know You can do anything.* Job's final recantation begins by a recognition of God's omnipotence, though it might be noted that he had conceded this attribute all along in his complaint against God, raising doubts not about divine power but about divine justice.

3. *"Who is this obscuring counsel without knowledge?"* Job is directly quoting God's first words to him in 38:2 (only substituting a synonymous verb). He does this in order to grant the validity of God's challenge to him.
    wonders beyond me that I did not know. The wonders are the spectacular vision of God's complex creation, from cosmogony to Leviathan, that has been vouchsafed to Job through the Voice from the Whirlwind.

4. *Let me ask you, that you may inform me.* Job again quotes from the beginning of God's speech to him, 38:2, in order to concede the justice of God's position.

By the ear's rumor I heard of You,   5
       and now my eye has seen You.
Therefore do I recant,   6
       And I repent in dust and ashes.

And it happened after the LORD had spoken these words to Job, that   7
the LORD said to Eliphaz the Temanite: "My wrath has flared against
you and your two companions because you have not spoken rightly of Me
as did My servant Job. And now, take for yourselves seven bulls and   8
seven rams and go to My servant Job, and offer a burnt-offering for yourselves, and Job My servant will pray on your behalf. To him only I shall
show favor, not to do a vile thing to you, for you have not spoken rightly
of Me as did my servant Job." And Eliphaz the Temanite and Bildad the   9
Shuhite and Zophar the Naamathite went out and did according to all

---

5. *By the ear's rumor I heard of You, / and now my eye has seen you.* "The ear's
rumor" is literally "the hearing of the ear," and picks up the imperative "hear" of
the previous line. The seeing of the eye is a testimony to the persuasive power
of the poetry that God has spoken to Job out of the whirlwind. Through that long
chain of vividly arresting images, from the swaddling bands of mist drifting over
the primordial sea at creation to the fearsomely armored Leviathan, whose eyes
are like the eyelids of dawn, Job has been led to see the multifarious character
of God's vast creation, its unfathomable fusion of beauty and cruelty, and
through this he has come to understand the incommensurability between his
human notions of right and wrong and the structure of reality. But he may not
see God Himself because God addresses him from a storm-cloud.

7. *you have not spoken rightly of Me as did My servant Job.* The three companions had repeatedly proffered lies—about Job and about the divine system of
justice—in order to preserve their pat notion of reward and punishment. They
were, in effect, corrupted witnesses on God's behalf. Though the LORD from
the whirlwind roundly rebuked Job for his presumption, Job in the debate,
unlike his three companions, had remained honest to his own observation of
reality and his awareness of his own acts; so, even in his presumption, he had
spoken "rightly" about God, had clung to his integrity. Thus God pointedly
continues here to call Job His "servant," as He did in his exchanges with the
Adversary.

that the Lord had spoken to them, and the Lord showed favor to Job.
10 And the Lord restored Job's fortunes when he prayed for his compan-
11 ions, and the Lord increased twofold all that Job had. And all his male
and female kinfolk and all who had known him before came and broke
bread with him in his house and grieved with him and comforted him for
all the harm that the Lord had brought on him. And each of them gave
12 him one kesitah and one golden ring. And the Lord blessed Job's latter
days more than his former days, and he had fourteen thousand sheep and
six thousand camels and a thousand yoke of oxen and a thousand she-

---

9. *the Lord showed favor to Job.* That is, God accepted Job's intercession on
behalf of the three companions because of Job's integrity.

10. *the Lord increased twofold all that Job had.* As countless readers have
objected, this doubling of property is scarcely adequate compensation for all
Job's sufferings, and even more so, the ten new children scarcely heal the
wound of the loss of the first ten lives. But the book ends in the folktale world
of the frame-story, where everything is reduced to schematic patterns and formulaic numbers, and perhaps in this world such a question cannot properly be
asked.

11. *all his male and female kinfolk.* The Hebrew says "all his brothers and his
sisters," but the narrative context suggests that the broader biblical meaning of
this kinship term is likely here.
    broke bread. Literally, "ate bread [that is, food]."
    grieved with him and comforted him. These are precisely the actions per-
formed by the three companions in 2:12, but here they are actually restorative,
and breaking bread together marks the return of the pariah Job to the human
community.
    kesitah. An evidently valuable coin mentioned in several other biblical texts,
though nothing more is known about it.
    one golden ring. The *nezem* is a large ring, worn on the ear or nose, not on a
finger.

asses. And he had seven sons and three daughters. And he called the 13,14
name of the first one Dove and the name of the second Cinnamon and
the name of the third Horn of Eyeshade. And there were no women in 15
the land so beautiful as Job's daughters. And their father gave them an
estate among their brothers. And Job lived a hundred and forty years after 16
this, and he saw his children and his children's children, four generations. And Job died, aged and sated in years. 17

---

14. *Dove . . . Cinnamon . . . Horn of Eyeshade.* These strange and lovely names
(the sons remain anonymous and no names were assigned to Job's children in
the opening frame-story) are mystifying. The Hebrew names *Yemimah,
Qetsi'yah, Qeren hapukh* have no currency elsewhere in the Bible. The writer
may have wanted to intimate that after all Job's suffering, which included hid-
eous disfigurement as well as violent loss, a principle of grace and beauty enters
his life in the restoration of his fortunes. Thus, the three daughters have names
associated with feminine delicacy and the arts of attraction, and they are said
to be the most beautiful women in the land.

15. *gave them an estate among their brothers.* This was not the standard biblical
practice of inheritance.

16. *children. Banim* can mean either "sons" or "children," but the prominent
attention just given to Job's three daughters suggests that the more inclusive
sense is intended. It may be especially fitting that Job, having begun his complaint by wishing that his own birth could be eradicated, at the end is witness
to a chain of births of his offspring.

PROVERBS

INTRODUCTION

lthough Proverbs, in contrast to Job and Qohelet, strikes certain recurrent notes of traditional piety and evinces great confidence in a rational moral order that dependably produces concrete rewards for virtue and wisdom, it is in some ways, like Job and Qohelet, not altogether a likely book for inclusion in the canon. The Babylonian Talmud (Shabbat 30B) in fact brackets Proverbs with Qohelet as a text that perhaps might have been excluded from the canon—in particular because it comprises contradictory assertions. The sequence of verses 4 and 5 in Chapter 26 is a vivid case in point: "Do not answer a dolt by his folly / lest you, too, be like him. // Answer the dolt by his folly, / lest he seem wise in his own eyes." What, then, the earnest reader may wonder, is one to do about answering a dolt? It is probably misguided to argue for a dialectic or subtly complementary relationship between these two admonitions. The contradiction between them stems from the anthological character of the book: the two sayings have been culled either from folk-tradition or from the verbal repertory of Wisdom schools and have been set in immediate sequence by the anthologist because of the identical wording—first in the negative and then in the positive—of the initial clause of each saying.

The Book of Proverbs is not merely an anthology but an anthology of anthologies. It is made up of six discrete units, each marked editorially as such at the beginning, with notable differences of emphasis and style among the units. Chapters 1–9 form a kind of general prologue to the subject of the instruction of wisdom. Michael V. Fox, in his two indispensable Proverbs volumes in the Anchor Bible Series, argues persuasively that this first unit was the last one composed, either in the Persian period or in the Hellenistic period. It is strikingly different from the collections of one-line, two-verset proverbs that follow in deploying poems that extend to all or a good part of a chapter. These include the vivid narrative about the seductress that takes up Chapter 7 and the allegorical representation of Lady Wisdom in Chapter 8 and of the contrasting figures of Lady Wisdom and Lady Folly in Chapter 9. The recurring theme in this initial unit that the fear of the LORD is the beginning of wisdom also sets it apart from the subsequent collections, in which wisdom is more typically thought of without theological trappings as a transmissible human craft. Finally, the prominence here of the Mentor and the inexperienced youth he seeks to instruct recedes or disappears as the book moves on to the one-line proverbs.

The second grouping, introduced like the first with the phrase "the proverbs of Solomon," runs from the beginning of Chapter 10 to 22:16. Many scholars think that this double ascription of the book to Solomon, celebrated in 1 Kings 5:12 for his prodigious production of proverbs, may have encouraged its inclusion in the canon, though that claim is hard to assess. In the one-line proverb, the symmetrical logic of poetic parallelism predominates, with most of the proverbs exhibiting either neatly matching statements in the two versets or emphatic antitheses. After this unit, which is the longest collection in the anthology of anthologies, a short unit begins that is marked with the exhortation, "Bend your ear and hear the words of the wise," the phrase "the words of the wise" evidently serving as a kind of title. This grouping provides the most vivid evidence of the international character of Wisdom literature because a large part of it, as scholars have long recognized, is a recasting of the sayings of Amenemope, a second-millennium Egyptian text, which may have reached the Hebrew writer through the mediation of an Aramaic version. After this, 24:23 begins with the declaration, "These, too, are from the wise," which indicates a new source, of which perhaps only a fragment is included because it ends or breaks off after eleven verses.

The first verse of Chapter 25 then provides a valuable historical clue about the editorial process of these collections: "These, too, are the proverbs of Solomon, which the men of Hezekiah king of Judea transcribed." Hezekiah reigned in Jerusalem in the late decades of the eighth century BCE. The men of Hezekiah would have been court scribes, and in fact there is a good deal of emphasis in this unit, which runs to the end of Chapter 29, on kings and how one should comport oneself in their presence. The verb "transcribed," *he'etiqu*, does not imply original composition but rather an activity such as collating and copying or transferring from another source, which means that the original formulation of at least some of these proverbs might have occurred generations, perhaps even quite a few generations, before the time of Hezekiah, however unlikely the ascription to Solomon.

Finally, Chapters 30 and 31 comprise, as Fox aptly calls them, a series of four "appendices" to the book proper. Each is quite different in style and emphasis from everything that precedes it in the completed anthology, and though the appendices are clearly drawn from different literary sources, there is no confident way of concluding whether they are later sources or just exotic ones. The first appendix, 30:1–14, is "The words of Agur, son of Yaqeh," a figure about whom nothing is known. The style is vatic, and the idea that God alone possesses wisdom runs counter to the prevailing notion in the rest of the book of wisdom as a teachable craft. The second appendix (30:15–38) is made up of a series of riddling epigrams cast in a three-four numerical pattern ("Three things are there that are not sated, / four that do not say 'Enough!' ") occasionally found elsewhere in biblical poetry and ultimately going back to Canaanite poetic style. The third appendix, 31:1–9, "The words of Lemuel, king of Massa," is a set of instructions of a queen mother to her royal son. At the very end of the book (31:10–31), we have an alphabetic acrostic poem celebrating the ideal wife—an interesting editorial choice for the conclusion of a book that has featured male mentors instructing young men and has repeatedly warned against seductresses and complained of shrewish wives.

The Book of Proverbs, then, is by no means cut from whole cloth, and consequently generalizations about its outlook and literary character will not hold for all parts of the anthology. By and large, the underlying conception of wisdom is thoroughly pragmatic, and, in keeping with the characteristic direction of Wisdom literature, it does not reflect particular Israelite interests. The recurring term *torah* does not refer to any divinely inspired text but simply means "teaching" or "instruction" and is closely coordinated with the constantly reiterated *musar*, "reproof" or "discipline." This basically untheological orientation, in which neither revelation nor covenant has any role, might conceivably have been another potential obstacle to the book's inclusion in the canon that was nevertheless overcome by the rabbinic sages. (The one brief component of the anthology that does sound fully "canonical" in this regard is Agur's pious poem exalting God's transcendent greatness and affirming the nullity of human wisdom.)

The book is poetry from end to end, but what kind of poetry is it? In line with its composite nature, it is not the same in all its segments. The acrostic poem at the end praising the "worthy woman" is a rapid sequence of narrative vignettes exhibiting the good woman in a chain of energetic actions on behalf of her household, acquiring flax and wool and weaving them, rising before daybreak to set out on her rounds of commerce, and so forth. The poems of the first nine chapters abound in incipiently narrative developments—Lady Wisdom calling out from the heights to invite the throngs to attend to her instruction, the Mentor spelling out step-by-step the disasters to which the Stranger Woman (presumably, a lascivious married woman) will lead a young man, the antithetical evocation in an extended metaphor of the delights of conjugal love.

The large central core of the book, however, from Chapter 10 to the end of Chapter 29, which gathers together one-line proverbs from a variety of sources, is the part of the book in which the poetry is liable to pose the greatest difficulties for modern readers. The one-line proverbs are either didactic admonitions or, somewhat less frequently, observations about social and ethical behavior. Some of the sayings in the second category are quite shrewd and evince lively satiric perceptions. The admonitions, on the other hand, show a good deal of predictability, founded as they are on what the writers assume to be tried-and-true principles for guiding a person through life. As a result, the poetry is sometimes boilerplate language, a rehearsal of traditional formulas. This is a limitation that the author of Job, perhaps the most original of biblical poets, obviously noticed, putting in the mouths of the three friends many complacent pronouncements about the rightness of the moral order that sound like this line from Proverbs (10:3): "The LORD will not make the righteous man hunger, / but the desire of the wicked He rebuffs." Poetry in all cultures serves a mnemonic function—in systems that have rhyme, the rhyme helps you remember the line that comes after its rhyming counterpart. In the semantic parallelism of biblical poetry, the match in meaning (and often in rhythm and syntax) helps you remember the second verset after the first. If there were in fact

Wisdom schools in ancient Israel, it is easy enough to imagine how the formulation of ethical and pragmatic principles in poetry helped students to memorize them. Thus, the line "Cheating scales are the LORD's loathing, / and a true weight-stone His pleasure" (11:1) occurs several times with minor variations. Unlike the sundry claims about the righteous and the wicked, it is unassailable as an ethical principle. One would hardly call it great poetry, but the poetic parallelism does serve to inscribe the saying in memory with the aim of being a kind of ethical prophylaxis: should you ever be tempted to enhance your profits in a sale of goods by using a crooked scale or an underweight marked stone, this saying is meant to come to mind and dissuade you.

Many other proverbs are grounded not in ethics but in purely prudential considerations, such as the reiterated exhortations not to give your bond for someone you don't know—for example, "He will surely be shattered who gives bond for a stranger, / but he who hates offering pledge is secure" (11:15). Here, too, the rather mechanical parallelism is an aid to memory, serving a prophylactic function in the economic sphere rather than in the ethical realm. The least interesting of the proverbs, as the one just cited may suggest, amount to poetic formulations of truisms. It seems scarcely necessary, for example, to be reminded, as we are by several different proverbs, that warfare needs to be conducted with considered strategy and expert military advisers, or that a person too lazy to provide for himself will end up in want.

This last instance of the lazy man, however, also illustrates how poetry in the Book of Proverbs often goes beyond a purely mnemonic function to serve as a vehicle of enlivening perception. Within the tight formal constraints of the one-line aphorism, dynamic and revelatory relationships emerge between the two halves of the line, generating what I have elsewhere called a poetry of wit. (The frequent celebrations in the book of the power of language invite from the audience a fine attentiveness to the play of language in the poetry.) Very often in biblical poetry, the second verset does not simply echo the first verset, as it does in the three lines quoted above, but instead introduces some sort of heightening or focusing development of it, which in Proverbs frequently is a small surprise or discovery. "A door turns on its hinge / and a sluggard on his bed" (26:14). Here, as in many other proverbs, the relation between the first verset and the second is that of a riddle to its solution.

That is, the assertion in the first half of the line is either so obvious (of course, a door turns on its hinge) that one wonders why it needs to be said at all, or it is perplexing, which makes one wonder for a different reason. The second half of the line then provides a sharply focused (and sometimes satirical) explanation. In this instance, the sluggard is revealed turning back and forth on his bed and getting nowhere, like the door, while the comparison also invites us to think of the contrast between people going in and out of the doorway as the door opens and closes and the sluggard unwilling to move from his bed. Here is a different riddle-proverb about the lazy man, in which the riddling first verset is enigmatic, to be explained in the second verset: "Like vinegar to the teeth and smoke to the eyes, / thus the sluggard to those who send him" (10:26). In formulations of this sort, the riddle form of the line is especially prominent: what is as noxious or irritating as vinegar to the teeth and smoke to the eyes?—a lazy man whom you have the misfortune to use on an errand. A third proverb on the sluggard illustrates the lively variety of the riddle form. The line begins, "The sluggard hides his hand in the dish." This action sounds bizarre, and one wonders why anyone would want to do such a thing. Then the second half of the line explains, "he won't even bring it up to his mouth" (19:24). This is, of course, an extravagant and amusing satiric hyperbole: the man is so lazy that, having plunged his hand into the dish, he is incapable of exerting the effort required to bring the food to his mouth. Thus, the fantastically exaggerated image becomes a representation of how laziness leads to a failure to provide for one's own basic needs, a notion couched in more realistic terms, such as having nothing to harvest when crops are not planted, in other proverbs.

The satiric perspective, to round out this sampling of proverbs on the sluggard, is not limited to riddling but can be brought to bear through a technique of miniaturist caricature: "The sluggard said, 'A lion's outside / in the square. I shall be murdered!' " (22:13). These words, of course, are a trumped-up excuse for his not leaving his house (or, perhaps, his bed): in the wonderful extravagance of the dialogue that the poet puts in the mouth of the sluggard, he fears that the fictitious lion prowling in the streets threatens not to devour but to murder him, as though it were a malevolent assassin and not merely a beast of prey.

Many of the proverbs set out an antithesis between the first verset and the second, and the tight confines of the one-line aphorism often generate a powerful energy of assertion in the antithesis. Thus: "A worthy woman is her husband's crown, / but like rot in the bones she who shames" (12:4). The first verset praising the good wife verges on platitude, but then the antithetical second verset produces a small shock: a crown is a noble thing yet also an external ornament (perhaps an allusion to the fortunate husband's enhanced reputation); rot in the bones is something internal, and devastating. This whole effect is strongly reinforced by the antithetical chiasm: worthy woman (a) / crown (b) // bone-rot (b´) / shaming woman (a´). Sometimes, the contrasting second verset takes on a surprising vividness against the foil of the first verset: "Drawn-out longing sickens the heart, / but desire come true is a tree of life" (13:12). By itself, the second clause might seem a bland truism, but after the sickening of the heart of unfulfilled desire, it conveys a strong sense of how sustaining it is to have one's longings consummated. In some antithetical proverbs, there is also narrative development from the first verset to the second: "Bread got through fraud may be sweet to a man, / but in the end it fills his mouth with gravel" (20:17). The idea that pleasures reaped through wrongful acts will eventually be followed by a comeuppance for the wrongdoer is a cliché of Wisdom literature. Here, however, the powerfully concrete image of delectable food that turns into a mouthful of gravel endows the familiar idea with poetic force.

A traditional proverb pattern that occurs with some frequency in the collection is "better X" (first verset) "than Y" (second verset). This is actually a variation on the antithetically structured line and similarly draws its expressive power from the bold juxtaposition of opposites. Here are two characteristic examples: "Better a meal of greens where there is love / than a fatted ox where there is hatred" (15:17) and "Better a dry crust with tranquility / than a house filled with feasting and quarrel" (17:1). Though some of these proverbs may give the impression of the rehearsal of rote learning, many others—perhaps the two instances just cited among them—are arresting not just because of the concise poetic wit but also because they appear to derive from shrewd and considered reflection on moral behavior and human nature and sometimes from introspection as well. If some of these maxims may seem too pat, one is startled to come across this proverb: "The heart knows its own bitterness, / and in its joy no stranger mingles" (14:10). The book as a whole, after all, works on the assumption that knowledge and experience are eminently transmissible and teachable and that everyone draws on the same fund of set moral principles. In this instance, however, the anthologists have included a very different perception—that each person's experience is ultimately incommensurable, that one's inward sorrows and delights have no adequate reflection in the lexicon of the social realm. Occasionally, despite the general adherence of the collection to moral certitude, one encounters a proverb that registers the stubborn ambiguity of human experience, as in this densely packed line: "Like water face to face / thus the heart of man to man" (27:19). The first verset evidently means to say that water gives back a person his own reflected image, and so the second verset would seem to assert that a man may know the heart of another by pondering what is in his own heart. But water, after all, is an unstable mirror, its surface liable to be troubled by wind or tide, its chromatic layers darkening or transforming the image, and hence the reflection of heart to heart may be a tricky or undependable business.

Rendering these pithy Hebrew maxims in English presents a special challenge. The distinctive lexical stamp of the Book of Proverbs is marked by its use of a set of overlapping terms for wisdom on the one hand and for foolishness or stupidity on the other. Michael V. Fox has exerted heroic scholarly effort to make nice distinctions among these approximate synonyms, but it is doubtful that the precise semantic contours of each of the recurring terms can be recovered with much confidence. The general term for wisdom is *hokhmah*, which has a practical orientation, being used in other contexts for the "wise" application of a craft by a skilled worker, but which in Chapters 8 and 9 is given cosmic resonance. Three other terms, *'ormah*, *mezimah*, and *tahbulah*, usually have connotations of calculation, shrewdness, or cunning, here put in a positive light. Of the sundry terms for the lack of wisdom, the one that has a clear connotation is *peti*, represented in this translation as "dupe," because it derives from a verbal root associated with seduction and hence suggests gullibility. By and large, the present translation uses the same English equivalent for each member of these two clusters of related terms, although there are moments when the immediate context has necessitated abandoning consistency.

The more pervasive challenge to the translator of Proverbs is that the expressive vigor of these sayings depends to such a large degree on their wonderful compactness, an effect reinforced by sound-play (alliteration, assonance, an occasional ad-hoc internal rhyme). Most of this sound-play inevitably disappears in the English, though some efforts have been made in this version to reproduce it, at least approximately. Because of the fundamental structural difference between biblical Hebrew and modern English, it often takes eight to ten words to say in English what is expressed in four Hebrew words. There is no escape from this linguistic quandary, but I have sought to narrow the gap between the two languages by avoiding (with just a few exceptions) polysyllabic words, by trying wherever possible to keep the number of accents—typically, three per verset—close to that in the Hebrew, and by reproducing something of the compression of formulation of the Hebrew without resort to explanatory or paraphrastic maneuvers in the translation. However imperfect the results, I would hope these procedures will bring readers closer than do earlier English versions to the concise forcefulness of the Hebrew. The speed, the occasional abruptness, the gnomic character of the original seem worth emulating—hence renderings such as "like water face to face, / so the heart of man to man."

1

The proverbs of Solomon, son of David, king of Israel.   1
To know wisdom and reproof,   2
        to understand discerning maxims.
To accept the reproof of insight,   3
        righteousness, justice, and uprightness.

---

1. *The proverbs of Solomon, son of David, king of Israel.* This editorial headnote
for the book follows the Late Biblical practice of ascribing texts to famous figures from the national past. In this case, the ascription was obviously encouraged by the legendary wisdom reported of Solomon in 1 Kings, including his
having composed many proverbs. In fact, the collections of sayings and longer
poems assembled in the book were written in all probability centuries after
Solomon, with the earliest stratum going back, perhaps, to the eighth century
BCE, though some individual proverbs may well have been older.

    proverbs. The Hebrew *mishley*—which actually means "proverbs of"—
became the prevalent title for the book in Jewish tradition. The term, which
suggests some sort of artful expression, usually poetic, has no entirely satisfactory English equivalent because it variously means proverb, parable, poetic
theme, rhapsodic utterance.

2. *To know wisdom and reproof.* The series of infinitive phrases, which runs
from here to the end of verse 4 and is picked up again in verse 6, is quite untypi-
cal of literary syntax in the Bible. It is presumably used because it lays out an
agenda for the book, with everything from the beginning through verse 9 con-
stituting a formal prelude to the book proper. "Reproof," *musar*, and the matching term "rebuke," *tokheḥah*, are prominently featured because the pedagogical
assumption of the book is that the unsuspecting young need to be warned of
life's dangers and scolded for their susceptibility to temptation—a process that
will be repeatedly evident, beginning here in verses 10–19.

4   To give shrewdness to the simple,
             to a lad, knowledge and cunning.
5   Let the wise man hear and gain learning,
             and the discerning acquire designs.
6   To understand proverbs and adages,
             the words of the wise and their riddles.
7   The fear of the LORD is the beginning of knowledge.
             Wisdom and reproof dolts despise.

8   Hear, my son, your father's reproof,
             and do not forsake your mother's teaching.
9   For they are a garland of grace on your head
             and a necklace round your throat.

---

4. *shrewdness . . . cunning.* This book uses in a positive sense a cluster of
terms—"designs" in the next verse belongs to the cluster—that in other contexts have a connotation of deviousness and scheming. ("Shrewdness," *'ormah,*
for example, is the word used for the primeval serpent in Genesis 3:1.) Such
usage fits in with the pragmatic curriculum of Proverbs. Intelligence of the
most practical sort, involving an alertness to potential deceptions and seduc-
tions, is seen as an indispensable tool for the safe, satisfying, and ethical life,
and a fool is repeatedly thought of as a dupe.

6. *riddles.* This is the same term, *ḥidah,* that is used in the Samson story. Some
of the one-line proverbs, as we shall see, are actually cast as riddles, with the
first verset posing the riddle and the second verset the solution. The burden of
the entire line is that fine attentiveness is required to take in fully the words of
the wise, and that idea is borne out by the compressed wit exhibited in many
of the proverbs.

7. *The fear of the LORD is the beginning of knowledge.* This summarizing statement reflects a distinctive Israelite emphasis not evident in analogous Wisdom
texts in Egypt and Mesopotamia.

8. *Hear, my son.* The persona of the Mentor now emerges, addressing his inexperienced disciple—as he will repeatedly do later—as "son," in keeping with
the precedent of Egyptian Wisdom writings.

My son, should offenders seduce you,   10
>> do not be willing.

Should they say,   11
>> "Go with us, let us lie in wait for blood,
>>> stalk the innocent for no reason.

Let us swallow them live like Sheol,   12
>> and the blameless like those gone down to the Pit.

All precious treasure we shall find,   13
>> we shall fill our houses with loot.

Your lot you should throw in with us,   14
>> one purse we all shall have."

My son, do not go on a road with them,   15
>> hold back your foot from their path.

---

10. *offenders.* One immediately sees why the traditional rendering of *ḥataʾim* as "sinners," perpetuated in many modern translations, is not quite right. These are offenders in the strict criminal sense, a gang of violent thugs. This monitory poem runs to the end of verse 19, followed by Wisdom's first speech, which takes up fourteen verses till the end of the chapter. Continuous poems of roughly this length constitute the first nine-chapter unit of the book. Then there is a shift to one-line proverbs.

do not be willing. The two-word Hebrew verset looks textually suspect, reflecting a rhythmic imbalance with the first verset.

11. *Should they say.* This formula for introducing speech, as elsewhere in biblical poetry, seems to be extra-metrical.

Blood . . . innocent. These two terms, distributed between the two versets, are, as Michael V. Fox neatly observes, a breakup of a bound collocation, "blood of the innocent," *dam naqi.*

12. *swallow them live like Sheol.* The implication of "blood" in the previous line is spelled out: the thugs' plan is to murder their victims and then seize their wealth.

14. *one purse we all shall have.* The thugs appeal to the young man not only on the basis of profit ("precious treasure") to be had but also for the camaraderie in crime that they offer.

15. *road . . . path.* Though these terms and related synonyms are a figure for a way of behavior, they are also literal here: the bandits want to draw the young man with them on a road where they will lie in wait for victims.

16   For their feet run to evil,
                and they hurry to shed blood.
17   For the net is spread out for no reason
                in the eyes of each wingèd thing.
18   Yet they lie in wait for their own blood,
                they lurk for their own lives.
19   Thus are the ways of all who chase gain,
                its possessor's life it will take.

20   Wisdom cries out in the streets,
                in the squares she lifts her voice.
21   At the bustling crossroads she calls,
                at the entrance to the town's gate says her sayings:

---

17. *For the net is spread out for no reason.* The unwitting birds do not imagine that the fowlers' net spread below them is meant to entrap them.

18. *Yet they lie in wait for their own blood.* Most interpreters, seeing an implied analogy between the unwitting birds and the naïve young drawn into crime, understand this to mean that the criminals do not imagine that they will be caught by the dire consequences of their own crime, do not realize that they are their own ambushers. This would be in keeping with an idea stressed in Proverbs—and vehemently rejected in Job—that there is a built-in moral mechanism that leads from crime to disaster for its perpetrators. Similarly in the next verse, ill-gotten gain is said to take "its possessor's life."

20. *Wisdom cries out in the streets.* Lady Wisdom, an important personage in the first large unit of Proverbs, is as close to an allegorical figure as the Hebrew Bible comes. Attempts to derive her from the Greek *Sophia* are questionable, and it is by no means clear that any of this book was written as late as the Hellenistic period. Female figures as symbols of nations—most notably, Zion—are common in biblical literature, but not as embodiments of abstractions. Perhaps the centrality of the quality of wisdom in this poetic book led to a feminine personification. The Hebrew *ḥokhmah* is a feminine noun, though here it appears in a plural form, *ḥokhmot*, construed grammatically as a singular (like Behemoth in Job). This could be a plural of intensification or an archaic form.

21. *bustling crossroads.* This translation follows a proposal by Fox. The literal sense is "chief [or head] of the bustlings," which he plausibly construes as an ellipsis.

How long, dupes, will you love being duped,   22
        and scoffers lust scoffing,
               and fools hate knowledge?
Turn back to my rebuke.   23
        Look, I would pour out my spirit to you,
               I would make my words known with you.
Because I called and you resisted,   24
        I reached out my hand and none paid heed,
and you flung aside all my counsel,   25
        and you did not want my rebuke.
I, too, shall laugh at your ruin,   26
        I shall mock when what you feared comes,
when what you feared comes like disaster,   27
        and your ruin like a whirlwind descends,
               when straits and distress come upon you.
Then they will call me and I shall not answer,   28
        they will seek me and they will not find me.
Because they have hated knowledge,   29
        and the LORD's fear they did not choose.
They did not want my counsel,   30
        they spurned all my rebuke.
And they ate from the fruit of their way,   31
        and from their own counsels they were sated.

---

25. *flung aside*. The verb is elsewhere used for unbinding the hair, so it literally means something like to put in disarray.

27. *straits and distress*. The Hebrew similarly features alliteration, **tsarah** *umetsukah*.

31. *ate from the fruit of their way*. As in verses 18 and 19, the idea is that they had to taste the bitter consequences of their own evil acts.
    from their own counsels they were sated. This verset extends the idea of eating the dire consequences of crime. "Counsels," *mo'etsot*, antithetically picks up the "counsel" of Wisdom (verse 30) that was spurned, the two words here being different noun formations from the same root.

32   For the waywardness of dupes will kill them
           and the smugness of fools will destroy them.
33   But who heeds me will dwell secure,
           and tranquil from the fear of harm.

---

33. *who heeds me will dwell secure*. Again and again, Proverbs pushes the notion that there is a pragmatic payoff for following the precepts of wisdom: those who do so will enjoy untroubled lives, secure from harm.

2

My son, if you take up my sayings,   1
    and my commands you store within you,
to make your ear hearken to wisdom,   2
    incline your heart to discernment,
for if you call out to understanding,   3
    raise your voice to discernment,
if you seek it like silver,   4
    search for it like treasure,
then will you understand the LORD's fear,   5
    and you will find the knowledge of God.
For the LORD gives wisdom,   6
    from His mouth, discerning knowledge.
He stores for the upright prudence,   7
    a shield to those who walk blameless,

---

1. *take up my sayings.* Here, as elsewhere, the Mentor presents himself as an authoritative figure who is the dependable source of wisdom for his as yet untutored disciple.

5. *then will you understand the LORD's fear.* Since the fear of the LORD is represented definitionally as the beginning of wisdom, the converse is also true: a person, by making a strenuous and sincere effort to discover wisdom, will come to understand what fear of the LORD is, for He (verse 6) is the one who ultimately imparts all wisdom.

7. *a shield.* The notion that wisdom protects one from mishaps is of a piece with the general conception of wisdom's possessing pragmatic advantages.

8   to keep the paths of justice
         and He watches the way of His faithful.

9   Then you will understand righteousness, justice,
         and uprightness, each pathway of good.

10   For wisdom will enter your heart,
         and knowledge be sweet to your palate.

11   Cunning will watch over you,
         discernment will keep you,

12   to save you from a way of evil,
         from a man who speaks perversely.

13   They forsake the paths of uprightness
         to go in the ways of darkness,

14   they rejoice to do evil,
         delight in evil's perverseness,

15   whose paths are crooked,
         and twisted in their pathways.

---

10. *for wisdom will enter your heart.* Here and above, in verse 2, the English reader should recall that the heart is conceived as the seat of understanding (rather like "mind"), though it also is associated with emotion.

11. *cunning.* See the comment on 1:4. It may be useful to keep in mind that "cunning" in English is not always a negative term. Consider, for example, such usages as "cunning design."

12. *perversely.* The Hebrew *tahapukhot* suggests things topsy-turvy, upended from their proper place. Proverbs repeatedly uses antithetical spatial metaphors for the good and the evil life. The former is a straight way; the latter is perverse, topsy-turvy, or, as in verse 15, crooked and twisted.

13. *They forsake the paths of uprightness.* The Hebrew here and in the next verse uses a plural participial form: "forsaking the paths." This entire first piece of admonition to the young man is quite general, warning him to stay away from bad people. The unit that begins with verse 16 is more specific—a warning of the dangers of the sexual seductress.

15. *twisted.* That is, both the paths and the men who go on them are twisted.

To save you from a stranger-woman,   16
     from a smooth-talking alien woman,
who forsakes the guide of her youth   17
     and the pact of her God forgets.
For her house leads down to death   18
     and to the shades, her pathways.

---

16. *stranger-woman.* The meaning of the Hebrew *zarah* has been much debated. The usual English designation, "strange woman," is misleading because it implies that she is strange—that is, somehow bizarre. She is not, as some have claimed, a prostitute because verse 17 indicates that she is married. There is also scant suggestion that, as others have argued, she is a foreigner, even though the parallel term in this line, *nokhriyah*, "alien woman," often means foreigner. In cultic contexts, a *zar* is someone prohibited from entering the sacred zone of the sanctuary because he is not a priest. That sense is relevant to our text: the married woman, because she is contracted to another man, is prohibited to the susceptible youth. The paired term *nokhriyah*, then, in the poetic parallelism, probably has the force of "another man's wife"—alien in a sexual rather than a national sense.

17. *the guide of her youth.* Though some render *'aluf* as "companion," the point is, in this patriarchal society, that the husband is expected to provide moral guidance for his wife, which in this case she has flagrantly ignored. The verbal root of the Hebrew noun means "to instruct" and has no association with companionability.

the pact of her God. Given the context of abandoning her husband-guide, the most likely reference is to the marriage contract, or perhaps, by extension, to the divine prohibition of adultery.

18. *her house leads down to death.* More literally, "stoops down" or "tilts down." It is unnecessary to emend *beytah*, "her house," to *netivatah*, "her path," as some have proposed, because the phrase offers a vivid image of the house of the adulteress—her husband may be away on business, as in Chapter 7—as a death trap: you enter it and find yourself on a chute sliding down into the realm of death. The writer seems to assume that adultery leads to death as a condign punishment, though he might have in mind the consequence of the husband's vengeance (compare 7:23).

19   All who come to her will not return,
               and will not attain the paths of life.

20   So that you walk in the way of the good,
               and the paths of the just you keep.

21   For the upright will dwell on earth
               and the blameless survive on it.

22   But the wicked are cut off from the earth,
               and traitors torn away from it.

---

19. *All who come to.* The Hebrew makes a pointed pun because to come into a woman means to have sex with her. The house leading down to death is thus metonymically linked with the woman's body leading to death.

21. *the upright will dwell on earth.* The multivalent Hebrew *'erets* here has the sense of "earth," not "land," because what is at issue is survival in life: the person who follows the ethical path marked out by wisdom will live long on earth while the wicked die before their time (the next verse), like the men who succumb to the wiles of the seductress.

3

My son, do not forget my teaching,   1
          and let your heart keep my commands.
For length of days and years of life   2
          and peace they will add for you.
Kindness and truth will not forsake you.   3
          Bind them round your neck,
                    write them on your heart's tablet,
and find favor and good regard   4
          in the eyes of God and man.
Trust in the Lord with all your heart,   5
          and do not lean on your discernment.

---

2. *length of days . . . years of life*. This pronouncement continues the central pragmatic theme in Proverbs: that following the path of wisdom leads to physical well-being, prosperity, and longevity.

3. *round your neck . . . on your heart's tablet*. The teachings of wisdom are both an external ornament and something to be internalized and permanently retained.

4. *good regard*. The Hebrew *sekhel* can also mean "intelligence" (a usage carried forward in modern Hebrew, where it suggests something like "common sense"). But the verbal root means "to see"—in many languages, there is a link between seeing and understanding—as in Genesis 3:6, "the tree was lovely to look at [*lehaskil*]." In the present context, where the opinions of others is at issue, "regard" seems the likely meaning. Fox comes to the same conclusion.

6　Through all your ways know Him,
　　　　　　and He will make your paths straight.

7　Do not be wise in your own eyes,
　　　　　　fear the LORD and swerve from evil.

8　Let it be healing for your flesh
　　　　　　and a balm to your bones.

9　Honor the LORD more than your wealth
　　　　　　and than the first fruits of your crop,

10　and your barns will be filled with abundance,
　　　　　　your vats will burst with new wine.

11　The LORD's reproof, my son, do not spurn,
　　　　　　and do not despise His rebuke.

12　For whom the LORD loves He rebukes,
　　　　　　and like a father his son, regards him kindly.

13　Happy the man who has found wisdom,
　　　　　　and the man who acquires discernment.

---

6. *make your paths straight.* The verb could also mean "level," meaning you can walk on your paths without obstruction, but the antithesis of crooked paths (see 2:15) may make straightening the more likely meaning.

7. *Do not be wise in your own eyes, / fear the* LORD. Behind this admonition is the key idea that fear of the LORD is the beginning of wisdom.

8. *your flesh.* The Masoretic text reads *shorekha,* "your navel," which sounds bizarre, the navel not being known as a focus of bodily well-being. The Septuagint evidently used a Hebrew text that read, far more probably, *she'eirkha,* "your flesh," and it seems likely that the medial *'aleph* was inadvertently dropped in scribal transmission.

10. *abundance.* Literally, "satiety." The reference is to abundant grain, paired with new wine in the second verset.

13. *Happy the man.* After the general exhortation to follow the words of the wise that takes up verses 1–12, a new unit begins here. The *'ashrey* formula, "happy the man," often marks the beginning of a textual unit, as in the Wisdom psalm (Psalm 1) that stands at the head of the canonical collection. The subject

For her worth is better than silver's worth,   14
    and her yield better than fine gold.
More precious is she than rubies,   15
    and all your cherished things could not equal her.
Length of days are in her right hand,   16
    in her left hand wealth and honor.
Her ways are ways of pleasantness,   17
    and all her paths are peace.
A tree of life is she to those who grasp her,   18
    and those who hold her are deemed happy.
The LORD through wisdom founded earth,   19
    set heavens firm through discernment.
Through His knowledge the deeps burst open,   20
    and the skies dripped dew.

---

of this poetic sequence, which ends at verse 20, is a celebration of the transcendent powers of wisdom.

14. *her worth*. Although wisdom is not explicitly personified in 1:20–33, she is nevertheless represented as a feminine figure, possessing two hands (verse 16). The term for "worth" here, *saḥar*, implies market value.

15. *rubies*. As with most precious stones in the biblical lexicon, the precise identification is uncertain. In modern Hebrew, *peninim* means "pearls," which might possibly be its biblical sense.

18. *deemed happy*. The word "deemed" has been added because the passive verb *me'ushar* is the condition of the person of whom others say *'ashrey*, "happy is he."

19. *The LORD through wisdom founded earth*. Though this could be read as a poetic flourish, it begins to move toward the idea cultivated by Kabbalists and others that wisdom is a cosmic principle by which God works out the design of creation.

20. *the deeps burst open . . . the skies dripped dew*. This figuration of fructifying creation is a benign reversal of the Flood story, where "all the wellsprings of the great deep burst / and the casements of the heavens were opened" (Genesis 7:11).

21   My son, let these things not slip away from your eyes,
              keep prudence and cunning,
22   and they will be life to your neck
              and grace to your throat.
23   Then you shall walk secure on your way,
              and your foot shall not be bruised.
24   If you lie down, you shall not be afraid.
              You shall lie down, and your sleep shall be sweet.
25   You shall not fear any sudden fright,
              nor the plight of the wicked when it comes.
26   For the LORD will be your trust,
              and will guard your foot from the snare.

27   Don't hold back bounty from him who earned it
              when it's within your hand's power to perform.
28   Don't say to your friend, "Go and come back,
              and tomorrow I'll give," when you have it.

---

21. *My son, let these things not slip away from your eyes.* This unit of the text, which runs to verse 26, is a series of exhortations to cling to wisdom and thus enjoy its benefits, which parallels the similar series in verses 1–12, forming a kind of frame around the celebration of the supernal force of wisdom in verses 13–20.

22. *life to your neck . . . grace to your throat.* Because of the poetic parallelism, the probable sense of the multivalent *nefesh* here, as frequently in Psalms (see, for example, Psalm 69:2), is "neck." The idea of wisdom as an ornament around the neck (compare verse 3) is common in Proverbs, but "life to your neck" sounds odd. The reference might conceivably be to a life-protecting amulet, worn around the neck.

25. *plight of the wicked.* That is, sooner or later, disaster will inevitably overtake the wicked, but a person who follows the ways of wisdom will have no reason to fear such catastrophe.

27. *Don't hold back bounty.* These words initiate a fourth textual unit, which is a miscellany of negative injunctions regarding behavior toward one's fellow man. It must be said that this whole series borders on platitude, rather like Polonius's advice to Hamlet.

Don't plot harm against your fellow,   29
  when he dwells secure alongside you.
Don't quarrel with a man for no reason   30
  if he has done you no harm.
Don't envy a man of violence   31
  and don't choose any of his ways.
For a crooked man is the Lord's loathing,   32
  and the upright are His intimates.
The Lord's blight is on the house of the wicked,   33
  and the abode of the righteous He blesses.
As for the scoffers, He scoffs at them,   34
  but to the humble He grants favor.
The wise inherit honor,   35
  and fools take away disgrace.

---

32. *crooked . . . upright.* The two Hebrew terms are pointed antonyms because "upright," *yesharim*, is literally "straight."

 and the upright are His intimates. The literal sense of the Hebrew is "and the upright are with [or "part of"] His intimate circle."

35. *honor . . . disgrace.* The two Hebrew terms are antonyms not only semantically but also etymologically: the word for "honor," *kavod*, derives from a root that means "weighty" or "heavy," and the word for "disgrace," *qalon*, derives from a root that means "light," which is to say, of no importance.

 take away. The Hebrew *merim* (ostensibly, "raises") is anomalous and also a singular verb where the plural is required. Efforts to recover an original term by emendation have been unavailing, but the poetic parallelism indicates that a word meaning "to take possession" was intended.

4

H ear, O sons, a father's reproof,
     and listen to discerning knowledge.

2 For good learning I have given you,
     do not forsake my teaching.

3 For I was a son to my father,
     a tender only child for my mother.

4 And he taught me and said to me:
     "Let your heart hold on to my words.
        Keep my commands and live.

5 Get wisdom, get discernment.
     Do not forget nor swerve from my mouth's sayings.

6 Do not forsake her and she will guard you.
     Love her and she will keep you.

---

3. *For I was a son to my father.* In the tradition-oriented framework of Proverbs, wisdom is a quality that age imparts to youth (a theme repeatedly struck by Job's companions), father to son. That idea is reinforced here by the introduction of a third generation, the grandfather of the young man who is the object of instruction. Just as the Mentor was taught by his father, whose words he goes on to quote, he will teach the young man.

A tender only child. As an only child, he would have been a special object of parental attention and of solicitude for his moral education.

6. *Do not forsake her.* The feminine pronoun refers to wisdom, which, even without explicit personification, is imagined as a female figure.

The beginning of wisdom is—get wisdom, 7
     and in all that you get, get discernment.
Dandle her and she will exalt you, 8
     will honor you when you embrace her.
She will put on your head a garland of grace, 9
     a crown of splendor she will hand you."

Hear, my son, and take my sayings, 10
     that the years of your life be many.
In the way of wisdom I teach you, 11
     I guide you on pathways of rightness.
When you walk, your step is not straitened. 12
     If you run, you will not stumble.
Hold fast to reproof, don't let go. 13
     Keep it, for it is your life.
On the wicked's path do not enter, 14
     and do not stride on the way of the evil.

---

7. *The beginning of wisdom is—get wisdom.* This sounds tautological, but Fox plausibly explains that it means one must acquire the precepts of wisdom even if at first it may be only by rote, with true comprehension dawning later.

8. *Dandle her.* There has been some exegetical dispute about the precise meaning of the verb *salsel* (the root probably suggests "curling"), but the manifest chiastic structure of the line argues for some physical expression of affection: dandle (a), exalt (b), honor (b´), embrace (a´). The next line exhibits a similar chiastic pattern.

10. *Hear, my son.* This formulaic exhortation, after the citation of the grandfather's admonitions to embrace wisdom, marks the beginning of a new unit. The subject of this unit is the imperative need to avoid the company of the wicked, and its governing metaphor is the two paths—the way of wisdom (verses 11–13) and the way of the wicked (verses 14–19).

12. *your step is not straitened.* The translation picks up a hint from the King James Version, which follows the alliterative effect of the Hebrew, *lo'-yeitsar tsa'adekha.*

14. *On the wicked's path do not enter.* The use of "enter" suggests that you should not even think of setting foot on that path.

15   Shun it, don't pass upon it,
        turn away from it and pass on.

16   For they do not sleep if they've done no evil,
        and they're robbed of sleep if they trip no one up.

17   For they break the bread of wickedness,
        and the wine of outrage they drink.

18   But the path of the righteous is like light's radiance,
        ever brighter till day has come.

19   The way of the wicked is like darkness.
        They know not on what they stumble.

20   My son, listen to my words,
        to my sayings bend your ear.

21   Let them not slip away from your eyes,
        guard them within your heart.

22   For they are life to those who find them,
        and healing to all their flesh.

---

17. *the bread of wickedness . . . the wine of outrage.* Unwilling to rest until they have done harm, they make their ill-gotten gains their daily diet.

18. *like light's radiance, / ever brighter till day has come.* This translation agrees with Fox, and against many interpreters, that *nekhon hayom* (literally, "the establishment of day") does not refer to noon but to the moment in the morning when the sun is fully risen and the daylight is strong. However, there is no warrant for construing *'or*, the primary biblical term for light, as "dawn," as Fox proposes, nor can one accept his understanding of the accompanying term, *nogah*, as a "derivative luminescence," since there are many biblical texts in which it is clearly a bright shining.

20. *My son, listen to my words.* Again this formula signals the beginning of a new textual unit. In this instance it is a miscellany of moral advice, involving the need to cling to the teachings of wisdom (verses 21–23), the avoidance of duplicitous speech (verse 24), and the importance of concentrating on the goal in front of you without glancing at the temptations on all sides (verses 25–27).

More than anything watched guard your heart,   23
     for from it are the ways out to life.
Put away from you twisted speech   24
     and lips' contortion keep far from you.
Let your eyes look in front,   25
     and your gaze straight before you.
Level the pathway of your foot,   26
     and all your ways will be sound.
Do not veer to the right or the left.   27
     Keep your foot away from evil.

---

23. *More than anything watched guard your heart*. The heart is the seat of understanding or, as we might say, the center of conscious intellection, and so it becomes the repository of the wisdom the young person will imbibe, and it needs to be zealously guarded.

the ways out to life. This expression, which has an antithetical counterpart in Psalm 68:21, "the ways out from death," has a certain mythological resonance, reinforcing the tremendous power of the human heart.

24. *twisted speech*. Literally, "mouth's twistedness."

25. *Let your eyes look in front*. The burden of this and the two subsequent lines that conclude the unit is that since moral dangers and temptations swarm on all sides, one must keep looking straight ahead and also choose a safe level path on which to walk in life. This prudential advice points toward a puritanical outlook, as in the cognate injunction in the Mishnah (Avot), "He who walks on a road and says 'How lovely this tree, how lovely this field,' incurs mortal guilt." The idea of looking only straight ahead of you is also the exact opposite of Qohelet's endeavor to explore all the realms of experience in search of wisdom.

gaze. The literal sense of the Hebrew is "eyelids." The claim of some interpreters, from Late Antiquity to the present, that the term means "eyeballs" is dubious. Because poetic parallelism requires a synonym for "eyes," the word for "eyelids" was enlisted: though one doesn't see with the eyelids, by metonymic extension the word becomes in poetry a stand-in for eyes.

1   M y son, to my wisdom hearken,
             to my discernment bend your ear,

2   to guard cunning
             so that your lips may keep knowledge.

3   For the stranger-woman's lips drip honey,
             smoother than oil her open mouth.

4   But in the end she's as bitter as wormwood,
             sharp as a double-edged sword.

---

1. *My son, to my wisdom hearken.* This poem begins with the usual formula of exhortation by the Mentor (this verse and the next). In this case, we have one continuous poem till the end of the chapter, a warning about the wiles of the stranger-woman and a celebration of the joys of conjugal sex. The poem is not quite narrative, like the matching poem of Chapter 7, despite certain narrative elements, but it is remarkable in the way it elaborates its argument through metaphor.

3. *the stranger-woman's lips drip honey.* The sensual ripeness of the alliteration in the Hebrew **nofet titofna** *siftey zarah* has a nearly identical counterpart in Song of Songs 4:11. In the translation, "lips drip" is a gesture toward this cluster of sound. The seductive lips are a counterpart to the lips that should keep knowledge in the preceding line.

    open mouth. The literal meaning of *ḥeikh* is "palate." Since it is in all likelihood not speech but kisses that are referred to in both halves of the line, the translation adds "open" in keeping with the erotic enticement that the poet surely had in mind. The Hebrew term used, as we shall see, sets up a strategic pun that occurs later in the poem.

4. *double-edged sword.* The literal sense of the Hebrew is "sword of [two] mouths," thus called because in biblical idiom the edge of the sword consumes.

Her feet go down to Death, 5
        in Sheol her steps take hold.
No path of life she traces, 6
        her pathways wander, and she does not know.
And now, sons, hear me, 7
        and do not swerve from my mouth's sayings.
Keep your way far from her 8
        and do not go near the entrance of her house,
lest you give to others your glory 9
        and your years to a ruthless man,
lest strangers sate themselves with your vigor, 10
        and your toil—in an alien's house,
and in the end you roar 11
        when your body and flesh waste away.

The idiom in this way shrewdly loops back, in an antithesis, to the lips and mouth (or palate) of the seductress.

6. *she does not know.* Focused as she is on sexual pleasure and the arts of seduction, she has no sense that she is embarked on a disastrous course, far from the straight way.

7. *and now, sons.* The Mentor temporarily switches to the plural, perhaps to generalize the case of this particular young man, but he then switches back to the singular in the next verse.

8. *the entrance of her house.* More literally, this would be "the opening of her house." Though the admonition is literally spatial—steer clear of her house, don't even think of approaching the door—an analogy is intimated between the woman's house and her body. (In the Talmud, this Hebrew term, *petaḥ,* becomes a designation of the vagina in some discussions of marital law.)

10. *lest strangers sate themselves with your vigor.* The causal mechanism is ambiguous. If the woman is married, like the stranger-woman in Chapter 7, the young man might be stripped of his resources by a husband's suit for damages. If she is single, she could turn out to be a gold digger who, exploiting his sexual obsession, would take him for all he's worth.

11. *your body and flesh waste away.* Presumably, this would be the consequence of his lacking the wherewithal to nourish himself properly, though the possibility of venereal disease should not be excluded.

12 And you will say, "How I hated reproof,
   and my heart despised rebuke.
13 And I did not heed my teachers' voice,
   to my instructors I did not bend my ear.
14 Soon I fell into every sort of harm
   in the midst of the assembled crowd."
15 Drink water from your own well,
   fresh water from your cistern.
16 Your springs will spread to the street,
   in the squares, streams of water.
17 Let them be yours alone
   and not for strangers alongside you.
18 Let your fountain be blessed,
   and rejoice in the wife of your youth.

---

14. *the assembled crowd.* Literally, "the assembly and congregation," which is here construed as a hendiadys. The idea is that the real harm suffered because of the stranger-woman will be compounded by public shaming.

15. *Drink water from your own well.* The association of the well with female fertility and especially with the womb (or vagina) is reflected both in the Song of Songs and in the recurrent betrothal type-scene, where the young man encounters his future bride by a well. The pure waters of the well are an antithesis to the sweet honey and smooth oil of the seductress's mouth. It is not clear whether the young man is already married or is being urged to enter marriage and its pleasures before he succumbs to the lure of the stranger-woman.

16. *Your springs will spread to the street.* Many critics prefer to follow the reading of the Septuagint, "Lest your springs spread to the street" because of the idea that the husband should enjoy his own private well, within the confines of his house. But since the spring or well is associated with the woman, it is not altogether clear what this would refer to—perhaps, by a stretch, to a prospect that the wife would become promiscuous because of her husband's infidelity, which is not entirely plausible. The line might mean, as we have proposed, that the consequences of the man's drinking from his own well—which perhaps would be his offspring—will be felt in the public realm. The next verse, however, would seem to argue for the Septuagint reading.

Love's doe, a graceful gazelle,   19
> her breasts ever slake your thirst,
> > you will always dote in her love.
And why dote, my son, on a stranger-woman,   20
> clasp an alien woman's lap?
For before the LORD's eyes are the ways of a man,   21
> He traces all his pathways.
The crimes of the wicked ensnare him,   22
> in the ropes of his offense he is held.
He will die for want of reproof,   23
> in his great doltishness he will dote.

---

19. *Love's doe, a graceful gazelle.* These delicate animal images are drawn from the same repertory the animal images repeatedly used in the Song of Songs. The "love," attached to "doe," *'ahavim,* suggests lovemaking rather than the emotional relationship, *'ahavah.*

her breasts ever slake your thirst. Some interpreters revocalize *dadim,* "breasts," as *dodim,* "lovemaking," in keeping with the language of the Song of Songs. But given the emphasis in this poem on drinking, the physical image of drinking from the breasts may be more likely.

20. *why dote.* It is a characteristic maneuver of biblical poetry and of biblical narrative to effect the move from one segment of the text to the next by repeating a key word used in a different sense. Here, the core meaning of *sh-g-h,* to give oneself to excess or wild feeling, is retained, but there is a switch from a positive valence (the beloved wife) to a negative one (the stranger-woman).

lap. The Hebrew *ḥeiq* is obviously a metonymy for the woman's sexual part, and it puns on the term for another orifice, *ḥeikh* ("palate" or "mouth"), used at the beginning of the poem and thus registers a small narrative progression. The allure of the seductress's mouth leads to dangerous sexual intimacy.

23. *he will dote.* This concluding verb closes the circle in the representation of the foolish young man who makes the mistake of falling for the seductress: the Hebrew, like the English, is ambiguous, leaving the reader to decide whether he is doting on the stranger-woman in his foolishness or simply doting on the condition of foolishness.

6

1   **M**y son, if you stood pledge for your fellow man,
               gave your handshake to a stranger,
2   you've been ensnared by your mouth's sayings,
               trapped by your mouth's sayings.
3   Do this, then, my son, and escape,
               for you have fallen into your fellow man's grasp,
                       go grovel, and pester your fellow man.
4   Give no sleep to your eyes
               nor slumber to your eyelids.

---

1. *if you stood pledge.* The first unit of this chapter, ending with verse 5, is another of the Mentor's pragmatic admonitions to the young man—in this instance, not to guarantee loans for others, an imprudent act that could easily lead one to financial ruin.

2. *mouth's sayings . . . mouth's sayings.* The characteristic pattern of biblical poetry would be to use a synonymous phrase in the second verset instead of the selfsame words. In fact, the Syriac translation reads for the second verset "by the word of your lips," and that may well have been the original version.

3. *escape.* Literally, "be saved" (in a physical, not spiritual, sense).
   go grovel, and pester your fellow man. The advice proffered is practical though scarcely edifying: if you have been foolish enough to get yourself into this sort of fix, use whatever means you can, even if they are humiliating or unpleasant, to extricate yourself from your obligation.

Escape like the deer from the hunter,   5
      and the bird from the fowler's hand.

Go to the ant, you sluggard,   6
      see its ways and get wisdom.
For she has no foreman,   7
      no taskmaster nor ruler.
She readies her bread in summer,   8
      stores up her food at the harvest.
How long, O sluggard, will you lie there.   9
      When will you rise from your sleep?
A bit more sleep, a bit more slumber,   10
      a bit more lying with folded arms,
and your privation will come like a wayfarer,   11
      your want like a shield-bearing man.

---

5. *hunter*. The Masoretic text reads *miyad*, "from a hand." This translation follows the Septuagint, which used a Hebrew text that seems to have had *mit-sayad*, "from a hunter."

9. *How long, O sluggard, will you lie there*. The lazybones sprawled inert on his couch is of course a sharp counterpoint to the ants scurrying about to gather their food, with no need of a taskmaster to urge them on.

11. *your privation will come like a wayfarer*. The inevitable consequence of the sluggard's unwillingness to bestir himself and provide for his own needs is destitution. The term used here for poverty, *reish*, is relatively uncommon, and may derive from the verbal stem *y-r-sh*, which can mean to take over someone else's possessions (hence the translation choice of "privation"). "Wayfarer" represents the Hebrew *mehalekh*, which means "one who walks about." The most probable reference is to a passerby or vagabond who breaks into an unprotected house.

    a shield-bearing man. This would be an intensification, as is the general case for parallel terms in the second verset, of "wayfarer," probably referring to an armed brigand.

12 A worthless fellow, a wrongdoing man,
    goes about with a crooked mouth,
13 winking his eyes, shuffling his feet,
    pointing with his fingers,
14 perverseness in his heart, plotting evil,
    ever fomenting strife.
15 Therefore his ruin will come suddenly,
    he'll be broken all at once beyond cure.
16 Six things are there that the LORD hates,
    and seven He utterly loathes.
17 Haughty eyes, a lying tongue,
    and hands shedding innocent blood,
18 a heart plotting wicked designs,
    feet hurrying to run to evil,
19 a lying deposer, a false witness,
    fomenting strife among brothers.

---

12. *crooked mouth.* Though the phrase indicates perverted speech, it also launches the pattern of distorted body parts that is continued in the next line.

13. *eyes . . . feet . . . fingers.* These gestures are evidently expressions of attempted seduction or deception, but as they are catalogued, they clearly represent the worthless fellow as someone who makes himself look grotesque.

16. *Six things . . . seven.* This numerical pattern—six, or indeed seven, and elsewhere, three, or indeed four—is used several times in Proverbs and occasionally in the Prophets. The miscellaneous character of the list accords with the miscellaneous character of this whole unit, which runs from verse 12 through verse 19.

17–18. *eyes . . . tongue . . . hands . . . heart . . . feet.* These lines pick up the use of body parts in verses 12 and 13 to create a small catalogue of immoral acts and stances, each associated with the agency of a particular physical organ or member.

Keep, my son, your father's command,   20
      and do not abandon your mother's teaching.
Bind them on your heart at all times,   21
      garland them round your neck.
When you walk about, it will guide you,   22
      when you lie down, it will guard you,
          when you wake, it will converse with you.
For a command is a lamp and teaching a light,   23
      and the way of life—stern rebukes.
To keep you from your fellow man's wife,   24
      from the smooth tongue of an alien woman.

---

20. *Keep, my son, your father's command.* The unit that begins here, a warning against the dangers of adultery, is relatively long and has a formal exordium that takes up four verses (20–23). The adding of mother to father points to a solid conjugal couple contrasting to adulterers.

22. *walk about . . . lie down . . . wake.* The language alludes to Deuteronomy 18:19, where it is the words of God's teaching (not, as here, that of human mentors) that must be remembered at all times.

23. *stern rebukes.* The literal sense of the Hebrew is "rebukes of reproof," but, as elsewhere, the effect of joining synonyms in the construct state is an intensification, hence "stern."

24. *your fellow man's wife.* The Masoretic text reads *'eshet ra'*, "wife of an evil man," but the phrase is semantically problematic. The Septuagint has *re'a* (merely a difference of vocalization), "fellow man," which is quite convincing as the authentic version.

    smooth tongue. Literally, "smoothness of tongue." The clear reference is to her seductive words.

25   Do not covet her beauty in your heart,
              and let her not take you with her eyelids.

26   For a whore's price is no more than a loaf of bread,
              but a married woman stalks a precious life.

27   Can a man scoop fire into his lap
              without his garments burning?

28   Can a man walk on glowing coals
              without his feet being scorched?

29   Thus who comes to bed with his fellow man's wife,
              whoever touches her will not go scot-free.

30   Let one not scorn the thief when he robs
              to fill his belly when he hungers.

---

25. *covet*. The Hebrew verb probably has the force here of "lust," but it is the same verb used in the Decalogue in the prohibition of adultery, and so it is appropriate to follow the translation choice adopted for the Decalogue.

her eyelids. Here the common poetic synonym for "eyes" has special relevance—the fluttering of the eyelids seductively.

26. *a whore's price . . . a loaf of bread*. The expression is no doubt hyperbolic (in Genesis 38 Tamar stipulates a kid—rather more valuable than a loaf of bread—as the price of her sexual favors): if you want sex, you could get it from a whore for mere pennies, whereas the real cost of sex with a married woman will be the destruction of your life ("a married woman stalks a precious life"). The poet is not suggesting that the adulteress is a deliberate killer, but rather that her cheating on her spouse will bring down the murderous wrath of her husband (verses 34 and 35) on her lover.

27. *scoop fire into his lap*. Pointedly, "lap" is linked by metonymy to the sexual organ. Fox neatly notes that "the line's assonance and alliteration are evocative of the hissing and crackling of fire"—*hayaḥeteh 'ish 'esh beḥeiqo*.

29. *who comes to bed with*. Literally, "who comes into." The idiom, however, refers not just to penetration but to the full sexual act, with the usual implication of a man's having sex with a woman for the first time.

not go scot-free. Literally, "not be innocent."

30. *Let one not scorn the thief*. The two verses here on the thief seem to interrupt the disquisition on the dangers of adultery, which resumes with verse 32. The connection may be in the next verset, "to fill his belly [literally, "throat" or

If he is caught, he must pay sevenfold,   31
    all the wealth of his house he must give.
Who commits adultery with a woman is senseless,   32
    ruining his life, it is he who does it.
Blight and disgrace he will find,   33
    and his shame will not be wiped out.
For jealousy turns into a man's wrath,   34
    he will show no pity on the day of vengeance.
He will take no account of ransom,   35
    and will not be content, though you offer large bribes.

"appetite"] when he hungers" and the prospect of impoverishment invoked in the next line: the thief takes what does not belong to him because he is hungry, a more elemental appetite than the lust that impels the adulterer, who takes a woman who is not his; the likely consequence for the thief is being stripped of all he possesses, whereas the adulterer's fate is shame, possible destitution (if the husband demands damages), and even death (if the husband's jealous rage turns lethal).

32. *adultery with a woman.* The redundant "with a woman" in the Hebrew creates metrical balance with the second verset, but the word also brings us back to the evocation of the seductive married woman in verses 24–26.
    senseless. Literally, "lacking heart," the heart here figuring as the seat of reason.

34. *jealousy turns into a man's wrath.* Literally, "jealousy is a man's wrath."

7

M y son, keep my sayings,
1
          and store up my commands within you.
2   Keep my commands and live,
          my teaching like the apple of your eye.
3   Bind them on your fingers,
          write them on the tablet of your heart.
4   Say to Wisdom, "You are my sister,"
          and call Discernment a friend.
5   To keep you from a stranger-woman,
          from a smooth-talking alien woman.
6   For from the window of my house,
          through my lattice I looked down,
7   and I saw among the dupes,
          discerned among the young men a witless lad,

---

1. *My son, keep my sayings.* This poem, a unified structure that takes up the entire chapter, is framed by a five-line exordium, with the specific topic introduced in verse 5, and a four-line conclusion (verses 24–27), in which the speaker points the moral of his story. What unfolds in between these frames is the closest to a sustained narrative that one finds in Proverbs.

6. *from the window of my house, / through my lattice I looked down.* The Mentor enjoys a spatially superior position, able to survey the street scene below where sexual dangers await the unwitting, he himself sheltered from curious eyes by the lattice through which he peers. As he goes on with his story, however, he moves from visual observation to novelistic invention in the vivid dialogue he provides for the seductress. His post of observation in his house is a counterpoint to the house of the stranger-woman with its lethal dangers. The narrative will be defined in part by the two thematic key words, "house" and "way."

passing through streets, by the corner,   8
      on the way to her house he strides,
at twilight, as evening descends,   9
      in pitch-black night and darkness.
And, look, a woman to meet him,   10
      whore's attire and hidden intent.
Bustling she is and wayward,   11
      in her house her feet do not stay.
Now outside, now in the square,   12
      and by every corner she lurks.
She seizes him and kisses him,   13
      impudently says to him:

---

9. *at twilight . . . in pitch-black night and darkness.* This line is a vivid instance of the deployment of narrative development from the first verset to the second in lines of biblical poetry. When the young man goes into the streets, heading in the direction of the seductress's house—whether intentionally or inadvertently—evening is falling. In the next moment—one might recall that sunset is quick in the latitude of the Land of Israel—it is already night, under the cloak of which the arts of seduction can be exercised with impunity. The word for "pitch black" is *'ishon*, otherwise the apple of the eye (as in verse 2)—that is, the darkest part of the eye. It is a characteristic procedure of biblical narrative and poetry to repeat the same word with a different meaning as a move is effected from one segment of the text to the next.

10. *whore's attire.* Since she is a married woman, not a professional prostitute, the reference is probably to provocative attire, not to clothing explicitly marked for the practice of prostitution.
    hidden intent. Literally, "guarded of heart." The translation follows an apt suggestion by Fox.

11. *in her house her feet do not stay.* In this society, a woman's place is in her home. Her going out into the streets is an expression of her sexual restlessness (no doubt encouraged by the extended absence of her husband).

13. *She seizes him and kisses him.* Her role as sexual aggressor is manifest.

14 "I had to make well-being offerings,
            today I've fulfilled my vows.
15 And so I've come out to meet you,
            to seek you, and I've found you.
16 With coverlets I've spread my couch,
            dyed cloths of Egyptian linen.
17 I've sprinkled my bed with myrrh,
            with aloes and cinnamon.
18 Come, let us drink deep of loving till morn,
            let us revel in love's delights.
19 For the man is not in his house,
            he's gone on a far-off way.

---

14. *I had to make well-being offerings.* The point is not merely her hypocrisy in launching an overture to adultery fresh from the temple service but also that she is proposing to him a sumptuous meat dinner as a prelude to sex. The *shelamim*, well-being offerings, would have only in part been burnt on the altar with another part of the animal reserved for feasting.

16. *With coverlets I've spread my couch, / dyed cloths of Egyptian linen.* Now she moves to the site of sexual consummation, explaining that she has lavishly prepared her bed with luxurious cloths imported from Egypt, scented with aromatic spices (verse 17) imported from Arabia and the East (probably India). It is clear that the seductress has means of affluence at her disposal, in all likelihood provided by her husband's activities as a merchant (see verse 20).

18. *let us drink deep of loving till morn.* The word for "loving," *dodim*, refers explicitly to lovemaking, and the drinking of *dodim* is a phrase used in the Song of Songs. Counting on his youthful vigor, she is offering him a whole night of continuous sex.

19. *For the man is not in his house.* This reference to her husband—not "my man" or "my husband" but "the man"—is vaguely contemptuous. This line neatly counterparts the two thematic key words, "house" and "way." While the man is on a far-off way, his house can become a love nest of adultery.

The purse of silver he took in his hand,   20
     at the new moon he'll return to his house."
She sways him with all her talk,   21
     with her smooth speech she leads him astray.
He goes after her in a trice,   22
     as an ox goes off to the slaughter,
         as a stag prances into a halter.
Till an arrow pierces his liver,   23
     as a bird hastens to the snare,
         not knowing the cost is his life.

---

20. *The purse of silver.* This detail equally suggests that the husband is a pros-
perous merchant and that he will be away for a long time. Some interpreters
see in it a hint that she is requesting money from the young man, though that
is not a necessary inference.

at the new moon. Many understand the Hebrew *keseh* to mean full moon,
but the term clearly reflects the verbal root that means "to cover," which would
accord far better with the new moon. If this assumption is correct, the story
would unfold in the early days of the lunar month, when the moon is still a
sliver and it is quite dark at night. That would give the wayward wife and the
young man almost four weeks to drink deep of love's pleasures.

22. *a stag prances into a halter.* The received text at this point is garbled. The
New Jewish Publication Society, for example, renders it "as a fool for the stocks
of punishment," not translating the first, incomprehensible word *ukhe'ekhes*,
and producing an unlikely parallel to the preceding verset about the ox going to
slaughter. Instead of the Masoretic *ukhe'ekhes 'el-musar 'ewil*, this translation
adopts a proposed emendation *ukhe'akes 'el-musar 'eyal*, which involves merely
a revocalization of the first word and deleting the *waw* in the last word, with
revocalization. *Musar* in this animal context would not mean "reproof," as it
does elsewhere in Proverbs, but "rope" or "halter" (the meaning of this word in
Job 13:18).

23. *an arrow pierces his liver.* This may be simply an image of a fatal wound,
though biblical Hebrew links the liver with sexual desire, so it could conceivably refer to venereal disease. Otherwise, the fate of death would be at the
hands of the vengeful husband. It is a reflection of the pragmatic orientation of
Proverbs that the Mentor warns against adultery not as a violation of a divine
commandment but as an act that can have lethal consequences.

24   And now, sons, listen to me,
                   and attend to my mouth's sayings.
25   Let your heart not veer to her ways,
                   and do not go astray on her paths.
26   For many the victims she has felled,
                   innumerable all whom she has killed.
27   Through her house are the ways to Sheol,
                   going down to the chambers of Death.

---

27. *Through her house are the ways to Sheol.* Here at the end, the key terms
"house" and "way" are pointedly brought together. Her house turns out to hide
a kind of metaphoric trapdoor—perhaps underneath that bed with its fancy
linens—opening on a chute that takes one down to the realm of death.

8

Look, Wisdom calls out,   1
        and Discernment lifts her voice.
At the top of the heights, on the way,   2
        at the crossroads, she takes her stand,
by the gates, at the city's entrance,   3
        at the approach to the portals, she shouts:
To you, men, I call out,   4
        and my voice, to humankind.
Understand shrewdness, you dupes,   5
        and fools, make your heart understand.
Listen, for I speak noble things,   6
        my mouth's utterance—uprightness.
For my tongue declares truth   7
        and my lips loathe wickedness.

---

2. *At the top of the heights, on the way*. The figure of Lady Wisdom positions herself up above—evidently, in a variety of places—where she can be widely heard down below, and she stands by the crossroads and at the entrance to the city (verse 3), where there are many passersby who will hear her voice. The implication is that wisdom is not a hidden or esoteric treasure but something plainly accessible—in the metaphor used here, proclaimed—to all.

6. *my mouth's utterance*. More literally, "my mouth's opening."

7. *my lips loathe wickedness*. Literally, "the loathing of my lips is wickedness."

8   In the right are all my mouth's sayings,
                nothing in them is twisted or crooked.

9   They are all plain to the discerning
                and straightforward for those who find knowledge.

10   Take my reproof rather than silver,
                and knowledge is choicer than fine gold.

11   For wisdom is better than rubies,
                all precious things can't match her worth.

12   I, Wisdom, dwell in shrewdness,
                and cunning knowledge I find.

13   Fear of the Lord is hating evil.
                Pride, haughtiness, an evil way,
                      and perverse speech do I hate.

14   Mine is counsel and prudence,
                I am Discernment, mine is might.

15   Through me kings reign,
                and rulers decree righteous laws.

---

8. *twisted or crooked*. Throughout the speech of Lady Wisdom, as elsewhere in Proverbs, there is an emphatic thematic contrast between the crooked and the straight.

9. *plain . . . straightforward*. Again, the notion is stressed that wisdom is universally accessible—indeed, transparent. The term rendered as "straightforward" could also be translated rather literally as "what is straight" or "straightness."

12. *I, Wisdom, dwell in shrewdness*. This is not really tautological. The quality of wisdom is predicated on the exercise of a kind of savvyness—shrewdness or cunning. See the comment on 1:4.

13. *perverse speech*. Literally, "a mouth of perversities."

15. *through me kings reign*. Here begins a new emphasis about the importance of wisdom, prepared for by the mention of "might" at the end of the previous line. Wisdom is a crucial prerequisite for statecraft, and only through it are rulers able to exercise effective governance.

Through me princes hold sway,   16
    and nobles, all the judges of earth.
I, all my lovers I love,   17
    and my seekers do find me.
Riches and honor are with me,   18
    long-lasting wealth and righteousness.
My fruit is better than all fine gold,   19
    and my yield, than the choicest silver.
On the path of righteousness I walk,   20
    within the ways of justice,
to pass substance on to my lovers,   21
    and their storehouses to fill.

---

16. *all the judges of earth.* The Masoretic text reads "all the judges of justice [*tsedeq*]," but many Hebrew manuscripts as well as two ancient translations show instead "earth" (*'erets*), which sounds better in context. It seems likely that a scribe inadvertently reproduced *tsedeq* from the end of the previous line.

19. *all fine gold.* The Hebrew uses two synonyms for gold, neither of them the standard word.

21. *to pass substance on to my lovers.* As elsewhere, Proverbs assumes that the exercise of wisdom leads to prosperity, among other good things.

22   The Lord created me at the outset of His way,
            the very first of His works of old.
23   In remote eons I was shaped,
            at the start of the first things of earth.
24   When there were no deeps I was spawned,
            when there were no wellsprings, water-sources.

---

22. *The Lord created me at the outset of His way.* Although Lady Wisdom is still speaking, the section from here through verse 31 looks like a new poem or, at the very least, a distinct new segment of the same poem. The speech from verse 1 through verse 21 is a celebration by Wisdom of her powers—her gift of plain and accessible discourse, the preciousness of her words, her indispensability as a guide to all who govern, the material benefits she conveys to her followers. It must be said that much of the poetry of this section deploys boilerplate language, echoing quite similar formulations—or even formulas—that one encounters elsewhere in Proverbs. The poem that begins with verse 22 has a cosmic framework rather than a pragmatic one: Lady Wisdom's self-celebration goes back to the role she played as God's intimate before He launched on the work of creation. This cosmic and cosmogonic prominence of Wisdom may well have provided a generative clue for the prose-poem about the Logos ("In the beginning was the word . . .") in the first chapter of John's Gospel. In rabbinic tradition, it was a trigger for the idea that God made the world by following the blueprint of the Torah, which pre-existed creation; and later the Kabbalah would elaborate this notion with a theosophic apparatus. This cosmic vision, moreover, is articulated in soaring poetry that seems quite unlike the poetry of the preceding section.

the very first of His works of old. Or "before His works of old." It is not entirely clear whether the poet intends this as a literal account of the order of creation, which is how this line was understood by later Jewish and Christian tradition, or whether this whole idea of the primordial presence of Wisdom is a kind of mythic hyperbole to express Wisdom's crucial importance in the order of things.

24. *When there were no deeps.* The story of creation in Genesis 1, of course, begins with God's breath hovering over the face of the deep, so Lady Wisdom wants to take us back to the moment of her gestation that is antecedent to the beginning of creation proper.

water-sources. This translation emends the Masoretic *nikhbedey mayim* (heavy with [?] water) to *nivkhey mayim*.

Before mountains were anchored down, 25
    before hills I was spawned.
He had yet not made earth and open land, 26
    and the world's first clods of soil.
When He founded the heavens, I was there, 27
    when He traced a circle on the face of the deep,
when He propped up the skies above, 28
    when He powered the springs of the deep,
when He set to the sea its limit, 29
    that the waters not flout His command,
        when He strengthened the earth's foundations.

---

25. *anchored down*. The denotation of the Hebrew verb is to set something in its sockets or on its foundations.

27. *traced a circle on the face of the deep*. The reference is probably to the horizon that surrounds the sea, visually marking its limits.

28. *propped up*. Literally, "fortified," "strengthened."

29. *that the waters not flout His command*. The literal configuration of the Hebrew idiom is "not cross His mouth." This is a recurrent notion of cosmogonic poetry in the Bible, ultimately harking back to the Canaanite creation myth in which the sea-god, Yamm, is subdued by the weather-god, Baal. As in the Voice from the Whirlwind in Job 38 and in many psalms, the LORD pronounces a decree, setting a boundary to the sea and not allowing it to go up on the dry land.

    strengthened. The Masoretic text reads *beḥuqo*, "traced" (or "inscribed"), which looks suspiciously like an inadvertent replication of *beḥuqo* in 27B and is not a verb that makes much sense with "foundations" as its object. The Septuagint evidently had a Hebrew text that read *beḥazqo*, "when He strengthened," the difference between the two readings being a single consonant.

30   And I was by Him, an intimate,
                 I was His delight day after day,
                       playing before Him at all times,
31   playing in the world, His earth,
                 and my delight with humankind.

32   And now, sons, listen to me,
                 happy who keeps my ways.
33   Listen to reproof and get wisdom,
                 and do not cast it aside.
34   Happy the man who listens to me,
                 to wait at my doors day after day,
                       to watch the posts of my portals.
35   For who finds me has found life,
                 and will be favored by the LORD.
36   And who offends me lays waste his life,
                 all who hate me love death.

---

30. *an intimate . . . His delight . . . playing before Him.* This line and the next
are the most original—and charming—turn that the poet gives to his cosmo-
gonic myth of the origins of Wisdom. Before there were creatures to occupy
God's attention, Wisdom was His delightful and entertaining bosom companion. As Fox aptly notes, Wisdom does not only possess great utility (the burden
of the preceding poem) but it is fun—as, say, the scholar takes great pleasure
in his research, the naturalist in discovering the intricacies of nature.

31. *playing in the world . . . and my delight with humankind.* The same delights
that winsome Lady Wisdom offered to her Creator she makes available in the
created world to those who embrace her. In all likelihood, the possessive "my"
attached to delight refers to the capacity to delight that Lady Wisdom possesses
and conveys to humankind, though it might also mean the delight she takes in
humanity.

32. *And, now, sons, listen to me.* This formulaic language marks the beginning
of a four-line formal conclusion, perhaps serving both poems.

34. *to wait at my doors day after day, / to watch the posts of my portals.* This
image, as a few interpreters have proposed, hints at the actions of a devoted
suitor, whom we might expect to find at the residence of a charmer like Lady
Wisdom.

9

Wisdom has built her house,   1
        she has hewn her pillars, seven.
She has slaughtered her meat,   2
        has mixed her wine,
                also laid out her table.
She has sent out her young women,   3
        calls loud from the city's heights:
Whoever the dupe, let him turn aside here,   4
        the senseless—she said to him.

---

1. *Wisdom has built her house.* The poem that constitutes this chapter comprises two antithetical units, the invitation of Lady Wisdom and the invitation of Lady Folly. Wisdom builds a grand, welcoming house with seven pillars. That number is not necessarily a reflection of architectural practice but rather of the formulaic and sacred character of the number seven.

her pillars, seven. The inverted order reflects the poetic flourish of the Hebrew syntax.

2. *slaughtered her meat.* Literally, "slaughtered her slaughter." Meat was not typically everyday fare but was reserved for sumptuous feasts.

3. *her young women.* These are her maidservants. But in the second verset, it is Wisdom herself who calls out her invitation from the heights.

4. *Whoever the dupe.* Wisdom offers her transformative services to the naive and the foolish who are very much in need of them.

she said to him. A small emendation, with warrant in the Septuagint, turns this into "I said to him," thus eliminating the third-person interruption of Lady Wisdom's speech.

5   Come, partake of my bread,
             and drink the wine I have mixed.
6   Forsake foolishness and live,
             and stride on the way of discernment.
7   Who reproves the scoffer takes on disgrace,
             who rebukes the wicked is maimed.
8   Rebuke not the scoffer lest he hate you.
             Rebuke the wise and he will love you.
9   Give to the wise, he will get more wisdom,
             inform the righteous, he will increase instruction.
10   The beginning of wisdom is fear of the LORD,
             and knowing the Holy One is discernment.
11   For through Me your days will be many,
             and the years of your life will increase.
12   If you get wisdom, you get yourself wisdom,
             but if you scoff, you bear it alone.
13   The foolish woman bustles about.
             Gullibility!—and she knows nothing of it.

---

5. *bread . . . wine*. These primary items of food and drink are, of course, symbolic of the feast of wisdom she is offering.

7. *is maimed*. The literal sense would be "it's his maiming [or blemish]."

9. *Give to the wise*. This phrase, which follows on the second verset of the preceding line, is clearly elliptical for "give instruction to the wise."

10. *the Holy One*. The Hebrew uses a plural ("holy ones"), which most interpreters understand as a plural of majesty referring to God. This is not a usage conclusively visible elsewhere, and in some instances *qedoshim* is an epithet for angels. The plural ending might be a scribal error.

12. *If you get wisdom, you get yourself wisdom*. The sense of this seeming tautology is that wisdom is an enduring acquisition, enjoyed by the wise person and benefiting those around him, whereas scoffing isolates a person in self-disgrace and confers no benefit. It should be said that this entire verse, coming after the line of peroration in verse 11, looks out of place.

13. *The foolish woman*. Momentarily, it seems as though the figure invoked is an exemplary instance of human behavior, as in many lines in Proverbs, but the

And she sits at the entrance of her house   14
       in a chair on the city's heights,
to call out to the wayfarers   15
       who go on straight paths:
Whoever the dupe, let him turn aside here,   16
       and the senseless—she said to him.
Stolen waters are sweet,   17
       and purloined bread is delicious.
And he does not know that shades are there,   18
       in the depths of Sheol, her guests.

---

next verse makes clear that, like Lady Wisdom, she is an allegorical representation of a general quality.

14. *she sits at the entrance of her house.* Though she is strictly symmetrical with Lady Wisdom in calling out from a house on the heights of the city, nothing is said about the splendor of a many-pillared house because, understandably, the residence of Folly is not likely to be a grand edifice.

15. *who go on straight paths.* Literally, "who make their paths straight." Lady Wisdom calls out to the foolish in order to make them wise. Lady Folly calls out to those going on the right path in order to lead them astray.

16. *Whoever the dupe . . . and the senseless.* Lady Folly's words repeat verbatim those of Lady Wisdom in verse 4 but with an opposite intent. Wisdom calls to the dupes and the thoughtless with the aim of extricating them from their hapless condition through her instruction. Folly calls to them—though in her case she would not plausibly have uttered these derogatory terms but rather thought them, counting on the gullibility of those she addresses—because she intends to exploit their naivete.

17. *Stolen waters are sweet, / and purloined bread is delicious.* These often quoted words actually constitute an anti-proverb, cast in the compact aphoristic form, with neat poetic parallelism, of the traditional proverb. The line epitomizes Lady Folly's seductive message: if you want to have a really good time, nothing works better than illicit behavior.
    purloined bread. Literally, "secret bread."

18. *shades are there.* The seemingly inviting house of Lady Folly with her seductive speech spells disaster for whoever goes there, and so is a gateway to death, concealing a trapdoor to the underworld, like the house of the seductress in Chapter 7.

10

1   The proverbs of Solomon.
      A wise son gladdens his father,
            but a foolish son is his mother's sorrow.
2   The treasures of wickedness will not avail,
            but righteousness saves from death.
3   The LORD will not make the righteous man hunger,
            but He rebuffs the desire of the wicked.

---

1. *The proverbs of Solomon.* This is a headnote or title for the collection of say-ings that runs from here to the end of Chapter 23. As is true of the Late Biblical practice of ascription of texts to famous figures, it is by no means clear that the compiler was claiming actual authorship for King Solomon. The superscription might merely be saying that these proverbs are in the manner of Solomon, the legendary composer of many proverbs. Unlike Chapters 1–9, which comprise extended poems, some of them taking up a whole chapter and some of them exhibiting narrative or quasi-dramatic elements, this collection consists of a miscellany of one-line proverbs, often with no connection from one line to the next. Much of the language is rather pat, consisting of neatly antithetical con-trasts from the first verset to the second between the wise man and the fool, the righteous and the wicked, by and large cast in stereotypical terms. Much of this will require scant comment.

A wise son . . . a foolish son. This initial proverb is a perfect illustration of the neatness of antithetical formulation: wise / foolish, father / mother, gladdens / sorrow.

2. *righteousness saves from death.* This verset would come to be chanted in Jew-ish funeral processions, though the meaning of *tsedaqah*, "righteousness," had shifted to "charity," which mourners were invited to offer.

3. *desire.* The Hebrew *hawah*, elsewhere "disaster," is here either an equivalent of or a mistake for *'awah*, "desire."

A deceitful palm brings privation,   4
          but the diligent hand enriches.
A clever son stores up in the summer,   5
          a disgraceful son slumbers at harvest-time.
Blessings on the righteous man's head,   6
          but outrage will cover the mouth of the wicked.
The memory of the righteous is for a blessing,   7
          but the name of the wicked will rot.
The wise of heart takes commands,   8
          but who speaks stupidly comes to grief.
Who walks in innocence walks secure,   9
          but who walks crooked ways is exposed.
Who winks with his eye gives pain,   10
          and who speaks stupidly comes to grief.
The righteous man's mouth is a wellspring of life, 11
          but outrage will cover the mouth of the wicked.
Hatred foments strife,   12
          but love covers up all misdeeds.
On the discerning man's lips wisdom is found, 13
          but a rod for the back of the senseless!
Wise men lay up knowledge,   14
          but the dolt's mouth is impending disaster.

---

5. *A clever son stores up in the summer.* As we have seen elsewhere—most notably, in the observation of the ant in 6:6–8—diligence as well as honesty or probity is seen as a cardinal virtue in Proverbs.

6. *the mouth of the wicked.* Some emend "mouth," *pi,* to "face," *peney.*

8. *who speaks stupidly.* The literal sense of the Hebrew is "the stupid of lips."

9. *who walks crooked ways.* Literally, "who makes his ways crooked."
is exposed. Literally, "is known."

10. *winks with his eye.* The reference is either to a lascivious gesture or a merely grotesque one. According to Fox, it is an expression of hostility.

14. *the dolt's mouth is impending disaster.* This is the case because, by saying stupid things, he brings disaster down on himself and perhaps on those around him as well.

15 The rich man's wealth is his fortress-city,
    the disaster of the poor, their privation.

16 The effort of the righteous is for life,
    the wicked's yield is for offense.

17 A path for life who observes reproof,
    but who forsakes rebuke leads astray.

18 Who covers up hatred has lying lips,
    he who slanders is a fool.

19 Through much talk misdeed will not cease,
    but the shrewd man holds his tongue.

20 Choice silver—a righteous man's tongue,
    but the heart of the wicked is worthless.

21 The righteous man's lips guide the many,
    but dolts die for lack of sense.

22 The Lord's blessing will enrich,
    and one increases no pain through it.

23 As doing foul things is sport for the fool,
    so is wisdom for the man of discernment.

24 What the wicked dreads will come upon him,
    and the desire of the righteous is granted.

---

15. *The rich man . . . the poor.* This verse illustrates how the conventionality of wisdom in these proverbs tumbles into truism since what is said here, after all, is that the rich man can depend on his wealth for security whereas the poor man's poverty makes him miserable.

18. *has lying lips.* The Hebrew merely implies "has."

19. *holds his tongue.* More literally, "holds his lips."

22. *one increases no pain.* Many interpreters understand the Hebrew noun *'etsev* to mean "toil" or "labor" because in Genesis 3:17 this word is linked with the pain of working the soil, but *'etsev* everywhere else means "pain" or "pang." This translation therefore understands it not to mean "no toil will increase it [the LORD's blessing]" but that through the LORD's blessing one is painlessly enriched.

When the storm passes, the wicked is gone,   25
      but the righteous is a lasting foundation.
Like vinegar to the teeth and smoke to the eyes,   26
      thus the sluggard to those who send him.
Fear of the LORD lengthens one's days,   27
      but the years of the wicked are short.
The longing of the righteous is a joy,   28
      but the hope of the wicked will perish.
A stronghold for the blameless is the LORD's way,   29
      but disaster for the workers of crime.
The righteous man never stumbles,   30
      but the wicked will not dwell on earth.
The mouth of the righteous puts forth wisdom,   31
      but a perverse tongue will be cut off.
The lips of the righteous will know to please,   32
      and the mouth of the wicked—perverseness.

---

25. *When the storm passes.* This is a bedrock assumption of Proverbs— vehemently contested by Job—that adversity sweeps away the wicked while the righteous endure. A different formulation of the same idea occurs in verse 27.

26. *Like vinegar to the teeth and smoke to the eyes.* This verse exhibits a different, and more interesting, pattern from the neat antithetical parallelism that governs almost all the lines up to this point: the first verset lays out a simile and the second verset reveals the referent of the simile. This looks rather like a riddle form: what is it that is like vinegar to the teeth and smoke to the eyes, discoloring the former and making the latter smart? The answer to the riddle is: a fool sent on an errand, who is bound to exasperate whoever has sent him.

29. *for the blameless.* The translation, following the precedent of several of the ancient versions, revocalizes the Masoretic *latom,* "for blamelessness," as *latam,* "for the blameless." This small change yields an otherwise missing parallelism: the LORD's way is a stronghold for the blameless but sheer terror for the wicked.

32. *to please . . . perverseness.* The antithetical parallelism here provides a clue to one of the connotations of *tahapukhot,* "perverseness," in Proverbs. It involves not only acting or speaking in a wrongheaded or contorted way but disconcerting or dismaying others through such behavior, in contrast to the righteous man, whose speech has the capacity to please others and win their goodwill.

11

1 Cheating scales are the LORD's loathing,
        and a true weight-stone His pleasure.
2 With a bold face, there comes disgrace,
        but wisdom is with the humble.
3 The upright's innocence guides them,
        but the falseness of traitors destroys them.
4 Wealth avails not on the day of wrath,
        but righteousness saves from death.
5 The innocent's righteousness makes his way smooth,
        but in his wickedness the wicked man falls.

---

1. *Cheating scales . . . a true weight-stone.* Much of the wisdom of Proverbs, as in this verse, is oriented pragmatically toward the world of commerce or labor. Stones marked with a fixed weight were placed on one of the two pans of the scale and the merchandise to be sold on the other pan.

2. *bold face . . . disgrace.* The translation emulates the rhyme in the Hebrew of *zadon* (literally, "arrogance") and *qalon*, "disgrace."

3. *traitors.* The Hebrew *bogdim* is used not in a political sense but to describe treacherous or untrustworthy people.

4. *righteousness saves from death.* This verset is identical with 10:2, leading one to suspect that some of these lines are modular constructs from traditional sayings.

5. *makes his way smooth.* The verb *yasher* can mean either to make straight horizontally (that is, in contrast to crooked) or vertically (in contrast to rough, uneven). Not falling into a pot-hole, like the wicked in the second verset, suggests the vertical sense.

The upright's innocence saves them,   6
    but in disasters are traitors ensnared.
When a wicked man dies, hope perishes,   7
    and the longing of villains will perish.
The righteous is rescued from straits,   8
    and the wicked man comes in his stead.
Through speech the tainted man ruins his fellow,   9
    but through knowledge the righteous are rescued.
When the righteous do well, the city exults,   10
    and when the wicked perish—glad song.
Through the upright's blessing a city soars,   11
    and by the mouth of the wicked it is razed.
Who scorns his fellow man has no sense,   12
    but a man of discernment keeps silent.
The gossip lays bare secrets,   13
    but the trustworthy conceals an affair.
For want of designs a people falls,   14
    but there is rescue through many counselors.

---

8. *The righteous is rescued from straits, / and the wicked man comes in his stead.* In this instance, the two versets create a miniature narrative with an almost comical didactic effect: the just man is rescued or, more precisely, extricated (*neḥelats*) from a tight spot in which he was jammed, and the wicked is promptly popped into that spot. This little narrative, of course, does not readily correspond to observable reality.

9. *Through speech . . . through knowledge.* There is a pointed contrast between thoughtless or perhaps devious speech (literally, "mouth") and the knowledge of the wise, which perhaps may not involve speech.

12. *but a man of discernment keeps silent.* The antithesis to the first verset suggests that there are cases where a discerning person may well feel scorn toward someone but is discreet enough not to express it.

14. *a people falls.* Some construe the Hebrew *'am* here in the military sense that it sometimes has in narrative prose, where it can mean "troops." In that case, "rescue," *teshuʿah*, in the second verset would reflect its related meaning of "victory."

15   He will surely be shattered who gives bond for a stranger,
              but he who hates offering pledge is secure.
16   A gracious woman holds fast to honor,
              but the arrogant hold fast to wealth.
17   A kindly man does good for himself,
              but a cruel man blights his own flesh.
18   The wicked man makes a false profit,
              but who sows righteousness reaps true reward.
19   A righteous son is for life,
              but the pursuer of evil—for his death.
20   The LORD's loathing are the crooked of heart,
              but His pleasure, whose way is blameless.
21   Count on it, the evil will not go scot-free,
              but the seed of the righteous escapes.
22   A golden ring in the snout of a pig,
              a lovely woman who lacks good sense.

---

16. *honor . . . wealth*. Elsewhere in Proverbs, these are coordinated terms, not antitheses.

18. *reaps*. The verb is only implied in the Hebrew.

19. *a righteous son*. The Masoretic text reads *ken tsedaqah*, "thus righteousness," which does not make much sense and produces a poor parallelism with the second verset in a series of proverbs where the parallelism is usually neat, even pat. This translation adopts a reading shown in some Hebrew manuscripts as well as in the Septuagint and Syriac: *ben tsedaqah* (literally, "son of righteousness").

20. *whose way is blameless*. Literally, "the blameless of way."

21. *Count on it*. Literally, "hand to hand." This appears to be a gesture of shaking hands in order to guarantee something.

22. *A golden ring in the snout of a pig*. This is another proverb cast in riddle form. This first verse gives us a bizarre and rather shocking image. The second verset spells out the referent of the image, the beautiful woman devoid of sense, and thus becomes a kind of punch line.

The desire of the righteous is only good.   23
        The hope of the wicked is wrath.
One man is spendthrift and gains all the more,   24
        another saves honestly but comes to want.
A benign person will flourish,   25
        and he who slakes others' thirst, his own thirst is slaked.
Who holds back grain the nation will damn,   26
        but blessing on the provider's head.
Who seeks out good pursues favor,   27
        but who looks for evil, it will come to him.
Who trusts in his wealth, he will fall,   28
        but like a leaf the righteous will burgeon.
Who blights his house will inherit the wind,   29
        and the dolt is a slave to the wise of heart.

---

23. *The hope of the wicked is wrath.* Although this clause makes a certain amount of sense as it stands in the Masoretic text, many scholars adopt the reading of some manuscripts and of the Septuagint, *'avdah,* "perishes," instead of *'evrah,* "wrath." This would bring the verset in line with 10:28B, which has nearly identical wording.

25. *benign person.* Literally, "person of blessing."
    he who slakes. Though this is what the Hebrew verb usually means, the verset is obscure, and the second verb rendered as "slaked" looks textually suspect.

26. *grain . . . provider.* Both these terms recall the story of Joseph as viceroy of Egypt providing grain in the famine.

28. *he will fall.* Some prefer to read instead of the Masoretic *yipol* a verb differing by one consonant, *yibol,* "he will wither," which produces a neater antithesis to the burgeoning leaf in the second verset.

30   The fruit of the righteous is a tree of life,
            and the wise man draws in people.
31   If the righteous on earth is requited,
            how much more the wicked offender.

---

30. *The fruit of the righteous is a tree of life.* It is a little problematic that fruit becomes tree, but perhaps the poet was drawn into a certain slackness because "fruit" in biblical usage is so often a lexicalized metaphor for "consequences," what one produces through his acts.

12

Who loves reproof loves knowledge,   1
        but who hates rebuke is a brute.
The good man finds favor from the Lord,   2
        but He will condemn the cunning schemer.
A man will not be firm-founded in wickedness,   3
        but the root of the righteous is not shaken.
A worthy woman is her husband's crown,   4
        but like rot in his bones a shameful wife.
The plans of the righteous are justice;   5
        the designs of the wicked, deceit.
The words of the wicked are a bloody ambush,   6
        but the mouth of the upright will save them.

---

4. *a worthy woman.* Fox, hewing to the etymology, renders this as "a woman of strength."

her husband's crown . . . rot in his bones. In this instance, the antithesis of the two versets diverges from the general pattern of stereotypical predictability, as in the three preceding lines, to exhibit an energy of biting satiric wit. After the crown image, which is conventional and decorous, the antithetical second verset moves from an adornment sitting on the head to something eating away the bones from within, suggesting that the badness of a bad wife has a more intense effect on the negative side than the goodness of a good wife on the positive side. The object of this strong simile, moreover, "a shameful wife" (one Hebrew word, *mevishah*), is held back to the very end of the line, thus becoming a kind of punch word.

6. *save them.* The vague pronominal object would be the victims of the wicked who appear in the first verset.

7   Overturn the wicked and they are gone,
          but the house of the righteous will stand.

8   By his insight will a man be praised,
          but the crooked of heart is despised.

9   Better a scorned man who has a slave
          than one who fancies himself honored and lacks bread.

10   The righteous man knows the life of his beast,
          but the mercy of the wicked is cruel.

11   Who works his soil is sated with bread,
          but who pursues empty things lacks sense.

12   The wicked covets the evil men's trap,
          but the root of the righteous stands firm.

13   In the crime of lips is an evil snare,
          but the righteous comes out from straits.

14   From the fruit of a man's mouth he is sated with good,
          a man gets recompense for his acts.

15   The way of a dolt seems right in his eyes,
          but who listens to counsel is wise.

16   The anger of a dolt becomes known in a trice,
          but the shrewd man conceals his disgrace.

---

9. *Better a scorned man . . . than one who fancies himself.* This formulation of "better X than Y" is a classic proverb pattern in biblical Hebrew.

10. *the mercy of the wicked is cruel.* Here the antithesis between versets takes an interesting turn. The righteous man is so compassionate that he has an intuitive sense of the needs and discomforts of his beast. The wicked person, on the other hand, is so utterly devoid of compassion that even what he affects to be an expression of mercy turns out to be cruel.

12. *The wicked covets the evil men's trap.* The Hebrew is a little obscure. It could mean that he covets whatever is caught in the evil men's trap, or perhaps that he envies the malicious ingenuity that is manifested in contriving the trap.
    stands firm. This translation reads, with the Septuagint, *yikon* for the Masoretic *yitein*, "will give."

A faithful deposer will tell what is right,   17
      but a lying witness—deceit.
One may speak out like sword-stabs,   18
      but the tongue of the wise is healing.
True speech stands firm always,   19
      but a mere moment—a lying tongue.
Deceit is in the heart of plotters of evil,   20
      but counselors of peace have joy.
No wrong will befall the righteous,   21
      but the wicked are filled with harm.
The Lord's loathing—lying lips,   22
      but who act in good faith are His pleasure.
A shrewd man conceals what he knows,   23
      but the heart of dullards proclaims folly.
The diligent's hand will rule,   24
      and the shiftless put to forced labor.
Worry in a man's heart brings him low,   25
      but a good word will gladden him.
The righteous exceeds his fellow man,   26
      but the wicked's way leads him astray.

---

17. *a lying witness—deceit.* The verb "tell" in the first verset does double duty for this verset, too.

18. *sword-stabs . . . healing.* Though the image of malicious speech as a cutting sword is conventional, the antithesis between stabbing and healing at the end of the respective versets produces a striking effect.

23. *what he knows.* Literally, "knowledge." It is notable in this verse that discretion is thought of as a cardinal virtue of wisdom.

24. *the shiftless.* The Hebrew *remiyah* usually means "deceit," but the context requires something like slackness. Perhaps someone failing to do a job he is given is thought to be deceitful for not honoring his commitment out of laziness.

26. *exceeds his fellow man.* Though this is a reasonable construction of the original, the Hebrew looks a little odd and has often invited emendation.

27   The shiftless will not roast his game,
                but a man's wealth is precious gold.
28   On the path of righteousness is life,
                but the way of mischief is to death.

---

27. *The shiftless will not roast his game.* Though the idea may well be that a slacker will never enjoy the fruits of his highly dubious labor, the Hebrew is cryptic and the text may be suspect.

a man's wealth is precious gold. In the implied antithesis, the assiduous person knows how to hang on to his substance.

28. *but the way of mischief is to death.* The Masoretic text, *wederekh netivah 'al-mawet*, seems to say literally "and the way of path un-death." This does not sound like intelligible Hebrew. This translation, following a hint from three ancient versions, reads *meshuvah*, "mischief" (or "waywardness"), for *netivah*, "path," and, in accordance with many Hebrew manuscripts, revocalizes *'al* ("not" or "un") as *'el*, "to."

13

A wise son—through a father's reproof,   1
        but a scoffer does not heed rebuke.
From the fruit of a man's mouth he eats goodly things,   2
        but from the throat of traitors comes outrage.
Who watches his mouth guards his own life,   3
        who cracks open his lips knows disaster.
He desires and has naught, the sluggard,   4
        but the life of the diligent thrives.
A lying word the righteous hates,   5
        but the wicked is stinking and vile.
Righteousness keeps the blameless,   6
        but wickedness perverts the offender.

---

1. *A wise son—through a father's reproof.* The Hebrew is still more gnomic, just four words without a verb or a preposition—literally, "wise son father's reproof."

2. *throat.* The parallelism with "mouth" in the first verset and the contrast between virtuous and vicious speech suggests that the multivalent *nefesh* here has the meaning of "throat." The verb "comes" has been added to clarify the Hebrew, which has no verb, or the merely implied verb "is."

3. *who cracks open his lips knows disaster.* Talking can get you into serious trouble, so the prudent man keeps his mouth shut.

4. *thrives.* More literally, "is luxuriant."

6. *the offender.* Reading *hata'* for the Masoretic *hata't*, "offense."

7   One man feigns riches having nothing at all,
           another plays poor, with great wealth.

8   The ransom for a man's life are his riches,
           but the poor man will hear no rebuke.

9   The light of the righteous shines,
           but the lamp of the wicked gutters.

10   The empty man in arrogance foments strife,
           but with those who take counsel is wisdom.

11   Wealth can be less than mere breath,
           but who gathers bit by bit makes it grow.

12   Drawn-out longing sickens the heart,
           but desire come true is a tree of life.

---

7. *feigns riches . . . plays poor.* This proverb is less explicitly didactic than most of the others in the collection: it merely registers, as a warning not to be taken in by appearances, that in the economic realm some people are not what they seem to be.

8. *the poor man will hear no rebuke.* If the received text is correct, this would mean that whereas the rich man may have to call on his wealth to ransom himself from predators, no one bothers a poor man. Nevertheless, "rebuke," *ge'arah*, is a little odd, and some emend it to *ge'ulah*, "redemption," yielding the sense that the poor man, when he is in a fix, has no resources with which to redeem himself.

9. *shines.* This translation reads *yizraḥ*, "shines," instead of the Masoretic *yismaḥ*, "rejoices," because light rejoicing doesn't make much sense. Others claim that *yismaḥ* has a secondary sense of "shine."

10. *empty man.* With Fox, the translation revocalizes the Masoretic *raq*, "only," to read *reiq*, "empty" or "worthless."

11. *Wealth can be less than mere breath.* Wealth can be evanescent, vanishing overnight, but the person who assiduously gathers it bit by bit—presumably, without undertaking risky ventures with what he has accumulated—will see his resources steadily grow.

Who scorns a word will be hurt,   13
    but who fears a command is rewarded.
A wise man's teaching is a wellspring of life,   14
    to swerve from the snares of death.
Good insight gives grace,   15
    but the way of traitors is their ruin.
Every shrewd man acts through knowledge,   16
    but a dullard broadcasts folly.
A wicked messenger falls into harm,   17
    but a trusty envoy brings healing.
Privation and disgrace for one spurning reproof,   18
    but he who takes in rebuke will be honored.
Desire fulfilled is sweet to the palate,   19
    but fools' loathing is swerving from evil.
Who walks with the wise gets wisdom,   20
    but who chases fools is crushed.
Harm pursues offenders,   21
    but the righteous are paid back with good.
A good man bequeaths to the sons of his sons,   22
    and stored for the righteous—the wealth of offenders.

---

13. *Who scorns a word.* The clear implication is that this is a word of reproof.

15. *is their ruin.* The received text reads, oddly, *'eytan*, "is staunch [or "strong"]." The translation follows the Septuagint and the Syriac, which appear to have had *'eydam*, "their ruin," in the Hebrew text from which they translated.

17. *brings healing.* The Hebrew says literally "is healing."

19. *to the palate.* The Hebrew *nefesh* would be literally "throat," or at least that is the meaning assumed here because of the verb *ye'erav*, "is sweet." But it could also mean "to the essential being."

22. *offenders.* The Hebrew uses a singular noun.

23   Much food from the furrows of the destitute,
          and some are swept away without justice.

24   Who spares his rod hates his son,
          but who loves him seeks him out for reproof.

25   The righteous man eats to satiety,
          but the belly of the wicked will want.

---

23. *Much food from the furrows of the destitute.* This proverb is cryptic. Perhaps, like verse 7, it might be a worldly observation on the contradictory nature of reality: destitute people have fields from which an abundant yield could be extracted, but they can't figure out how to do it; others are suddenly destroyed by disease or disaster for no good reason. The burden of this line sounds more like Qohelet than Proverbs. Fox emends the text to yield "the great devour the tillage of the poor."

24. *who spares his rod hates his son.* The Hebrew exhibits a pointed compactness, underscored by internal rhyme and assonance, that defies translation: *ḥoseikh shivto sonei' beno.*

25. *to satiety.* The literal sense of the Hebrew is "for the sating of his appetite [or "gullet," *nafsho*]."

Wisdom has built her house,   1
        and Folly with her own hands destroys it.
Who walks in uprightness fears the LORD,   2
        and he of twisted ways does despise Him.
In the mouth of the dolt is a rod of pride,   3
        but the lips of the wise will guard them.
Without any oxen the manger is clean,   4
        but there is much yield in the bull's strength.
A trustworthy witness does not lie,   5
        but the lying deposer is a false witness.

---

1. *Wisdom has built her house.* This verset is identical with the first verset of 9:1, except that here the Masoretic text adds *nashim*, "women" or "of women," after "Wisdom." That word looks suspect as idiomatic usage, and one may concur in the proposal of R. B. Y. Scott that it is a scribal gloss. Accordingly, it is omitted in the translation. In any case, the momentary appearance in this section of Proverbs of the allegorical apparatus from the preceding (but presumably later) section, Chapters 1–9, is anomalous.

3. *the mouth of the dolt . . . the lips of the wise.* The contrast is between arrogantly aggressive speech (the "rod of pride") and prudent, self-protective speech.

4. *Without any oxen the manger is clean.* This entire line has the ring of a canny folk-saying: your manger may remain clean when you have no oxen to feed, but it is the strength of the ox, however he dirties manger and barn, that enables you to reap a harvest.

5. *A trustworthy witness . . . the lying deposer.* This is one of those proverbs that verges on tautology.

6   The scoffer seeks wisdom in vain,
            but knowledge for the discerning is easy.

7   Go before a foolish man,
            you will not learn from him knowing speech.

8   The shrewd man's wisdom is to understand his own way,
            but the folly of dullards deceives them.

9   Guilt dwells in the tents of scoffers,
            but among the upright—favor.

10   The heart knows its own bitterness,
            and in its joy no stranger mingles.

11   The house of the wicked will be destroyed,
            and the tent of the upright will flourish.

12 .   There may be a straight way before a man,
            but its end is the ways of death.

13   Even in laughter the heart may ache,
            and the end of joy is sorrow.

---

7. *knowing speech.* Literally, "lips of knowledge."

8. *the folly of dullards deceives them.* Literally, "the folly of dullards is deceit."
Given the antithetical parallelism with the first verset, this has to mean not that
they are deceitful but that they deceive themselves.

9. *Guilt dwells in the tents of scoffers.* The received text looks defective here. It
reads, literally, "dolts scoffs [*sic*] [or "intercedes"] guilt," *'ewilim yelits 'asham.*
Taking a hint from the Septuagint, this translation instead reads *be'ohaley letsim
yalin 'asham.*

10. *The heart knows its own bitterness.* In the midst of didactic platitudes, we
suddenly get an arresting aphorism about the incommensurability of each person's private experience.

12. *its end is the ways of death.* The repetition of "way" from the first verset is a
little awkward. That effect might be at least mitigated if one adopted Tur-
Sinai's proposed emendation of *'aharit* to *'orhotaw*, yielding "its paths are the
ways to death."

13. *the end of.* The Masoretic text has "its end."

From his ways the impure of heart is sated, 14
     and the good man from his deeds.
A dupe will believe everything, 15
     but the shrewd man understands where he steps.
A wise man is cautious and swerves from evil, 16
     but a fool rages and trusts too much.
A short-tempered man commits folly, 17
     but a cunning man will be raised high.
Dupes will inherit folly, 18
     but the shrewd wear a crown of knowledge.
The evil bow before the good, 19
     and the wicked at the gates of the righteous.
The poor man is hated even by his neighbor, 20
     but the rich man has many who love him.
Who scorns his neighbor offends, 21
     but happy he who pities the poor.
Surely those who plan evil do stray, 22
     but steadfast kindness for those who plan good.
In all hard labor there is profit, 23
     but word of the lips is sheer loss.

---

14. *ways . . . deeds.* It doesn't seem that an opposition is expressed. We are left with the rather bland statement that both the evil man and the good man live with the consequences of what they do.

17. *will be raised high.* The Masoretic text reads *yisanei'*, "will be hated," which is questionable. This translation reads, with the Septuagint, *yinasei'*, "will be lifted up" or "will be raised high," a simple transposition of consonants.

19. *at the gates of the righteous.* That is, they court them, bow down to them at the entrance of their homes.

24 The crown of the wise is shrewdness;
    the garland of dullards is folly.
25 A true witness saves lives,
    a lying deposer fosters deceit.
26 In fear of the LORD there is a stronghold,
    and for one's sons it is a shelter.
27 Fear of the LORD is a wellspring of life,
    to swerve from the snares of death.
28 In the people's multitude is the king's glory,
    but when the nation is absent—the ruler's disaster.
29 Patience means great discernment,
    but impatience multiplies folly.
30 A healing heart is life to the body,
    but envy is rot in the bones.

---

24. *shrewdness.* The received text reads *'oshram,* "their wealth," an improbable candidate as the crown of the wise. The Septuagint, more plausibly, has *'ormah,* "shrewdness."

 the garland. The received text reads "The folly of dullards is folly." Instead of this tautology, this translation, following many critics, reads *liwyat,* "garland of," instead of *'iwelet,* "folly."

25. *fosters deceit.* The verb—there is none in the Hebrew—is added for clarification.

28. *ruler.* The translation reads *rozen* for the Masoretic *razon,* "famine."

29. *multiplies.* The received text has "lifts up," *merim,* but three ancient versions show *marbeh,* "multiplies."

30. *a healing heart.* Presumably, the heart is healing because it feels something like equanimity, in contrast to the corrosive envy in the antithetical second verset.

Who oppresses the poor insults his Maker,   31
      but he honors Him who pities the wretched.
In his evil the wicked is driven off,   32
      but the righteous finds shelter in his innocence.
In a discerning heart wisdom rests   33
      but is not known in the midst of fools.
Righteousness raises a nation,   34
      but offense leads to want among peoples.
A king's pleasure is a discerning servant,   35
      but his wrath is the shameful man.

---

32. *the righteous finds shelter in his innocence.* The Masoretic text says "in his death," *bemoto*, which is problematic theologically and perhaps grammatically as well. The translation follows the Septuagint and the Syriac, which read *betumo*, "in his innocence," which is a simple transposition of consonants and thus an error a scribe could easily make, possibly induced by the motive of later piety.

33. *but is not known.* The Masoretic text lacks the "not," but this is surely a scribal error because it is hard to imagine that there would be a declaration in Proverbs that wisdom is known in the midst of fools.

34. *want.* Following scholarly consensus and the Septuagint, this translation replaces the Masoretic *ḥesed*, "kindness," with *ḥeser*, "want." The difference between the Hebrew graphemes for *d* and *r* is quite small. The phrase "leads to" has been added in the translation for clarification of the Hebrew, which has no verb.

15

I   *A* soft answer turns back wrath,
           but a hurtful word stirs anger.

2   The tongue of the wise improves knowledge,
           but the mouth of dullards bubbles with folly.

3   The eyes of the LORD are everywhere,
           watching the evil and the good.

4   Healing speech is a tree of life,
           but perverse speech breaks the spirit.

5   A dolt will spurn his father's reproof,
           but who heeds rebuke gains shrewdness.

6   Great treasure is in the righteous man's house,
           but the yield of the wicked is blighted.

7   The lips of the wise spread knowledge—
           not so, the heart of fools.

8   The wicked's sacrifice is the LORD's loathing,
           but the prayer of the upright, His pleasure.

9   The LORD's loathing is the way of the wicked man,
           but He loves the pursuer of righteousness.

---

4. *perverse speech breaks the spirit.* The Hebrew wording is crabbed, and there could be a textual problem in this verset. Here is a very literal rendering: "and a perversion in it is a break in the spirit." The translation for clarity repeats "speech" (more literally, "tongue") from the first verset because "in it," *bah,* refers to "speech."

6. *the yield.* The received text has "in the yield," but some Hebrew manuscripts, the Septuagint, and the Syriac do not show "in."

Harsh reproof for him who forsakes the path,   10
      who hates rebuke will die.
Sheol and Perdition are before the LORD,   11
      how much more so the hearts of men.
A scoffer does not love it when one rebukes him,   12
      to the wise he will not go.
A glad heart will brighten the face,   13
      but by the heart's pain the spirit is lamed.
A discerning heart seeks knowledge,   14
      but the mouth of dullards chases folly.
All the days of the poor man are miserable,   15
      but a cheerful man has a perpetual feast.
Better a pittance in the fear of the LORD   16
      than great treasure with turmoil.
Better a meal of greens where there is love   17
      than a fatted ox where there is hatred.
A hot-tempered man stirs up strife,   18
      but a patient man quiets quarrel.

---

11. *Sheol and Perdition are before the* LORD, / *how much more so the hearts of men*. This line departs from the predominant antithesis between the two versets to employ an *a fortiori* pattern: proposition (first verset) followed by how much more so (second verset). The effect here is quite striking. The vast depths of the realm of death (Sheol and Perdition are synonyms, not distinct entities) lie transparently exposed to the LORD's scrutiny, which therefore can penetrate the human heart with incomparably greater ease. This structure thus produces a powerful statement of how completely God knows all our most innermost thoughts.

13. *by the heart's pain the spirit is lamed*. More literally, "the heart's pain is a lamed spirit."

15. *a cheerful man*. The literal sense is "good-hearted," but in biblical idiom, to be of good heart does not mean kindness or benevolence but rather a good mood.

16. *treasure*. The Hebrew *'otsar* means either storehouse or, by metonymy, what it contains.

19   The sluggard's way is like a hedge of thorns,
             but the path of the upright is smooth.
20   A wise son gladdens his father,
             but a foolish man scorns his mother.
21   Folly is joy to the senseless,
             but a man of discernment walks straight.
22   Plans are thwarted where there is no counsel,
             but with many advisers they are carried out.
23   There is joy for a man in an apt answer,
             and how good is a timely word!
24   A path of life upward for the man of insight,
             that he may swerve from Sheol below.
25   The house of the proud will the LORD uproot,
             but He sets firm the widow's boundary-stone.
26   An evil man's plots are the LORD's loathing,
             but the sayings of the pure are sweet.
27   He blights his house whose gain is ill-gotten,
             but the hater of bribes shall live.

---

20. *a foolish man scorns his mother*. In light of the parallelism with the first verset, this does not mean that he deliberately scorns his mother because he is a fool but rather that his being a fool has the effect of humiliating his hapless mother.

22. *Plans are thwarted*. This verse, like several others in this chapter, pronounces a piece of prudential wisdom that verges on truism or banality.

23. *an apt answer*. Literally, "his mouth's answer."

25. *boundary-stone*. These were used to mark the borders of a person's property. Thus the possessions of the vulnerable widow are safeguarded by the Lord.

26. *but the sayings of the pure are sweet*. The Hebrew of the received text reads "and the sweet sayings are pure," *wetehorim 'imrey-no'am*. This translation adopts the reading of the Septuagint, which appears to reflect a Hebrew text that showed *we'imrey tehorim yin'amu*.

The righteous man's heart utters truth,   28
> but the mouth of the wicked bubbles with evils.

The Lord is far from the wicked,   29
> but the prayer of the righteous He hears.

What brightens the eyes gladdens the heart,   30
> and good news puts sap in the bones.

An ear hearing rebuke for life   31
> in the midst of the wise will abide.

Who casts off reproof despises himself,   32
> but he who heeds rebuke gets understanding.

The Lord's fear is wisdom's foundation,   33
> and humility comes before honor.

---

28. *utters truth*. The Masoretic text reads "utters to answer," but the Septuagint, the Syriac, and the Targum all seem to reflect a Hebrew text that read *'emunim*, "truth," "true things," "trustworthiness," instead of *la'anot*.

33. *wisdom's foundation*. The Masoretic text has *musar hokhmah*, "the reproof of wisdom," which is conceivable but odd. This translation adopts a small, widely proposed emendation, *musad*, "foundation," for *musar*. This would bring the verset in line with several statements in Proverbs that the fear of the Lord is the beginning of wisdom.

16

1 Man's is the ordering of thought,
        but from the Lord is the tongue's pronouncing.
2 All a man's ways are pure in his eyes,
        but the Lord takes the spirit's measure.
3 Turn over your deeds to the Lord,
        that your plans may be firm-founded.
4 Each act of the Lord has its own end;
        even the wicked, for an evil day.
5 The Lord's loathing is every haughty man,
        be sure of it, he will not go scot-free.
6 In faithful kindness a crime is atoned,
        and in the Lord's fear one swerves from evil.

---

1. *from the* Lord *is the tongue's pronouncing.* Throughout Proverbs, apt and articulate speech is conceived as a key to relationships among people and as the indispensable instrument of wisdom. Thus, a person orders his own thought because the autonomy of consciousness is not questioned, but it is a gift from God when thought is translated into fitting speech. The Hebrew rendered here as "pronouncing," *ma'aneh,* can mean either speaking out or answering.

4. *Each act . . . has its own end; / even the wicked.* Reality may seem contradictory or disturbing, but God determines a purpose for all things, so that even the wicked, however outrageous their acts, are destined to come to a bad end, thus confirming the just system of divine purpose in all things.

6. *In faithful kindness . . . in the* Lord's *fear.* The combination of complacent piety and platitude, one must say, is manifested in a good many of the proverbs and is especially salient in this chapter.

When the Lord is pleased with the ways of a man, 7
  even his enemies will make peace with him.
Better a pittance in righteousness, 8
  than abundant yield without justice.
A man's heart may plan his way, 9
  but the Lord will make his step firm.
There is magic on the lips of a king— 10
  his mouth won't betray in judgment.
A balance and just scale has the Lord, 11
  all the weights in His purse are His work.
Wicked acts are the loathing of kings, 12
  for in righteousness a throne stands firm.
Righteous lips are the pleasure of kings, 13
  and they love an honest speaker.
A king's wrath is like death's messengers, 14
  but a wise man may appease it.
In the light of a king's face is life, 15
  and his pleasure like a cloud with spring rain.
Getting wisdom, how much better than gold, 16
  to get discernment is choicer than silver.

---

9. *A man's heart may plan his way.* This proverb is closely analogous to the one in verse 1, except that here it is action ("step") rather than speech that is determined by God.

10. *There is magic on the lips of a king.* In Proverbs the faith in God's authority and justice is repeatedly accompanied by a confidence in the established political order—here the order of justice implemented by kings. This political stance is another one in Proverbs with which Qohelet takes issue.

11. *balance . . . scale . . . weights.* These instruments for conducting trade, elsewhere in Proverbs referred to literally, are here a metaphor for the fairness and precision with which God judges the world.

13. *they love.* The Hebrew verb is in the singular and should either be emended to read as a plural or revocalized to read as a passive ("is loved").

17   The upright's highway is to swerve from evil,
         who guards his life will watch his way.

18   Pride before a breakdown,
         and before stumbling, haughtiness.

19   Better abjectness with the humble
         than sharing spoils with the proud.

20   Who looks into a matter will come out well,
         and who trusts in the LORD is fortunate.

21   The wise of heart will be called discerning,
         and sweet speech will increase instruction.

22   Insight is a wellspring of life to its possessors,
         but the reproof of the foolish is folly.

23   A wise man's heart will make his mouth clever,
         and lips' sweetness increases instruction.

24   Pleasant sayings are honeycomb,
         sweet to the palate, and healing to the bones.

25   There may be a straight way before a man,
         but its end is the ways of death.'

26   The toiler's self toils away
         because his own mouth has compelled him.

---

17. *The uprights' highway is to swerve from evil.* This verset plays paradoxically with two spatial terms. The "upright" is literally "the straight ones," "those who go straight." Usually to "swerve" (*sur*) means to veer off from a straight path. Here, however, swerving from evil means going on the straight way.

20. *Who looks into a matter . . . who trusts in the* LORD. This verse is another instance of the joining of platitude with piety.

23. *make his mouth clever . . . lips' sweetness.* In a variation on the proverb of verse 1, here it is wisdom rather than God that produces apt and captivating speech.

24. *sweet to the palate.* The literal sense of the Hebrew noun *nefesh* in this context is "throat."

25. This verse is identical with 14:12.

26. *The toiler's self toils away.* This proverb is a little cryptic. Some interpreters understand "self," *nefesh*, in its sense of "appetite," and then construe "mouth"

A worthless man is a furnace of evil,   27
      and on his lips like burning fire.
A perverse man provokes a quarrel,   28
      and a sullen man drives off a friend.
A lawless man gulls his companion   29
      and leads him on a way that is not good.
He closes his eyes plotting perversions,   30
      purses his lips and fixes on evil.
Gray hair is a crown of splendor,   31
      through righteousness attained.
Better patience than a warrior,   32
      and who governs his spirit than a conqueror of towns.
In the lap the lot is cast,   33
      but from the LORD is all the disposing.

---

in the second verset as a metonymy for "hunger"—that is, the laborer is driven to toil by his own hunger. This translation construes the second half of the line as a reference to injudicious speech: because the worker has involved himself in debt by making an indiscreet commitment, he is obliged to labor in order to pay what he owes. This understanding would set this verse in contrast to the celebration of wise speech in verses 23 and 24.

27. *a furnace of evil.* The Masoretic text reads *koreh ra'ah,* "digs up evil." The translation adapts a widely accepted emendation, *kur* ("furnace of") *ra'ah.*

30. *closes his eyes . . . purses his lips.* Though there is some debate about the meaning of this verse, the likely intention is simply a kind of caricature of the wicked man who exhibits these facial gestures as he plots evil. The received text shows *'otseh,* which is not a comprehensible word, for "closes," but the widely accepted emendation of *'otsem* yields the ordinary Hebrew verb for closing the eyes.

31. *through righteousness.* The Hebrew says "through the way of righteousness." "The way" has been dropped from the translation to avoid cumbersomeness since it is in any case clearly implied.

33. *In the lap the lot is cast.* Although not much is known about the mechanics of casting lots in ancient Israel, it would seem that the lot was dropped into the lap of a seated person.

17

1 **B**etter a dry crust with tranquility
      than a house filled with feasting and quarrel.
2 A clever slave rules over a son who shames,
      and in the midst of brothers will share the inheritance.
3 Silver has a crucible and gold a kiln,
      and the LORD tries hearts.
4 An evildoer listens to wicked speech,
      a liar hearkens to calamitous talk.
5 Who mocks the poor insults his Maker,
      who rejoices in ruin will not go scot-free.
6 The crown of the elders is sons of sons,
      and the glory of sons, their fathers.
7 Unfit for a scoundrel, overweening speech,
      much less for a nobleman, lying speech.

---

1. *feasting*. Literally, "sacrifice," which is to say, choice cuts left over from the sacrifices. See the note on 7:14.

2. *slave . . . share the inheritance*. This declaration does not necessarily reflect social or economic reality but is better understood as a kind of hyperbole: cleverness trumps heredity if the heir in question is a fool or a scoundrel.

5. *rejoices in ruin*. On the basis of the phrase used here, *sameaḥ le'eyd*, modern Hebrew has appropriately adopted *simḥah le'eyd* as its term for *schadenfreude*.

7. *overweening speech*. The meaning of *yeter* (related to the term that means "more") is not entirely clear. It could mean something like "highfalutin," though the King James Version "excellent" is rather unlikely.

A bribe is a gemstone in the eyes of its user;   8
      wherever he turns he will prosper.
Who overlooks faults seeks love,   9
      and who repeats a speech drives off a friend.
A rebuke comes down on a discerning man,   10
      more than a hundred blows on a fool.
Sheer rebellion an evil man seeks,   11
      but a cruel agent will be against him.
Better meet a bear bereft of its cubs,   12
      than a dolt in his folly.
Who gives back evil for good,   13
      evil will not depart from his house.
Like opening a sluice is a quarrel's start—   14
      before strife flares up, let it go.
Who acquits the wicked or condemns the just,   15
      the LORD's loathing are they both.

16

---

8. *a gemstone . . . wherever he turns he will prosper.* Some interpreters claim, on tenuous contextual grounds, that the Hebrew noun means "magic stone." The more likely meaning is that the bribe, like a precious stone, provides a person a resource that opens doors for him. In any case, the resource is "in the eyes of" the briber, and hence the prospering is not a stated fact but what this person imagines.

10. *a rebuke . . . a hundred blows.* In this instance, the comparison is vividly effective: a sensitive, discerning person will feel the bite of a verbal rebuke more than the callous fool feels a severe beating.

11. *a cruel agent.* This whole verse reflects the cautiously pragmatic political conservatism of Proverbs: if you are imprudent enough to willfully rebel against the government, it will send its ruthless agents to eliminate you.

12. *Better meet a bear bereft of its cubs.* In this instance, the "better than" (the compact Hebrew lacks the usual *tov*) pattern combines with the riddle form: What could be worse than encountering a bear robbed of its cubs? Running into a fool.

16   Why is there a fee in the hand of the fool
            to buy wisdom when he has no sense?

17   At all times a companion is loving,
            and a brother was born for the hour of trouble.

18   A senseless man offers his hand,
            stands bond for his fellow man.

19   Who loves crime loves dissention,
            who builds a high doorway seeks a downfall.

20   A crooked man will come to no good,
            and the perverse of speech will fall into harm.

21   One begets a fool to one's own grief,
            and a scoundrel's father will not rejoice.

22   A joyful heart can effect a cure,
            but a lamed spirit dries up the bones.

23   Bribe from his bosom the wicked man takes
            to tilt the paths of justice.

24   Right in front of the discerning is wisdom,
            but the fool's eyes are on the ends of the earth.

25   Vexation to his father, a foolish son,
            and gall to her who bore him.

---

16. *a fee*. In other contexts, this Hebrew noun means "price." It has been plausibly inferred from this line that there was some general practice of paying teachers for Wisdom instruction of the kind one finds in Proverbs.

17. *the hour of trouble*. "Hour" has been added for the sake of intelligibility.

18. *offers his hand, / stands bond*. Both phrases refer to offering financial surety for someone, an act considered imprudent in Proverbs.

19. *a downfall*. More literally, "a break," which is to say, disaster.

24. *Right in front of the discerning*. The Hebrew says literally "with the face of [or with the presence of]." The idea is that wisdom is right before the eyes of the discerning, whereas fools misguidedly look for it at the ends of the earth.

To punish the just is surely not good,   26
        to flog nobles for uprightness.
Who is sparing in speech knows knowledge,   27
        and coolheaded is the man of discerning.
A silent dolt, too, may be reckoned wise,   28
        who seals his lips, may be deemed discerning.

---

27. *coolheaded*. Literally, "cool of spirit." This idiom is not otherwise attested, and hence the meaning is not entirely certain. The marginal gloss in the Masoretic text corrects *qar*, "cool," to *yeqar*, "precious" or "rare," which does not help matters. Attempts to make this phrase mean "reticent" rest on shaky premises.

28. *a silent dolt, too, may be reckoned wise*. This proverb builds on the preceding one: a wise person is sparing in speech out of good sense and prudence, but a fool may give the appearance of wisdom by keeping his mouth shut.

18

A loner seeks a pretext,
    where one needs prudence, he is exposed.

2   A fool does not care for discerning
    but for exposing his inner thoughts.

3   When a wicked man comes, scorn comes, too,
    and with disgrace, shame.

4   Deep waters the words a man utters,
    a flowing brook, the wellspring of wisdom.

5   To favor the wicked is not good,
    to skew the case of the innocent.

6   The lips of the fool lead to quarrels,
    and his mouth calls out for blows.

---

1. *A loner seeks a pretext.* The received text reads "desire," *ta'awah*. The translation follows the Septuagint, which reflects *to'einah*, "pretext."

where one needs prudence, he is exposed. The Hebrew says merely "wherever prudence, he bursts out," or "is exposed"; "one needs" has been added in translation as an interpretive guess. The sense of the whole verse might be: a person cut off from other people constantly looks for a quarrel and by so doing shamefully exposes his own weaknesses in the very situations that call for prudence.

2. *A fool does not care for discerning.* This proverb on the lack of discretion is paired thematically with the preceding proverb. There are several such pairings in this chapter.

his inner thoughts. Literally, "his heart."

4. *the words a man utters.* Literally, "the words of a man's mouth."

6. *lead to quarrels.* Literally, "enter into quarrel."

A fool's mouth is a disaster for him,   7
    and his lips a snare for his life.
The words of a grumbler are like pounding,   8
    and they go down to the belly's chambers.
He who is slack at his task   9
    is a brother to one who destroys.
The name of the LORD is a tower of strength,   10
    the righteous runs to it and is protected.
The rich man's wealth is his fortress city,   11
    like a high wall within its hedge.
Before a downfall a man's heart is proud,   12
    and before honor, humility.
Who answers a word before hearing it out,   13
    it is folly for him and disgrace.
A man's spirit sustains him in his illness,   14
    but a lamed spirit who can bear?
A discerning heart will get knowledge,   15
    and the ear of the wise will seek knowledge.
A man's gift clears the way for him,   16
    and leads him before the great.

---

7. *A fool's mouth is a disaster for him.* This proverb about the damaging consequences of ill-considered speech is explicitly paired with the preceding proverb.

11. *within its hedge.* This translation follows the Septuagint and three other
ancient versions in reading *bemesukato* for the Masoretic *bemaskito* ("in his
imagining"?).

14. *A man's spirit sustains him in his illness.* This is one of several declarations
in Proverbs about the therapeutic effect of mood or mind—a notion that still
seems medically relevant after two and a half millennia.

16. *a man's gift.* The gift in question might be a bribe, or perhaps something
resembling the contribution that a lobbyist makes to a legislator.

17   First to speak in his dispute seems right,
              till his fellow man comes and searches him out.

18   The lot puts an end to strife,
              and separates the disputants.

19   A brother wronged is like a fortress city,
              and strife like the bolt of a palace.

20   From the fruit of a man's mouth his belly is sated,
              he will sate the yield of his lips.

21   Death and life are in the tongue's power,
              and those who love it will eat its fruit.

---

17. *First to speak in his dispute.* "To speak" is merely implied in the Hebrew.

18. *The lot puts an end to strife.* The evident idea is that when there is a dispute with no clear way to resolve it, something like the toss of a coin can bring it to an end.

19. *A brother wronged.* The formulation in the original is a little cryptic. The most likely meaning: if you wrong someone close to you, he becomes bristlingly defensive, shutting himself off from you like a fortified city.

20. *the fruit of a man's mouth.* As elsewhere, the exercise of speech is seen as decisive, producing consequences for good or for ill with which the speaker must live. This proverb is clearly paired with the one that follows.

21. *those who love it will eat its fruit.* The choice of the verb "love" is revealing in regard to the underlying attitude toward language. A cultivated person delights in language and takes pleasure in its apt use, and this exercise of well-considered expression will redound to his profit. In this fashion, the ethic of articulate speech in Proverbs mirrors the form of the proverbs themselves, which, at least in intention, are finely honed articulations of wisdom, often exhibiting concise wit.

Who finds a wife, finds a good thing   22
>   and wins favor from the LORD.
Imploringly speaks the poor man,   23
>   and the rich man answers harshly.
There is a companionable man to keep company with,   24
>   and there's a friend closer than a brother.

---

23. *Imploringly . . . harshly.* The contrast between the hapless poor man and the rich man who has power over him is pointedly expressed in a tight antithetical chiasm (an instance of the use of the power of the tongue by one who loves it): abb´a´, imploringly / poor man // rich man / harshly.

24. *a companionable man . . . a friend closer than a brother.* Although the chapter divisions are not original to the text, the textual unit from verse 1 to verse 24 is neatly marked by an antithetical *inclusio*: in the first verse, we see someone who is isolated or separated from others, focusing on his own desire, and who consequently gets into trouble; this last verse affirms the sustaining power of friendship. Fox suggests a nuance of contrast between the first verset and the second: there are companionable people with whom one may enjoy social intercourse, but there are also intimate friends closer than a brother.

19

1 Better a poor man walking in his innocence,
    than a man twisted in speech who is a fool.
2 It is surely not good to lack knowledge,
    and who hurries with his feet offends.
3 A man's folly perverts his way,
    and his heart rages against the LORD.
4 Wealth will give one many friends,
    but the poor is parted from his friend.
5 A false witness will not go scot-free,
    and a lying deposer will not escape.
6 Many court the favor of a nobleman,
    and all are friends to a man with gifts.
7 All a poor man's brothers despise him,
    even more, his friends draw back from him.
    [They are not pursuers of sayings.]

---

1. *walking in innocence . . . twisted in speech*. Walking in innocence suggests the recurrent image of walking on a straight way and so becomes a neat antithesis of twisted speech.

    a fool. A few manuscripts read instead "rich."

2. *It is surely not good*. The Hebrew wording is cryptic.

4. *Wealth will give one many friends*. This whole line is one of the instances in which Proverbs offers not moral instruction but a disenchanted observation (like Qohelet) about the way things are: people flock around the rich and avoid the poor. Verse 6 makes essentially the same point.

7. *They are not pursuers of sayings*. The translation reflects the opaque wording of the Hebrew. The verset is textually suspect and may not belong at all because

Who acquires good sense cares for himself,   8
    who guards discernment will find good.
A false witness will not go scot-free,   9
    and a lying deposer will perish.
Unfit for the fool is pleasure,   10
    even more, for a slave to rule princes.
A man's insight gives him patience,   11
    and his glory, to overlook a fault.
A roar like a lion's, the wrath of a king,   12
    but like dew on the grass his favor.
Disaster to his father, a foolish son,   13
    and a maddening drip, a nagging wife.
House and wealth are deeded by parents,   14
    but a clever wife is from the LORD.
Sloth induces slumber,   15
    and a shiftless person will go hungry.

---

there are no triadic lines elsewhere in this whole section of Proverbs—hence the brackets here.

10. *Unfit for the fool is pleasure.* A wise person knows how to manage pleasure judiciously, but a fool will choose harmful pleasures or pursue pleasure to excess. This predisposition for the aristocracy of wisdom goes hand in glove with the affirmation of social hierarchy in the second verset.

12. *a roar like a lion's . . . dew on the grass.* The contrast between the king's wrath and his favorable disposition is effectively highlighted by the move from the simile of the carnivore roaring before it tears apart its prey to the gentle descent of dew on grass.

13. *maddening.* The literal sense of the Hebrew *tored* is "driving away."
    a nagging wife. The literal sense is "quarrels of a wife," but the context amply justifies the translation.

14. *a clever wife.* Though this phrase could also be construed as "a clever woman," the proverb suggests that a man may depend on his parents for the inheritance of wealth and house, but God alone can grant him the gift (or good luck) of a clever wife.

16   Who keeps a command keeps his own life,
          who scorns his own ways will die.

17   Who pities the poor makes a loan to the LORD,
          and his reward He will pay back to him.

18   Reprove your son while there is hope,
          and to his moaning pay no heed.

19   A very hotheaded man bears punishment,
          try to save him—you will make things worse.

20   Heed counsel and take reproof,
          that you get wisdom in the end.

21   Many are the plans in the heart of a man,
          but it's the LORD's counsel that is fulfilled.

22   A man's desire is his own lack,
          and better a poor man than a liar.

23   Fear of the LORD is for life,
          and one rests sated, untouched by harm.

---

19. *A very hotheaded man.* The translation follows the Masoretic marginal correction, *gedol,* instead of the unintelligible *gerol* of the consonantal text.

try to save him. This is another instance in which each Hebrew word of the received text is comprehensible but they make little sense together, so the translation is conjectural. A very literal rendering would be "but if you save and you still would add."

21. *Many are the plans in the heart of a man.* This proverb is manifestly a Hebrew equivalent of "man proposes and God disposes."

22. *his own lack.* The Masoretic text reads "his own kindness" (*ḥesed*). The translation adopts an emendation proposed by Tur-Sinai, *ḥeser,* "lack," mindful that there are many scribal confusions between the letter *reish* and the similar-looking *dalet.*

23. *one rests sated, untouched by harm.* Again, the Hebrew is rather cryptic and the translation an interpretive guess.

The sluggard hides his hand in the dish,   24
    he won't even bring it up to his mouth.
Beat the scoffer and the dupe becomes shrewd,   25
    rebuke the discerning and he gains knowledge.
Despoiling a father, putting a mother to flight,   26
    is the shaming disgraceful son.
A son ceases to heed reproof,   27
    murmuring evil sayings.
A worthless witness scoffs justice,   28
    and the mouth of the wicked swallows crime.
Retribution is readied for scoffers,   29
    and blows for the backs of fools.

---

24. *hides his hand in the dish.* In this proverb, one sees a satiric, and hyperbolic, relation between the first verset and the second. The reader initially wonders why the sluggard hides his hand—or, literally, "buries it"—in the dish, and then discovers that he's too lazy to lift it up to his mouth. The hyperbole in this way conveys the reiterated point that a lazy person fails to provide for his own basic needs.

25. *Beat the scoffer . . . rebuke the discerning.* This proverb is a variation on the idea expressed in 17:10—a whipping may beat sense into a fool, but a word of rebuke suffices for the wise.

27. *A son ceases.* The translation adopts the Septuagint here, reading *ḥadel ben* instead of the Masoretic *ḥadal beni*, "cease, my son."
    murmuring evil sayings. The received text reads *lishgot me'imrey da'at*, "to dote from [?] sayings of knowledge." The translation follows the Septuagint, which seems to have read in the Hebrew *lahagot ma'amarim ra'im*.

29. *Retribution.* Thus the Masoretic text. Many scholars prefer to emend *she-fatim* to *shevatim*, "rods," which is to say, "blows."

20

W̲ine is a scoffer, hard drink is rowdy,
        all who dote on them get no wisdom.

2   A roar like a lion—a king's terror,
        who provokes him mortally offends.

3   It honors a man to sit back from a quarrel,
        but any dolt will jump right in.

4   After winter the sluggard does not plow,
        he asks in the harvest and has nothing.

5   Deep waters the counsel in a man's heart,
        but a man of discernment draws them up.

6   Many a man is called faithful partner,
        but who can find a trustworthy person?

7   The righteous man goes about in his innocence.
        Happy his children after him!

8   A king seated on the throne of judgment
        sifts out all evil with his eyes.

---

1. *hard drink.* A persuasive argument has been made that the Hebrew *sheikhar* is a strong drink made from grapes, which is to say, grappa.

3. *will jump right in.* The general sense of the verb *yitgala'* is to burst out— here, perhaps, in rage. There is some doubt about its meaning in this context.

6. *who can find a trustworthy person.* This proverb is one of many that does not offer direct advice but instead registers a cautionary observation about human behavior. The trust in the moral perceptiveness of the king expressed in verse 8 and elsewhere is the antithesis to this realistic skepticism.

Who can say, "I declare my heart pure.   9
      I am clean of my offense"?
Two different weight-stones, two different measures—   10
      the LORD's loathing are they both.
In his deeds a lad may dissemble   11
      though his acts be upright and pure.
An ear that hears and an eye that sees,   12
      the LORD made them both.
Do not love sleep, lest you lose all your worth,   13
      keep your eyes open and be sated with bread.
"Bad, bad," says the buyer,   14
      and he goes away and then preens himself.
There is gold with abundance of rubies,   15
      but lips of knowledge are a precious vessel.
Take his garment, for he stood bond for another,   16
      and for strangers, take his pledge.

---

9. *I declare my heart pure.* It is also possible to construe the Hebrew verb here to mean "I have made my heart pure."

11. *In his deeds a lad may dissemble.* The proverb is understood in this translation to be a comment on a paradoxical possibility of human behavior: though a young person's acts may be perfectly honest, he may nevertheless use them to create a false impression.

14. *he goes away and then preens himself.* What appears to be involved is a satiric vignette of a particular kind of consumer: he dismisses the merchandise as utterly inferior, whether it is or not, and then goes off empty-handed, congratulating himself on his own acumen. Alternately, one could emend the verb *'ozel,* "goes away," to *huzal,* "is cheapened," as Heinrich Graetz proposed in the nineteenth century. This would yield the following miniature narrative: first the prospective buyer denigrates the merchandise; then the price comes down and he buys it, praising himself for his shrewdness.

16. *Take his garment.* Here the reiterated warning against offering bond for another is cast as an imperative: take his garment or whatever he has put up as security, seeing that he has been foolish enough to expose himself to this sort of risk.

17 Bread got through fraud may be sweet to a man,
          but in the end it fills his mouth with gravel.
18 Plans set through counsel will be fulfilled,
          and you should make war through designs.
19 Laying bare secrets the gossip goes round;
          don't trust yourself to a blabbermouth.
20 Who reviles his father and his mother,
          his lamp will gutter in pitch darkness.
21 An estate gained hastily from the start,
          its end will not be blessed.
22 Do not say, "Let me pay back evil."
          Hope for the LORD, that He give you victory.
23 Two different weight-stones are the LORD's loathing,
          and cheating scales are not good.
24 From the LORD are the steps of a man,
          and how can a person grasp his own way?
25 It's a snare for a man to utter "Sanctified,"
          and after the vows to reflect.
26 A wise king sifts out the wicked
          and turns the wheel over them.

---

22. *"Let me pay back evil." / Hope for the LORD, that He give you victory.* This admonition may recall the story of David and Abigail in 1 Samuel 25. David, enraged when his men are insulted by her husband Nabal, is on his way to wreak vengeance, but Abigail implores him not to shed blood and have his own hand "rescue" or "give victory" (the same verb as here) but to leave vengeance to the LORD.

25. *to utter "Sanctified," / and after the vows to reflect.* Though the general sense of the verse seems to be that one should not really pronounce vows of sacrifices for the temple, the Hebrew wording, and in particular the verb represented here as "utter," are obscure.

26. *the wheel.* The probable reference is to the wheels of a chariot with which a triumphant king would crush the defeated enemy.

The Lord's lamp is the life-breath of man,   27
      laying bare all the inward chambers.
Let a king keep faithful trust,   28
      that he uphold his throne in faithfulness.
The splendor of young men is their strength,   29
      and the glory of elders, gray hair.
With fearsome bruises scour away evil,   30
      and blows to the belly's chambers.

---

27. *laying bare.* The Hebrew verb *hofes* seems to say "searching out," which would work for God but not for a lamp, but it should either be read as *hosef* (a simple transposition of consonants) or understood to have the sense of *hosef,* such reversals of consonants with a retention of the meaning being not infrequent in biblical verbal stems.

    all the inward chambers. Literally, "all the belly's chambers."

28. *let a king keep.* The translation assumes a singular, *yitsor,* for the plural *yitsru* in the received text. This assumption is encouraged by the Masoretic linking of the verb with a hyphen to *melekh,* "king," suggesting that this singular noun is the grammatical subject of the verb.

30. *fearsome bruises.* The Hebrew joins two synonyms in the construct state ("bruises of wound"), which as elsewhere is an intensifier.

    scour away. There is some margin of doubt about the meaning of this term, especially since the consonantal text shows it as a verb, *tamriq* (which ordinarily does not appear in this particular conjugation), whereas the Masoretic marginal note corrects it to *tamruq* ("unguent"?). The most likely meaning, if one considers the repeated affirmation of corporal punishment in Proverbs, is that the only appropriate way of dealing with an evil person is to beat the living daylights out of him.

    the belly's chambers. This is the same Hebrew phrase that is used at the end of verse 27.

21

1 ater-streams, a king's heart in the hand of the LORD,
        wherever He desires, He diverts it.
2 A man's whole way is right in his eyes,
        but the LORD takes the measure of hearts.
3 Doing righteousness and justice
        is choicer to the LORD than a sacrifice.
4 Haughty eyes and overweening heart—
        the furrow of the wicked is offense.
5 The plans of the diligent—only for gain,
        and all who hasten—only for loss.
6 Attaining treasures with a lying tongue
        is vanished breath and snares of death.

---

1. *Water-streams, a king's heart.* This proverb appears to play on the idea expressed elsewhere (20:5) that there are deep waters in a man's heart. The proverb is also cast in riddling form: What could it mean that a king's heart is streams of water in God's hand (or power)?—that God, like an engineer, can divert the channels into whatever course He chooses.

4. *the furrow of the wicked is offense.* All their endeavors to reap are an offense.

5. *the diligent . . . all who hasten.* The contrast is between the person who carefully plans his projects and carries them out assiduously and those who do things precipitously, without deliberation. Again, the consequences are purely pragmatic: the diligent reaps a profit; the rash end up penniless.

6. *and snares of death.* The Masoretic text reads *mevaqshey mawet,* "seekers of death," a problematic reading because the phrase does not accord well with "vanished breath" and the plural creates a syntactic incoherence. The transla-

The plunder of the wicked drags them down,   7
      for they refuse to do justice.
Perverse is the way of a stranger-man,   8
      but a pure one, his deeds are straight.
Better to dwell in the corner of a roof,   9
      than with a quarrelsome wife in a spacious house.
The wicked longs for evil with all his being,   10
      his fellow man gets no pity from him.
When the scoffer is punished, the dupe gets wisdom,   11
      but when a wise man is taught, he gains knowledge.
The righteous fathoms the hearts of the wicked,   12
      subverts the wicked for evil.
Who stops up his ear to the cry of the poor,   13
      he, too, will call unanswered.
A gift in secret allays anger,   14
      and a stealthy bribe, fierce wrath.

---

tion follows a reading shown in some variant manuscripts, the Septuagint, and the Vulgate: *umoqshey mawet*, "and snares of death."

8. *a stranger-man.* The Hebrew, literally "man and stranger," looks suspect. Some emend *'ish wazar* to *'ish kazav*, "a lying man," which reads smoothly, though it has no textual warrant.

9. *Better to dwell in the corner of a roof.* The "better than" proverb form here is also a kind of riddle: What could possibly be worse than to have to perch (or live) in the corner of a roof? To live with a quarrelsome wife.
   a spacious house. The Hebrew *beyt haver* would be literally "house of a friend"—perhaps a welcoming house. But a reversal of the order of consonants yields *bayit rahav*, "a spacious house."

11. *dupe . . . wise man.* When the fool sees that the troublemaker has come to grief, he wises up, whereas the wise man needs only instruction to get wisdom.

12. *the hearts of the wicked.* The translation follows the Septuagint, which shows *libot*, "the hearts of," instead of the Masoretic *leveyt*, "to the house of."

14. *a stealthy bribe.* Literally, "a bribe in the bosom"—that is, a bribe that is slipped furtively into the bosom of the bribe-taker.

15 A joy to the righteous, the doing of justice,
    but disaster to wrongdoers.

16 A man who strays from insight's way
    will repose in the assembly of shades.

17 The lover of revels is a man in want,
    who loves wine and oil will not grow rich.

18 A ransom for the righteous, the wicked man,
    and in place of the upright, the traitor.

19 Better to dwell in a desert land
    than with a quarrelsome angry wife.

20 Rare treasure and oil in the wise man's abode,
    but a foolish man swallows them up.

21 Who pursues righteousness and kindness
    will find life, righteousness, and honor.

22 The wise man goes up against a town of warriors
    and takes down its mighty stronghold.

23 Who guards his mouth and his tongue
    guards his life from trouble.

24 The arrogant brazen—scoffer his name,
    he acts in arrogant anger.

---

16. *strays from insight's way / will repose in the assembly of shades*. A miniature narrative unfolds between the two versets: a person strays from the straight way of wisdom and then finds himself in the realm of the netherworld.

17. *wine and oil*. In the good life of the ancient Mediterranean, rubbing the body and head with fine olive oil was a valued luxury, hence its bracketing here with wine as a metonymy for hedonism.

18. A *ransom for the righteous . . . in place of the upright*. The idea is that whatever disasters might have overtaken the good person will fall instead on the wicked.

19. *Better to dwell in a desert land*. This proverb is thematically and structurally parallel to verse 9, with the desert replacing the roof corner as a miserable place to live that is preferable to life with a quarrelsome wife.

20. *Rare*. Literally, "desired."

The sluggard's desire will kill him,   25
      for his hands refuse to act.
All day long he aches with desire,   26
      but the righteous gives unstinting.
The sacrifice of the wicked is loathsome,   27
      even more, as he brings it depraved.
A lying witness will perish,   28
      but a man who listens to counsel will speak.
A wicked man is brazen-faced,   29
      but the upright understands his own way.
There is no wisdom and no discernment   30
      and no counsel before the Lord.
A horse is readied for the day of battle,   31
      but victory is the Lord's.

---

26. *he aches with desire.* Literally, "he desires a desire." The "he" would simply refer to the person who is slave to his own desires. The Septuagint reads "the dolt desires."

27. *depraved.* Literally, "in depravity." Fox argues for the sense of "with a scheme."

28. *a man who listens to counsel will speak.* The Masoretic text reads "a man who listens will forever [*lanetsaḥ*] speak," which scarcely seems the outcome one would want from an attentive person (presumably, attentive in a court of justice). The translation adopts the emendation of *le'etsah*, "to counsel."

31. *but victory is the Lord's.* The second verset springs a kind of revelatory surprise on the audience of the proverb. After the image of the horse readied for battle, either saddled for its rider or hitched to its chariot, we discover in two Hebrew words, two beats, against the four words and four beats of the first verset, that the outcome of the battle is determined by God alone.

22

1 A name is choicer than great wealth—
   than silver and gold, good favor.
2 The rich and the poor come together,
   the Lᴏʀᴅ is maker of both.
3 The shrewd man sees harm and hides,
   but dupes pass on and are punished.
4 What follows humility is fear of the Lᴏʀᴅ,
   wealth and honor and life.
5 Thorns and pitfalls in the way of the crooked,
   who guards his life keeps far from them.
6 Train up a lad in the way he should go,
   when he grows old he will still not swerve from it.

---

2. *come together.* More literally, "meet." Though exegetical energy has been lavished on the question of what it means for the rich and the poor to come together, the obvious sense, dictated by the second clause of this line, is that whatever social and economic differences separate the rich and the poor, in the end they are both God's creatures and equal before Him.

3. *pass on and are punished.* Evidently, the unreflective dupe passes on in the direction of harm, or moves right through it, not realizing the damage it is inflicting on him. "Punished" in this context suggests something like "come to grief."

6. *in the way he should go.* Though the literal sense is "according to his way," there is no reason to swerve from the formulation of the King James Version, which catches the intended meaning and has become proverbial.

The rich rules over the poor,   7
    and the borrower is slave to the man who lends.
Who sows wrongdoing will reap injustice,   8
    and the rod of his wrath will fail.
The generous one, he shall be blessed,   9
    for he gave of his bread to the wretched.
Banish the scoffer and strife will depart,   10
    dispute and demeaning will cease.
Who loves heart's purity,   11
    speaks graciously—the king is his friend.
The Lord's eyes watch over knowledge,   12
    and He confounds the traitor's words.
The sluggard said, "A lion's outside   13
    in the square. I shall be murdered!"
A deep pit is the mouth of stranger-women.   14
    The cursed of the Lord will fall into it.

---

8. *the rod of his wrath will fail.* The assumption is that the wrongdoer is hurt-fully aggressive toward others ("rod," *shevet,* is the same instrument wielded instructionally against sons, though in that case it is a "rod of reproof"). In the end, when he gets his comeuppance, his power to harm others will fail.

9. *The generous one.* Literally, "good of eye."

11. *speaks graciously.* The literal sense of the Hebrew, which has no verb, is "graciousness of his lips."

13. *I shall be murdered.* The inappropriate verb (instead of "eaten up" or "killed") is probably deliberate. The lazy man, giving free rein to his fantasy in order to find excuses for not leaving his house, imagines that the lion prowling the streets will viciously "murder" him, as though it were a malicious assassin.

14. *A deep pit is the mouth of stranger-women.* As elsewhere, the stranger-woman is somebody else's (seductive) wife. Her mouth is a dangerous pit because she uses it to speak the sweet talk of seduction (for a vivid example, see Chapter 7). It is also prelude and analogue to the lower "pit" in which she seeks to draw the gullible young man.

15   When folly is bound to the heart of a lad,
            the rod of rebuke will remove it from him.

16   One oppresses the wretched but makes him increase,
            one gives to the wealthy but he comes to want.

17   Bend your ear and hear the words of the wise,
            and set your heart on my knowledge.

18   For it is sweet that you keep them in your belly,
            that they all be fit on your lips.

19   For your trust to be in the Lord,
            I have informed you today, even you.

---

15. *When folly is bound to the heart of a lad.* In the rather brutal pedagogy of Proverbs, if your child shows foolish inclinations, you need to beat them out of him.

16. *One oppresses . . . one gives.* This is another proverb that is not a didactic maxim but rather an observation about the sometimes paradoxical nature of human reality: in some cases, a person may seek to take advantage of a poor man and yet the poor man thrives; in some cases, a person may give to someone who already has plenty and somehow the rich man ends up in want.

17. *Bend your ear and hear the words of the wise.* Here begins a formal exordium, running to verse 21, that marks the inception of a new collection of proverbs that comprises two sub-units, 22:22–23:11 and 23:12–24:22. The first of these sub-units, as most scholars for nearly a century have agreed, is an adaptation of an Egyptian Wisdom text, the Instruction of Amenemope, and thus bears witness to the international circulation of Wisdom literature. Fifteen of its twenty-four verses have notable parallels in Amenemope, and some of the sequencing of the proverbs is the same. In all likelihood, the Egyptian text was first translated into Aramaic, perhaps in the seventh century BCE, by which time Aramaic had become a diplomatic lingua franca in the Near East. Elite circles in Israel at this point certainly knew Aramaic, and so an adaptation from the Aramaic to Hebrew would have been perfectly likely. It is notable that the Hebrew of this section incorporates a number of Aramaic usages.

Have I not written for you thirty things   20
        in good counsel and knowledge?—
to inform you the utmost true sayings,   21
        to respond to those who send you.

Do not rob the wretched, for wretched is he,   22
        and do not crush the poor in the gate.
For the LORD will argue their case,   23
        and deprive those who deprived them of life.
Consort not with an irascible man,   24
        and do not join a hotheaded person,
lest you learn his ways   25
        and take on a snare for your life.
Do not be of those who give their hand in pledge,   26
        who back up extortionate loans.

---

20. *thirty things*. The Masoretic text has *shalishim* ("captains"?) in the *ketiv* (consonantal text) and *shelishim* ("threes"?) in the *qeri* (marginal gloss). Neither makes sense, and the translation adopts Fox's persuasive emendation to *sheloshim*. Amenemope has thirty maxims, and there are thirty maxims in this sub-unit, if one counts the exordium as the first maxim.

21. *the utmost true sayings*. The Hebrew strings together synonyms, *qosht* (a borrowing from Aramaic, meaning "truth"), *'imrey 'emet* ("sayings of truth"), with an effect of emphasis or intensification.

22. *do not crush the poor in the gate*. The gate was where courts of justice were held, and the sense of subverting the legal rights of the poor is spelled out in the first verset of the next line.

24. *a hotheaded person*. The Hebrew *'ish-ḥeimot* is unusual as an idiom but, Fox informs us, is a direct translation of the Egyptian phrase.

27   If you have nothing with which to pay,
              why should your bedding be taken from under you?
28   Do not shift the age-old boundary-stone
              that your forefathers set up.
29   Have you seen a man who is quick at his task?
              Before kings he shall stand.
                    He shall not stand before the lowly.

---

27. *why should your bedding be taken from under you.* As the law in Exodus 22:25–26 makes clear, the poor man's bedding was the cloak in which he wrapped himself for sleep—hence one is forbidden to take it away from him at night in pawn for a debt. A letter on behalf of a laborer, found at Yavneh Yam, and dating from the seventh century BCE, complains about the deprivation of the cloak for debt. The Hebrew seems to say "why should he take your bedding," but the third-person masculine singular is often used as the equivalent of a passive and thus is translated here as a passive.

28. *Do not shift the age-old boundary-stone.* This injunction, which has a close parallel in the Egyptian source-text, reflects the general view that real property should be inalienable.

29. *quick at his task.* The Hebrew adjective *mahir* suggests, as in a number of other occurrences, "adept" or "skilled."
    the lowly. A more literal rendering of the Hebrew *ḥashukhim* would be "the obscure," but the sense is not that they lack fame but rather that, unlike kings, they have no social standing.

23

When you sit to break bread with a ruler,   1
        understand well what is before you,
and put a knife to your gullet,   2
        if you are a gluttonous man.
Do not crave his delicacies,   3
        when they are bread of lies.
Do not strain to become rich,   4
        through your understanding, leave off.
Let your eyes but fly over it, it is gone,   5
        for it will surely sprout wings,
               like an eagle fly off to the heavens.

---

2. *put a knife to your gullet.* This admonition not to gorge oneself when dining with the powerful has numerous parallels in Egyptian Wisdom literature.

3. *they are bread of lies.* The powerful man may seem to be showering you with hospitality in laying out a grand spread before you, but he has his own calculations, and a guest who eats too eagerly may come to regret it.

4. *through your understanding, leave off.* Though the Hebrew is a bit cryptic, this may be the most plausible construction: use your good sense not to strive excessively for wealth. Fox understands this as "Leave off your staring," but construing the noun *binah* as "staring" is somewhat strained, even though the cognate verb sometimes means "to consider" or "to regard."

5. *over it.* The antecedent is an implied noun, "wealth."

6 Do not break bread with a stingy man,
   nor crave his delicacies.
7 For like one who gauges in his mind, so he is.
   "Eat and drink," he will say to you,
     but his heart is not with you.
8 Your crust that you eat you will vomit,
   and you will ruin your pleasant words.
9 In a fool's ears do not speak,
   for he will despise the insight of your words.
10 Do not shift the age-old boundary-stone,
   nor enter the fields of orphans.
11 For their redeemer is strong,
   he will argue their case against you.

12 Bring your heart to reproof,
   and your ear to sayings of truth.
13 Do not hold back reproof from a lad,
   when you strike him with the rod, he won't die.

---

7. *but his heart is not with you.* The stingy host, like the ruler, may make a gesture of hospitality, but what he has in mind is anything but generosity. The vivid image of vomiting in the verse that follows may suggest that he will offer his guest questionable food—say, three-day-old fish that has begun to go bad—which he has bought at a very cheap price.

11. *for their redeemer is strong.* Many understand this as a reference to God, Who protects the helpless orphans in their plight. "Redeemer," *go'el*, is a judicial term (this is how it is used in Job and in Ruth), and so it could refer here to a human redeemer, some hitherto unknown kinsman who will come forth and battle for the rights of the orphan.

12. *Bring your heart to reproof.* This very general admonition signals the beginning of another collection of sayings, not from Amenemope, though. As Fox points out, sundry other Egyptian sources are tapped.

You, with the rod you should strike him   14
      and save his life from Sheol.
My son, if your heart gets wisdom,   15
      my heart, too, will rejoice,
and my inward parts will exult   16
      when your lips speak uprightness.
Let your heart not envy offenders,   17
      but in fear of the Lord all day long.
For if you keep it, there is a future,   18
      and your hope will not be cut off.
Listen, my son, and get wisdom,   19
      and make your heart go straight on the way.

---

14. *save his life from Sheol.* The insistence here and elsewhere on vigorous corporal punishment is linked to the fear of the dire consequences for failing to discipline a young person. Either because he will become involved in dangerous activities or be punished by God, his swerving from the right path can lead to his death.

16. *inward parts.* The literal sense of the Hebrew is "kidneys" (hence the King James Version, "reins"), thought to be the seat of conscience.

17. *but in fear of the Lord all day long.* The Hebrew seems to imply an elided verb such as "dwell." Some scholars emend this phrase to "fearers of the Lord," but envy seems the wrong attitude toward such people.

18. *if you keep it.* The Hebrew lacks a verb, and the translation follows the Septuagint, which has a verb to this effect, evidently based on a Hebrew text that showed *tishemrena.* The antecedent of "it," a feminine suffix in the Hebrew, would be "fear of the Lord" in the previous line.

19. *make your heart go straight on the way.* The verb *'asher* means literally "make strides," though, as Fox suggests, it probably puns both on *yashar,* "straight," and on its other sense, to declare someone fortunate.

20   Do not be with the guzzlers of wine,
        with those who gorge on meat.

21   For the guzzler and gorger will lose all,
        and slumber will clothe him in rags.

22   Listen to your father who begot you,
        nor despise your mother when she grows old.

23   Get truth and do not sell it,
        wisdom, reproof, and discernment.

24   The righteous man's father will surely be gladdened,
        the wise man's begetter rejoices in him.

25   Your father and mother rejoice,
        and she who bore you will be gladdened.

26   Pay mind, my son, to me,
        and let your eyes keep my ways.

27   For a whore is a deep ditch,
        and a narrow well, the stranger-woman.

---

21. *slumber will clothe him in rags.* The Hebrew does not specify an object for the verb, but, contrary to many interpreters, it would have to be the glutton and drunkard, now seen lying in a sated stupor and thus neglecting his possessions, which he comes to lose.

26. *keep.* The translation adopts the correction of the marginal *qeri*. The text proper, reversing the consonants of the verb, erroneously reads "be pleased with."

27. *whore . . . stranger-woman.* These are complementary possibilities of dangerous liaisons, the prostitute and the adulteress. Each is a trap into which a foolish man can tumble, with the sexual sense of "ditch" and "well" manifest. Chapter 5 offers a contrasting image of conjugal sexuality as a pure well.

Why, like a kidnapper she lies in wait,   28
      and sweeps up the traitors among men.
For whom "alack," for whom "alas,"   29
      for whom strife, for whom complaint?
For whom needless wounds,
      For whom bloodshot eyes?
For those who linger over wine,   30
      who come to try mixed drink.
Do not regard wine in its redness,   31
      when it shows its hue in the cup,
         going down smoothly.
In the end it bites like a snake,   32
      and like a viper spews its poison.

---

28. *a kidnapper*. The Hebrew *ḥetef* is odd but derives from a verbal stem that means "to snatch."

sweeps up. The verb *tosif*, elsewhere meaning "to increase," here seems to derive, as many commentators have concluded, from *'asaf*, to take away or gather up.

traitors. At least here, the double standard for sexual behavior is not applied: the married men who frequent promiscuous women are traitors to their own wives, and their involvement with the adulterers will lead them to a bad end.

29. *For whom*. This interrogative phrase, which could equally be rendered as "who has?" begins an extended riddle form: only at the end of the second line here, with the reference to bloodshot eyes, is there an explicit hint that the object of all these mishaps is the drunkard, whose identity is then spelled out in the next verse.

31. *in its redness*. Literally, "as it shows red."

going down smoothly. The phrase *yithalekh bemeysharim* is elucidated by its use in Song of Songs 7:10 in reference to the beloved's palate, which is "like goodly wine." Amusingly, the language of this verse in Proverbs, intended as a warning against wine, is repeatedly used in the Hebrew drinking poems of medieval Andalusia as a celebration of the glories of wine.

33   Your eyes will see strange things,
                and your heart will speak perverseness,
34   and you will be like one who beds in the sea,
                who beds on the top of the rigging.
35   "They struck me—I felt no hurt;
                they beat me—I was unaware.
      When will I awake?
                I will look for it again."

---

33. *Your eyes will see strange things.* The hallucinations and mental confusion of drunkenness are the snake-bite of the drink.

34. *like one who beds in the sea / who beds on the top of the rigging.* The simile provides a striking satiric image of the wobbliness of the drunkard. In a characteristic move of intensification from the first verset to the second, the drunken person is not merely like someone trying to sleep in the surging sea but like someone lying up in the rigging as the ship pitches about.

35. *They struck me—I felt no hurt.* The drinker is too stupefied by alcohol to realize that he has been beaten. These words loop back to the riddle question, "For whom needless wounds?"
    When will I awake? / I will look for it again. At the end of this satiric vignette, the alcoholic remains true to his addiction: still in a half-stupor as he pronounces these words, he is in no condition to go out and get more wine, but as soon as his mind clears a bit, that is just what he means to do.

24

Do not envy evil men,   1
        and do not desire to be with them.
For their heart ponders plunder,   2
        and their lips speak trouble.
Through wisdom a house is built,   3
        and through discernment it is firm-founded.
And through knowledge rooms are filled   4
        with all precious and pleasant wealth.
A wise man is mightier than a strong one,   5
        and a man of knowledge than one of great power.
For through designs you should make war,   6
        and victory comes from abundant counsel.

---

4. *with all precious and pleasant wealth*. In this verset the poet diverges from the prevalent pattern of neat semantic parallelism between the two halves of the line, which is emphatically evident in the three preceding lines, to stipulate, in a little surprise, with what the rooms of the house are filled.

5. *mightier than the strong one . . . than one of great power*. The Masoretic text reads *gever ḥakham ba'oz*, "a wise man in [the?] strength," and *me'amets-koah*, "summons up power." The second phrase is intelligible though a poor parallelism; the first phrase is not intelligible. The translation follows the Septuagint, the Syriac, and the Targum, all of which seem to have read *gavar ḥakham mei'az* and *mei'amits-koah*, readings that yield the translation offered here.

7   Wisdom is too high for the dolt,
                   he won't open his mouth in the gate.
8   Who plots to do evil,
                   they will call him a master of cunning.
9   The foulness of foolishness is an offense,
                   the scoffer is loathed by people.
10   Should you be slack on the day of distress,
                   your strength will be constrained.
11   Save those who are taken to death,
                   and from those stumbling to slaughter do not hold back.
12   Should you say, "Why, we did not know of this."
                   Will not the Weigher of Hearts discern,
         and the Watcher of your life not know,
                   and pay back a man by his deeds?
13   Eat honey, my son, for it is good,
                   and honeycomb, sweet on your palate.
14   Thus know wisdom for yourself,
                   if you find it, there is a future,
                         and your hope will not be cut off.

---

7. *he won't open his mouth in the gate*. As elsewhere, the gate is where judicial discussions were conducted. The dolt, lacking all wisdom, will have no idea what to say in such deliberations.

9. *loathed by people*. More literally, "people's loathing."

11. *slaughter*. Or "a killing."

12. *we did not know of this*. These words refer back to the previous line: when people are about to be slaughtered, don't pretend that you had no notion of what was happening.
    not know. The "not" is unstated in the Hebrew but carried over from the previous clause.

13. *Eat honey, my son*. Though the urging to eat something that tastes sweet may sound momentarily superfluous, the equation between honey and wisdom was a familiar one, and it is promptly spelled out in the next verse, which is clearly bracketed with this one.

Do not enter the home of the righteous   15
       nor plunder the place where he beds his flock.

For seven times a righteous man falls and gets up   16
       but the wicked stumble in evil.

When your enemy falls, do not rejoice,   17
       and when he stumbles, let your heart be not gladdened,

lest the LORD see and it be evil in His eyes,   18
       and He deflect His wrath from him.

Do not be provoked by evildoers,   19
       do not envy the wicked.

For there is no future for the evil man,   20
       the lamp of the wicked will gutter.

Fear the LORD, my son, and the king,   21
       neither one nor the other vex.

For ruin from them rises suddenly;   22
       Who can know the disaster wreaked by both?

---

15. *Do not enter the home of the righteous.* The Masoretic text reads, "Do not lay in wait, wicked man, for the home of the righteous," *'al te'erov rasha' leneweh tsadiq.* This is odd because "lay in wait" is something done to a person, not to a place, and because vocatives addressed to the wicked are not part of the rhetorical strategy of Proverbs. The translation adapts an emendation proposed by Fox, based in part on the Septuagint: *tavo',* "enter," for *te'erov,* "lie in wait," and the deletion of *rasha',* "wicked man," as a probable gloss.

21. *neither one nor the other vex.* The Masoretic text reads, "And don't mix in (*tit'arav*) with *shonim.*" The meaning of *shonim* is in doubt. Some think it means "dissidents"; the King James Version guesses, desperately, "them that are given to change." There is no evidence that this verbal root, which can mean either "to repeat" or "to be different," had either of these senses in the Bible. The translation follows the Septuagint, which reads *sheneyhem,* "the two of them," for *shonim,* and *tit'abar* (or perhaps *te'aber*), a root having to do with anger, instead of *tit'arav,* "mix in." This two-line proverb, then, follows a recurring theme of the book in warning against provoking those in power, who can have a short fuse and a heavy hand.

23   These, too, are from the wise:
         showing favor in justice cannot be good.

24   Who says to the guilty, "You are innocent,"
         peoples will curse him,
            nations will damn him.

25   But for the rebukers it will be pleasant,
         upon them the blessing of good will come.

26   With lips does he kiss
         who answers in forthright words.

27   Prepare your task outside
         and ready it for yourself in the field.
            After, you will build your house.

28   Do not be a witness for no cause against your neighbor,
         that you should seduce with your lips.

29   Do not say, "As he did to me I will do to him,
         I will pay back the man by his deeds."

30   I passed by the field of the lazy man
         and by the vineyard of one without sense,

---

23. *These, too, are from the wise.* This is the brief formal introduction of a new selection of proverbs from a different source.

showing favor in justice. This second verset in fact begins the sequence on impartiality in justice that takes up the next two lines.

26. *kiss . . . forthright words.* The line flaunts a paradox: he who speaks straightforwardly—probably words of justified criticism—is as one who kisses, however harsh the words.

27. *Prepare your task outside.* This is another piece of purely pragmatic wisdom: first, a person must shore up his substance by working in the field, and then he will be in a position to build a house. This proverb is a pointed antithesis to the satiric portrait at the end of the chapter of the lazy man letting his possessions sink into ruin.

30. *I passed by the field of the lazy man.* The miniature first-person narrative that begins here is relatively rare in this part of the book, where hortatory second-person address predominates.

and, look, it had all sprouted thorns,   31
      its surface was covered with thistles,
        and its stone wall was in ruins.
And I beheld and I paid mind,   32
      I saw, I took reproof;
a bit more sleep, a bit more slumber,   33
      a bit more lying with folded arms,
and your privation will come like a wayfarer,   34
      your want like a shield-bearing man.

---

32. *I took reproof.* In this context, the recurring idiom has the sense of "I learned a lesson."

33–34. *a bit more sleep, a bit more slumber.* These two lines duplicate 6:10–11. See the comment there for an elucidation of the language.

25

¹ These, too, are proverbs of Solomon, which the men of Hezekiah king of Judea transcribed.

²   God's honor is to hide a matter,
           the honor of kings, to probe a matter.
³   The heavens for height and the earth for depth,
           but the heart of kings is beyond probing.

---

1. *which the men of Hezekiah king of Judea transcribed.* The historical claim is perfectly plausible. Hezekiah reigned during the last three decades of the eighth century BCE, and court scribes in this period might well have collated and redacted a small collection of proverbs. The use of "too," *gam*, clearly suggests that there was at least one earlier collection, the most likely candidate being the one that begins in Chapter 10.

2. *God's honor is to hide a matter.* God's purposes in history, nature, and individual lives are beyond human ken, and their hidden character enhances our sense of divine power.
    the honor of kings, to probe a matter. The king, as supreme judicial and executive authority, is obliged to sift out facts for the purposes of justice and policy. The emphasis on kings and on the comportment before nobility in all likelihood reflects the concerns of the court scribes responsible for this collection of proverbs. It continues through verse 7.

3. *The heavens for height and the earth for depth.* This line initiates the puzzle pattern that is especially prominent in this particular collection: a potentially enigmatic image in the first verset followed by its human referent or antithesis in the second verset.

Remove the dross from silver,   4
     and for the refiner the vessel comes out.
Remove the wicked man from the king's presence,   5
     and his throne is firm-founded in justice.
Do not preen before a king,   6
     and do not stand in the place of the great.
For better that he say to you, "Come up here,"   7
     than that he abase you before a noble
          whom your eyes have seen.
Do not go out quickly to a quarrel,   8
     for what will you do afterward
          when your neighbor puts you to shame?
Take up your quarrel with your neighbor,   9
     but another's secret do not reveal,
lest he who hears revile you,   10
     and your infamy not be withdrawn.
Golden apples in silver carvings,   11
     a word spoken in its own right way.
A ring of gold and a fine-gold bangle—   12
     the wise rebuker to an ear that heeds.

---

4. *Remove the dross from silver*. In this instance, the puzzle image takes up a whole line of poetry, and the explanation of its relevance to the affairs of men is unfolded in a second line (verse 5).

7. *whom your eyes have seen*. This clause sounds lame and may well be a mistaken scribal addition.

11. *golden apples in silver carvings*. This image of exquisite jewelry for apt speech reflects the high value placed in Proverbs on eloquent and beautifully framed speech.

12. *A ring of gold and a fine-gold bangle*. Here the enigmatic nature of the riddle image in the first verset is flaunted: it is rather a surprise that something as harsh and immaterial as rebuke should turn out to be the referent of these images of fine jewelry. The ring, *nezem*, would be worn either on the ear or the nose, and the former placement fits nicely with the listening ear.

13   Like the chill of snow on a harvest day,
                  a faithful messenger to his senders,
                        he revives his master's spirits.
14   Clouds and wind yet there is no rain—
                  a man who boasts of a deceptive gift.
15   Through patience a leader is duped,
                  and a gentle tongue breaks a bone.
16   If you find honey, eat just what you need,
                  lest you have your fill of it and throw it up.
17   Be sparing of your visits in your neighbor's house,
                  lest he have his fill of you and hate you.
18   A mace and a sword and a sharpened arrow—
                  a man who bears false witness against his neighbor.

---

13. *Like the chill of snow on a harvest day.* Of course, snow would never fall on a harvest day in the Land of Israel. The early harvest in late May is an especially hot period, but even during the late harvest at the beginning of October, it is relatively warm.

14. *Clouds and wind.* The combination of clouds and wind suggests that a heavy storm is brewing. The lack of rain then sets up the enigma of the riddle, to be solved in the second verset.

15. *Through patience a leader is duped.* If you take your time and calculate carefully, you can find a way to make a ruler serve your purposes. The verb could also be rendered as "beguiled," but the violence of the second verset argues for the more negative sense.
    a gentle tongue breaks a bone. This is a very vivid instance of the tendency to intensification in the second half of the line. Duping a ruler through patient strategy in the first verset is a plausibly realistic event; the second verset then deploys a strong hyperbole—gentle speech as an agency of terrific destruction, which is also an anatomical image, the soft tongue that paradoxically can break a bone.

17. *Be sparing of your visits.* The literal sense of the Hebrew is "make your foot rare."

18. *A mace and a sword and a sharpened arrow.* In this instance the riddling nature of the initial verset is compounded by this stringing together of three different weapons. For the first term, the received text shows *meifits* ("scatter"),

A shattered tooth and a shaky leg—   19
    treacherous refuge on a day of trouble.
Who takes off a garment on a cold day,   20
    vinegar on natron—
        thus the singer of songs to a downcast heart.
If your foe is hungry, feed him bread,   21
    and if he thirsts, give him water,
for you would heap live coals on his head,   22
    and the LORD will pay you back.
A north wind brings on rain,   23
    and an angry face—a secretive tongue.
Better to dwell in the corner of a roof   24
    than with a quarrelsome wife in a spacious house.

---

but this is almost certainly a mistake for *mapats*, "mace" or "club," as the evidence of the Septuagint indicates.

19. *shaky*. The translation reads *mo'edet*, "stumbling" or "shaky," for the Masoretic *mu'edet*, "designated" or "warned against," the difference being only the vocalization.

20. *vinegar on natron*. The effect of vinegar on natron (sodium carbonate) is to produce an acrid sizzle.

22. *the LORD will pay you back*. Some understand this to mean that the LORD will reward you—reward for showing humanity to your enemy. But the verb also means to requite or punish, and that sense is a better match with the idea of heaping coals on the foe's head in the first verset: if you are inhumane to your enemy, the LORD will requite it of you.

23. *an angry face—a secretive tongue*. Showing anger drives people to guard their words and not say what they mean.

24. *Better to dwell in the corner of a roof*. This verse duplicates 21:9. See the comment there.

25   Cool water to a famished throat—

        good news from a distant land.

26   A muddied fountain, a fouled-up spring—

        a righteous man toppling before the wicked.

27   To eat too much honey is not good,

        and to be sparing of speech is honor.

28   A breached city without a wall—

        a man with no restraint to his spirit.

---

27. *to be sparing of speech is honor.* The Masoretic text here makes little sense: *weḥeqer kevodam kavod*, "and the probing of their honor is honor." This translation follows the emendation formulated by Fox, *weḥoqer daber mekhubad*.

28. *a breached city without a wall.* This riddle image would have communicated a condition of terribly exposed vulnerability to the ancient audience, which was very familiar with fortified walls as an important means of protecting cities from invaders. In the second verset, then, the man of unrestrained spirit is seen as making himself painfully vulnerable to humiliation or harm.

26

Like snow in the summer, like rain in the harvest,   1
      so honor is unfit for a fool.
As a bird for wandering, as a swallow for flight,   2
      so a groundless curse won't come to pass.
A whip for the horse, a bridle for the donkey,   3
      and a rod for the back of fools.
Do not answer a dolt by his folly   4
      lest you, too, be like him.
Answer the dolt by his folly,   5
      lest he seem wise in his own eyes.

---

1. *Like snow in the summer.* This is part of a whole series here of riddle-form one-line proverbs. These are cast either as a paradoxical or a puzzling image in the first verset—in this instance: what could possibly be as anomalous as snow in a warm season?—or as an image so self-evident that the listener wonders why it should be mentioned (for example, verses 3, 7, 14, 20).

2. *a bird . . . a swallow.* Just as these winged creatures by their nature fly away, a groundless curse will not "come down on" its intended object but will dissipate, fly away.

4–5. *Do not answer a dolt . . . answer the dolt.* Ingenious exegetical effort has been exercised to set these two contradictory proverbs in a dialectic or complementary relationship with each other. It is more plausible to assume that they were bracketed together editorially because of the similarity of formulation while they reflect two quite different and originally independent perspectives. The first proverb counsels us to avoid contention with a fool because we are liable to get entangled in his own misguided or confused terms ("by [or according to] his folly"). The second proverb urges us to answer the fool so that he is compelled to recognize what a fool he is. In this English version, *kesil,* generally

6 He cuts off his own legs, drinking outrage,
        he who send words by a fool.
7 Thighs hang slack on the lame
        and a proverb in the mouth of fools.
8 Like one binding a stone in a sling,
        so he who gives a fool honor.
9 A thorn comes up in the hand of a drunk
        and a proverb in the mouth of fools.
10 A master brings all things about,
        but who hires a fool hires vagabonds.
11 Like a dog going back to his vomit
        a dolt repeats his folly.

---

rendered as "fool," has been translated as "dolt" because the word for "folly" here, *iwelet*, is an entirely different term.

6. *He cuts off his own legs, drinking outrage.* In this proverb, the riddle image is especially violent: like a man who terribly mutilates himself is he who entrusts a message to a fool.

8. *binding.* With the Septuagint, the translation reads *tsorer*, "binding" or "one who binds," instead of the Masoretic *tseror*, "bundle." The relation of image to referent is not entirely clear. Fox's explanation is that giving a fool honor "arms" him to do harm to others, like the loading of a slingshot with a stone.

9. *A thorn comes up in the hand of a drunk.* Presumably, he is staggering about in his drunken stupor and thus thrusts his hand unawares against thorns.
    a proverb in the mouth of fools. This means either that they will pronounce a warped proverb that may hurt others or, lacking the wisdom to pronounce wise sayings, in their effort to do so they will shame or do harm to themselves. The latter option may be more likely.

10. *A master brings all things about, / but who hires a fool hires vagabonds.* The Hebrew of the received text is obscure, but the sundry attempts to emend it involve major surgical operations on the text with no more than scant support in the ancient versions. This translation follows the general outline of the construction proposed in the New Jewish Publication Society translation.

11. *Like a dog going back to his vomit.* This is another case of a violent, and arresting, riddle image in the first half of the line.

Have you seen a man wise in his own eyes?   12
     There is more hope for the fool than for him.
The sluggard says, "A young lion is on the road,   13
     a lion is out in the squares."
A door turns on its hinge,   14
     and a sluggard on his bed.
The sluggard buries his hand in the dish,   15
     he cannot bring it back up to his mouth.
The sluggard is wiser in his own eyes   16
     than seven who answer with good sense.
Like one who seizes the ears of a passing dog   17
     is he who mixes in with a quarrel not his.
Like a lunatic shooting deadly firebrands   18
     is a man who deceives his neighbor   19
     and says, "Why, I was joking."

---

13. *The sluggard says.* This proverb is a virtual doublet of 22:13. See the comment there. The Hebrew uses two synonyms for "lion," and the translation resorts to a familiar fallback by rendering the first term, *shaḥal*, as "young lion."

14. *A door turns on its hinge.* This is a particularly witty deployment of a seemingly obvious image for the riddling part of the line. A door, of course, turns on its hinge; but then we are invited to link that to the sluggard, turning from one side to the other in bed and going nowhere, like the door. We may also imagine the door opening and shutting, with people going in and out, while the sluggard remains in bed.

15. *The sluggard buries his hand in the dish.* This proverb duplicates 19:24. See the comment there.

17. *seizes the ears of a passing dog.* The simile has a special edge because dogs were not domesticated in ancient Israel but rather wandered outside as semi-feral scavengers. The vivid implication is that a person who mixes into someone else's quarrel is liable to get badly bitten.
    mixes in. The translation reads *mit'arev* for the Masoretic *mit'aber* ("becomes angry").

18. *lunatic.* There is some question about the precise meaning of the Hebrew term.
    deadly firebrands. The literal sense of the Hebrew is "sparks, arrows, and death." "Arrows and death" may be a hendiadys for "deadly arrows."

20   When there is no wood, a fire goes out,
             and without a grumbler, strife falls silent.
21   Coal for embers and wood for fire
             and a belligerent man to stir up quarrel.
22   A grumbler's words are like pounding
             and they go down to the belly's chambers.
23   Silver with dross glazed on pottery
             are ardent lips and an evil heart.
24   By his lips a foe dissembles
             and within he lays out deceit.
25   Though he makes his speech fair, do not trust him,
             for seven loathsome things are in his heart.
26   Who covers hatred in deception,
             his evil will be exposed to all.
27   Who digs a pit will fall in it,
             and who rolls a stone, it will come back on him.
28   A lying tongue hates those it crushes,
             and a smooth mouth pushes one down.

---

22. *A grumbler's words*. This is another doublet. See 18:8.

23. *ardent lips*. An emendation of the first consonant of the Hebrew word rendered as "ardent" (or "burning") yields "smooth lips," which is the reading of the Septuagint.

25. *speech*. Literally, "voice."

26. *to all*. Literally, "in the assembly"—that is, in public.

28. *a lying tongue hates those it crushes*. The tongue is a synecdoche for the liar, but it accords with the potent agency assigned to speech in Proverbs that the tongue should be the subject of both verbs here. What the proverb seems to have in mind is a common psychological mechanism in which the victimizer comes to hate or despise the very person to whom he does wrong, perhaps feeling contempt because the victim has so pathetically exposed himself to harm. For a vivid sexual instance in the Bible, see the story of Amnon and Tamar in 2 Samuel 13.
       a smooth mouth. The reference is obviously to smooth speech, but the agency of the body part, as with the tongue in the first verset, is important for the poetic effect.

27

D̶o not boast about tomorrow,   1
       for you know not what the day will bring forth.
Let a stranger praise you and not your own mouth,   2
       another, and not your own lips.
The weight of a stone and the heft of sand—   3
       the dolt's anger is heavier than both.
The cruelty of fury and anger's rush—   4
       but who can stand up to envy?
Better open reproof   5
       than hidden love.
The wounds from a friend are faithful   6
       but the kisses of a foe are profuse.
A sated appetite disdains honeycomb   7
       but to a hungry appetite all bitter is sweet.
Like a bird wandering from its nest   8
       is a man wandering from his place.

---

3. *The weight of a stone and the heft of sand.* After the two preceding proverbs, which are prudential exhortations, this verse reverts to the riddle form, as does the next verse.

6. *The wounds from a friend are faithful.* Both the content of the second verset and the larger context of Proverbs suggest that "wounds" here means something like "cutting words of rebuke" (in contrast to the hypocritical kisses of an enemy). They are "faithful" in the sense that they are meant to serve one's best interest, and are an expression of loyal friendship.
profuse. This is what the Hebrew term means. The implication is that the kisses are excessive, and suspect.

9   Oil and incense gladden the heart,
                and a friend's sweetness more than inward counsel.
10   Do not forsake your friend or your father's friend
                nor enter your brother's house on the day of your ruin.
     Better a close neighbor
                than a distant brother.
11   Get wisdom, my son, and gladden my heart,
                that I may give back an answer to my insulter.
12   The shrewd man saw evil and hid.
                Dupes passed on and were punished.
13   Take his garment, for he stood bond for another,
                for an alien woman, take his pledge.
14   Who greets his neighbor in a loud voice
                first thing in the morning,
                        it is reckoned to him a curse.

---

9. *a friend's sweetness more than inward counsel.* The Hebrew is somewhat cryptic, or perhaps merely elliptical. "Sweetness" might be an ellipsis for "sweet
counsel." The phrase rendered as "inward counsel," or perhaps "one's own
counsel," is *'atsat nafesh,* which could mean literally "the counsel of the essential self," "the counsel of the spirit," or simply "a person's counsel."

10. *Do not forsake your friend.* Fox understands the verb in context to mean
"ignore," though the evidence for that sense of *'azav* elsewhere is scant.
     nor enter your brother's house. The implication is that a true friend is a better
resource in life than a brother.
     Better a close neighbor / than a distant brother. Despite the verse breaks, this
is obviously a separate proverb, bracketed editorially with the previous one
because of the comparison of friend and brother.

12. *The shrewd man.* This proverb duplicates 22:3.

13. *Take his garment.* This is still another doublet—of 20:16—with minor
changes.

14. *Who greets his neighbor in a loud voice.* This proverb is an amusing observation on social behavior: when you are barely awake in the morning, the last
thing you want is a bellowed—and perhaps ostentatious—greeting from a
neighbor.

A maddening drip on a cloudy day   15
    and a nagging wife are alike.
Who conceals her conceals the wind,   16
    and her name is called "right hand."
Iron together with iron,   17
    and a man together with his friend.
Who tends a fig tree will eat its fruit,   18
    and who guards his master will be honored.
Like water face to face   19
    thus the heart of man to man.
Sheol and Perdition are not sated,   20
    and the eyes of man are not sated.

---

15. *A maddening drip.* This proverb is a somewhat different formulation of 19:13.

16. *Who conceals her conceals the wind, / and her name is called "right hand."* The Hebrew is unintelligible, as the translation indicates, and even with emendation it is hard to make sense of this verse. The "her" may refer to the nagging wife of the previous verse, in which case the idea is that it is impossible to hide her because she is everywhere. (The verb for the initial "conceal" is plural in the Hebrew but has been emended to a singular to accord with the second "conceals.") The literal sense of the second verset in the received text is "and the oil of his right hand will call [or will be called]," *weshemen yemino yiqra'*. This has been emended, partly in accordance with the Septuagint, to read *weshemah yamin yiqarei'*. Even so, the meaning is unclear. Perhaps, by a stretch, it could mean, she is thought of as the right hand—that is, powerful—because there is no way to conceal or repress her. Amidst all this confusion, Fox interestingly detects a pun: *tsafan*, "conceal," suggests *tsafon*, "north"; and *yamin*, "right hand," is an alternate term for "south."

17. *Iron together with iron.* This is usually understood to refer to magnetized iron, which clings to iron, and so does a man to his friend. The force of the proverb is in its terrific compactness, which the translation tries to preserve.

19. *Like water face to face.* Again, the translation reproduces the strong compactness of the original. The reference is obviously to someone seeing his own reflection in water. But water is unstable and therefore an undependable or distorting mirror, unlike an actual mirror of polished bronze (there were no glass mirrors in this era). Thus one man's heart provides a tricky or deceptive image of what is in the heart of another.

21   Smelter for silver and kiln for gold,
        and a man according to his praise.

22   Though you grind down a dolt with a mortar,
        in the pestle among the groats,
            his folly will not swerve from him.

23   You must surely know the look of your flock,
        put your mind on the herds.

24   For wealth is not forever
        nor a crown for time to come.

25   The grass is gone, new grass appears,
        the mountains' grasses are gathered.

26   There are sheep for your clothing,
        he-goats, the price of a field.

27   Enough goat's milk for your food,
        for the food of your house,
            and viands for your young women.

---

21. *a man according to his praise.* A man's reputation tests him, burns out the dross, as a smelter tries silver or gold.

23. *You must surely know the look of your flock.* These words begin a multi-line proverb on the virtues of responsible pastoralism that runs to the end of verse 27.

24. *wealth.* In a pastoral economy, wealth would be measured chiefly in flocks.
    a crown. This term represents an intensification of the initial verset: not only is wealth transient, but even a crown (and the power and possessions that go with it) is not forever.
    for time to come. Literally, "for generation after generation."

25. *The grass is gone, new grass appears.* The grass, of course, is vital for feeding the flocks, and so it is important that there is a new growth each year.

26. *he-goats, the price of a field.* Fox's explanation seems plausible: you can always sell off some of your goats to purchase more fields to pasture the rest.

27. *goat's milk.* The word for goat means "she-goat" and is entirely different from the masculine term used in the previous verse.
    viands. The literal sense is "life." The usage may reflect an etymology analogous to "viands"—that which you live on.

28

   he wicked man flees with no pursuer,   1
        but the righteous are bold as a lion.
Through the crime of a land, its princes are many,   2
        but through a discerning man it is long-lasting.
A poor man oppressing the lowly—   3
        pounding rain without bread.

---

1. *The wicked man flees . . . the righteous are bold.* The wicked, plagued by a guilty conscience, live in constant fear of divine retribution or legal punishment, whereas the righteous live in confidence.

2. *Through the crime of a land, its princes are many.* The possible but by no means certain meaning is that when a country is lawless, it produces many different contenders for power.

but through a discerning man it is long-lasting. As the translation reflects, the Hebrew text that has come down to us makes virtually no sense. Here is a more literal rendering: and through a discerning knowing man thus he (it?) is long-lasting. In the translation, "knowing" has been dropped as an apparent scribal doublet for "discerning." Some interpreters claim that *ken*, "thus," means "honesty," which would then be the subject of "is long-lasting," but when *ken* does not mean "thus," it is an adjective, "honest," not a noun. Emendations of this line have been unavailing.

3. *A poor man oppressing the lowly.* In an unjust economic hierarchy, even a poor person can exploit other disadvantaged people, or perhaps be used as a tool by the powerful to exploit them. This is a rare proverb in which the riddle image ("pounding [more literally, "sweeping"] rain without bread") appears in the second verset—perhaps because there is also something of a riddle or at least a paradox in this first verset.

pounding rain without bread. Rain as a rule waters the soil, enabling the growth of grain. A torrential rain washes away the soil, making the growth of

4   Those who forsake teaching praise the wicked,
             but those who keep the teaching confront them.
5   Evil men do not understand justice,
             but the LORD's seekers understand all.
6   Better a destitute man walking blameless
             than one stubborn in his ways though rich.
7   A discerning son keeps the teaching,
             but one who consorts with gluttons shames his father.
8   Who increases his wealth through interest and usury
             will amass it for one kind to the poor.
9   Who turns his ear from listening to teaching,
             his very prayer is loathsomeness.
10   Who misleads the upright to an evil way,
             in his own pit he will fall,
                  and the blameless will inherit good.
11   Wise in his own eyes is the rich man,
             but the discerning poor will find him out.
12   When the righteous rejoice, grand is the splendor,
             but when the wicked rise up, man dons disguise.

---

grain impossible. The poor man's oppression of the lowly is purely destructive, and, in a kind of pun, he himself is without bread.

8. *interest and usury*. Though attempts have been made to discriminate between the two Hebrew terms, the distinction remains uncertain. The first of the terms, *neshekh*, etymologically means "bite" and so probably suggests excessive interest.
    will amass it for one kind to the poor. This notion that ill-gotten gains will end up in the hands of the charitable is clearly wishful thinking.

10. *and the blameless will inherit good*. This third verset looks suspiciously like an addition to the original line.

12. *man dons disguise*. The verb *yeḥupas* can mean either "will be sought for"—yielding the sense that under the regime of the wicked decent people are hard to find, perhaps have to hide—or "is disguised," that is, forced self-protectively to dissemble. Since the grand splendor of the first verset implies public display, the antithetical sense of disguise may be somewhat more likely.

Who covers his crimes will not prosper,   13
       but who admits and leaves off will be granted mercy.
Happy the man who fears at all times,   14
       but who hardens his heart will fall into harm.
A growling lion and a famished bear—   15
       a wicked ruler over a poor people,
              a prince lacking discernment and great in   16a
              oppression.
Who hates ill-gotten gains   16b
       will have length of days.
A man oppressing by blood guilt   17
       flees to a pit.
              Let none hold on to him.
Who walks in blamelessness will be rescued,   18
       but the crooked of ways will fall in a ditch.
Who tills his soil is sated with bread,   19
       but who pursues empty things is sated with poverty.
A trustworthy man abounds in blessings,   20
       but who hastens to enrich himself will not go scot-free.

---

14. *fears.* In context, this would be fear of doing evil or fear of retribution if evil is done.

16a. *a prince lacking discernment and great in oppression.* Despite the conventional verse break, influenced by the brevity of 16b, this verset, as Fox notes, is clearly the third element of a triadic line characterizing the unjust ruler that begins in verse 15.

16b. *Who hates ill-gotten gains / will have length of days.* This proverb is scanned here as an abbreviated line with two versets, each having two beats in the Hebrew. But it is equally possible to represent it as a one-verset truncated line of poetry.

17. *oppressing.* The translation assumes *'osheq,* an active verb, instead of the passive *'ashuq,* "oppressed," of the Masoretic text.

18. *in a ditch.* The received text reads *be'ehat* ("all at once"?), but the Syriac, more plausibly, reflects *beshahat,* "in a ditch."

21   Favoritism is not good,
            and for a crust of bread a man may do wrong.
22   The miserly man rushes off after wealth,
            unaware that want will befall him.
23   Who rebukes another man will find more favor
            than a smooth talker.
24   Who robs his father and mother saying "It is no crime"
            is a friend to a man who brings ruin.
25   The greedy man stirs up strife,
            but who trusts in the LORD flourishes.
26   Who trusts in his own heart, he is a fool,
            but who walks in wisdom, he will escape.
27   Who gives to the destitute knows not want,
            but who averts his eyes abounds in curses.
28   When the wicked rise up, man hides,
            and when they perish, the righteous are many.

---

21. *for a crust of bread a man may do wrong.* If the first verset suggests that in justice—that is what the term for "favoritism" generally implies—one should not show partiality to the rich and powerful, then this clause probably means that a judge should also have compassion for the poor man who may have stolen out of sheer desperate hunger.

23. *another man.* The translation emends *'adam aharay,* "a man after me," in the received text to *'adam 'aheir,* "another man."

26. *he is a fool.* This is an instance of what Fox calls a "gapped"—that is, elliptical—proverb. The wise man will escape from trouble, but the fool will not escape.

29

A man often rebuked who is stiff-necked,   1
    will be suddenly broken beyond healing.
When the righteous are many, a people rejoices,   2
    but when the wicked man rules, a people groans.
A man who loves wisdom will gladden his father,   3
    but a chaser of whores will destroy wealth.
A king makes a land stand firm through justice,   4
    but a deceitful man destroys it.
A man who flatters his fellow   5
    spreads a net at his feet.
In an evil man's crime is a snare,   6
    but the righteous is glad and rejoices.
The righteous man knows the cause of the poor.   7
    The wicked man does not grasp knowledge.
Scoffing men fan the flames of a city,   8
    but the wise will turn back wrath.

---

1. *A man often rebuked.* Literally, "a man of rebukes."

2. *When the righteous are many, a people rejoices.* This proverb, like the next one and several others in this chapter, is no more than a formulation in verse of a platitude.

3. *a chaser of whores will destroy wealth.* The objection to consorting with whores is pragmatic, not moral—they will drain all your financial resources.

7. *the cause of the poor.* "Cause" here is used in its legal sense: the righteous man concerns himself with the struggle of the poor to get justice.

9   When a wise man contends with a doltish man,
             the dolt rages and mocks, with no calm.

10   Bloody men hate the innocent,
             but the upright look out for his life.

11   The fool gives vent to his whole spirit,
             but the wise man quells it.

12   A ruler heeding a lying word—
             all his servants are wicked.

13   A pauper and a schemer meet—
             the Lord gives light to the eyes of both.

14   A king who judges the poor with honesty,
             his throne will stand firm for all time.

15   Rod and rebuke impart wisdom,
             but a lad run loose shames his mother.

16   When the wicked increase, crime increases,
             but the righteous will witness their downfall.

---

9. *the dolt rages.* The Hebrew merely says "he," but "dolt" has been added in the translation to avoid the ambiguity of the pronoun's antecedent.

10. *look out for his life.* The received text shows *yevaqshu nafsho*, "seek his life," an idiom that everywhere else means to try to kill a person. This translation emends the verb to *yevaqru*, a difference of one consonant, producing a verb that can have the sense shown in this English version.

11. *gives vent . . . quells.* This proverb articulates the view found elsewhere in the book that self-restraint and discretion are important attributes of wisdom.

13. *A pauper and a schemer meet.* The probable sense of "meet" here is that, for all the differences between these two categories of people, they share one point of commonality—that, whatever their intentions for evil or good and whatever the restrictions of their condition in life, they are equally dependent on God's illumination in order to achieve insight or a state of well-being (giving light to the eyes may imply both).

16. *the righteous will witness their downfall.* The literal sense of the verb is "see," reflecting a recurrent biblical idiom that implies triumph over one's enemies because one survives to watch them come to a bad end.

Reprove your son and he will give you ease,   17
     and offer delicacies for your palate.
Without vision a people turns wild,   18
     but happy is he who follows the teaching.
Through words a slave will not accept reproof,   19
     though he understand, there will be no answer.
Have you seen a man hasty in his words?   20
     There is more hope for the dolt than for him.
Who pampers his slave from youth,   21
     in the end there will be dismay.
An angry man stirs up strife,   22
     and a hothead abounds in crime.
A man's pride will bring him low,   23
     but the lowly of spirit will hold on to honor.

---

17. *your palate.* The literal sense of the noun *nefesh* in context is either "throat" or "appetite." The conjunction with "delicacies" argues against any other sense of this multivalent term.

19. *Through words a slave will not accept reproof.* The implication, unfortunately, is that the only way to reprove a slave effectively is to beat him. Egyptian Wisdom texts often reflect this idea.

though he understand, there will be no answer. The second verset spells out why it is that verbal reproof of a slave will be unavailing: even if he understands the criticism leveled against him, he will choose not to respond, given his refractory slave's character.

21. *dismay.* The Hebrew *manon* appears nowhere else and is not readily linked with any verbal root that would make sense in context, which makes it look very much like a scribal error. Three different ancient versions render it in ways that point to a Hebrew text that showed *manod.* That noun, literally "shaking," elliptical for "shaking of the head," is a gesture performed when witnessing some sort of disaster.

23. *low . . . lowly.* In both instances, the Hebrew uses the same verbal stem, *sh-p-l* (*tashpilenu, shefal-ruaḥ*), in a pointed antithesis.

24   Who shares with a thief hates himself,
            he will hear the curse and will not tell.

25   A man's fear becomes a snare,
            but he who trusts in the LORD will be safe.

26   Many seek a ruler's presence,
            but a man's judgment comes from the LORD.

27   A wrongdoer is the loathing of the righteous,
            and the wicked's loathing, the man of straight ways.

---

24. *he will hear the curse.* The curse, or imprecation, is probably a solemn curse publicly pronounced that will come down on the head of whosoever has evidence of the crime to offer in court yet remains silent.

25. *A man's fear becomes a snare.* The fearful man, in contradistinction to the man who trusts in the LORD, runs the danger of being tripped up by his own anxiety, imagining dangers where they are not and acting timorously where boldness is called for.

30

The words of Agur, son of Yaqeh, the oracle, utterance of the man, to 1
Ithiel, to Ithiel and Ukhal.
> For I am a brute among men, 2
>> and no human discernment have I.
> I have not learned wisdom, 3
>> nor the knowledge of the holy ones do I know.

---

1. *The words of Agur.* As this heading makes clear, the unit that follows (which probably ends with verse 9) is distinct from the rest of the Book of Proverbs. The two terms that follow, "oracle," *masa'*, and "utterance," *ne'um*, are usually reserved for vatic or prophetic speech, a kind of discourse uncharacteristic of Proverbs. What follows is a first-person, incipiently confessional statement unlike anything that has preceded in this book. The name Agur is otherwise unattested.

to Ithiel, to Ithiel and Ukhal. These names, and the repetition, are enigmatic. Many scholars revocalize them and change the word divisions of the consonantal text to yield three verbs. Thus Fox proposes the following: "I am weary, God, / I am weary, and have wasted away." Though it is possible that this was the original reading in the Hebrew, there is no warrant for it in the ancient versions, and it remains conjectural.

3. *I have not learned wisdom.* This proclamation is a counterpoint to the prevailing emphasis of Proverbs. Agur, humbly aware of his limitations before a transcendent God (see the next verse), says in effect that any wisdom he might have pretended to attain amounts to nothing.

the knowledge of the holy ones. Though an exegetical tradition going back to the Middle Ages understands *qedoshim* as "the Holy One," the Hebrew noun is plural. It is true that the most common name for God, *'elohim*, is plural in form though singular in meaning, but the evidence that *qedoshim* works in the same way is not altogether convincing. The most likely reference would be to angelic beings.

4   Who has gone up to the heavens and come down,
          who has scooped up the wind in his palms?
    Who has wrapped up the waters in a cloak.
          Who has raised up all ends of the earth?
    What is his name or the name of his son,
          That you should know?

5   Every saying of God is pure,
          He is a shield to all who shelter in Him.

6   Add nothing to His words,
          lest He rebuke you and you be given the lie.

7   Two things I have asked of You,
          do not withhold them from me before I die.

8   Falsehood and lying words keep far from me.
          Privation and wealth do not give me.
          Provide me my allotted bread.

---

4. *Who has gone up to the heavens and come down.* Only someone who could negotiate this trajectory, patently impossible for mortal man, would be capable of achieving divine wisdom.

the waters . . . the earth. These are the two principal elements of the biblical cosmogony.

What is his name or the name of his son. This formulation has obviously invited Christological readings that would not have been within the purview of the Hebrew poet, writing several centuries before the emergence of Christian doctrine. In the patrilineal society of ancient Israel, a man's full name was his given name and the name of his father (for example, Isaiah son of Amoz), as in our society it is the given name and the family name.

6. *Add nothing to His words.* This injunction is in keeping with Deuteronomy 4:2. The burden of this verse and the preceding one is a pious counterweight (perhaps for that reason appealing to the editor) to the idea of wisdom as a kind of craft with human instructors that predominates in the book: all wisdom comes from God through His revealed words, and no mere human should tamper with them.

7. *do not withhold them from me before I die.* This existential urgency is of a piece with Agur's distinctive confessional mode.

8. *Provide me my allotted bread.* This clause does not constitute a third thing but is simply the condition to which Agur aspires after his two wishes are

Lest I be sated and I renounce,   9
       and I say, "Who is the Lord?"
And lest I lose all and I steal
       and profane the name of my God.

Do not denounce a slave to his master,   10
       lest he revile you and you bear guilt.

A generation that reviles its father   11
       and its mother it does not bless.
A generation that is pure in its eyes   12
       though it has not been washed of its filth.
A generation, how haughty its eyes,   13
       and its eyelids, how arrogant.

---

granted—freedom from falsehood, neither privation nor wealth—and then he will be content with a modest material sufficiency.

9. *Lest I be sated and I renounce.* Too many worldly goods may lead a person to feel he has no need for God. Compare Deuteronomy 32:15.

And lest I lose all and I steal / and profane the name of my God. These words sketch out a miniature narrative: first the person dismisses God as he revels in his abundant possessions; then he becomes impoverished and resorts to crime, thus profaning God's name.

10. *Do not denounce a slave to his master.* This proverb, in the form of a negative injunction, is unlike the words of Agur in form and substance and also could not belong to the "generation" sequence that begins in the next verse. An editor may have inserted it here because, like both lines of verse 9, it has a "lest" clause.

11. *A generation that reviles its father.* Here begins an independent unit of four verses (five lines of poetry) that deploys "a generation" as an emphatic anaphora at the beginning of every line but the last. The content is purely denunciatory, in a style reminiscent of the Prophets, and there is nothing here but negative characterizations of the generation in a series of subordinate clauses, with no actual grammatical predicate.

12. *filth.* The Hebrew *tso'ah* implies excremental filth, though it is not really scatological.

14 A generation whose teeth are swords,
                 and meat-cleavers its jaws,
      to devour the lowly from the earth
                 and the impoverished from humankind.

15a The leech has two daughters: "Give!" "Give!"
                 Three things are there that are not sated,
15b four that do not say, "Enough!":
16   Sheol and a blocked womb,
                 the earth unsated with water
                      and fire, which does not say "Enough!"
17   An eye that mocks a father
                 and scorns submission to a mother,
      the rooks of the river will gouge it,
                 and the eagle's young will devour it.
18   Three things are there too wondrous for me,
                 and four that I cannot know:

---

14. *meat-cleavers.* The relatively rare term *ma'akhelet* (also used in the story of the Binding of Isaac) is not an ordinary knife but the kind of knife used to butcher meat.

15a. *The leech has two daughters.* This succinct aphorism is restricted to a single verset. One should probably assume, as most commentators have, that there is an implied human referent—a greedy person, or perhaps a greedy woman, because the Hebrew for "leech" is a feminine noun. Some interpreters see the two daughters as a reference to the two suckers of the leech.

15a–15b. *Three things . . . four.* This little numerical progression is traditional in a certain line of biblical poetry. Compare Amos 1:3: "For three crimes of Damascus / and for four, I will not revoke it."

16. *Sheol and a blocked womb.* A parallelism between Sheol (the biblical netherworld) and the womb appears elsewhere in biblical poetry. H. N. Bialik, the great modern Hebrew poet, in a poem expressing revulsion after a sexual encounter with a woman, refers to her "hidden treasures that like Sheol cannot be sated." Here, Sheol is never sated with the dead, always wanting more, and the blocked womb, in an ironic antithesis, is never satisfied with its condition of barrenness, always hungry to produce life.

the eagle's way in the heavens,   19
      the way of the snake on a rock,
the ship's way in the heart of the sea,
      and the way of a man in a young woman.
This is the way of an adulterous woman—   20
      she eats and wipes her mouth
        and says, "I did nothing wrong."
For three things does the earth shudder,   21
      and for four, it cannot bear it:
for a slave who rules   22
      and a scoundrel who is sated with bread,
for a hateful woman in the marriage bed,   23
      and a slave-girl who dispossesses her mistress.

---

19. *heavens . . . rock . . . sea . . . young woman*. There is a kind of wry wit in this sequence. The speaker imagines bird, reptile, and vessel passing through the remote regions of sky, earth, and sea that are beyond his ken. Then the fourth term invokes another place inaccessible to the imagination of the male speaker—a woman's sexual mystery, known only to her lover. The preposition "in" here before "a young woman" is meant to be understood literally—that is, in a physiological sense—as many interpreters through the ages have in fact understood it.

20. *this is the way of the adulterous woman*. This worldly observation interrupts the series of three-four sayings. It may have been inserted here because of "the way" and because of the sexual reference at the end of the preceding verse.
    she eats and wipes her mouth. Elsewhere in Proverbs, an analogy between mouth and vagina is implied (for example, Chapter 5).

23. *for a hateful woman in the marriage bed*. In the Hebrew, "in the marriage bed" is a passive verb, which means "is married / is sexually possessed." Fox's proposal to revocalize the verb *tiba'el* as *tiv'al* and to understand it as "gain mastery" is unconvincing because *b-'-l* does not appear in this sense as an intransitive verb elsewhere (despite the noun *ba'al*, which does mean "master" as well as "husband"). The transitive verb generally has the sexual sense indicated above. The hateful woman enjoying conjugal consummation is part of a series of figures whose fate is disturbingly not what it should be, after the slave who rules and the scoundrel who prospers, and before the slave-girl who dispossesses her mistress.

24   Four things are the smallest on earth,
          yet they are the very wisest:
25   the ants, a people not strong,
          who ready their bread in the summer,
26   the badgers, a people not mighty,
          who make their home in the cleft,
27   the locusts, who have no king,
          and march out all in a row,
28   the spider, who can be caught with hands,
          yet it is in the palace of kings.
29   Three things stride handsomely
          and four things handsomely walk:
30   the lion, mightiest of beasts,
          who does not turn back from anything,
31   the rooster and the he-goat,
          and the king against whom none can stand.

---

24. *smallest on earth, / yet they are the very wisest.* Though diminutive in size, they evince wisdom in how they dispose themselves. This proverb thus celebrates the value of wisdom over sheer size or strength and implies that people should learn from these small creatures.

27. *march out all in a row.* Though it is questionable whether locusts assemble themselves in such neat formation, the idea is suggested by the perception of the mass of locusts as an invading army that sweeps away everything in its path, despite the smallness of its individual constituents.

28. *the spider.* There is some doubt about the identity of this creature. In any case, it is something small and easily caught, probably some sort of insect, that nevertheless is able to do what no ordinary human can, penetrate the palaces of kings.
    the palace of kings. The Hebrew has a plural for "palace" and a singular for "kings."

31. *the rooster.* The Hebrew *zarzir* has been identified with several different creatures. Compounding the puzzle, it is attached here to the noun *motnayim,* "loins," and nobody has come up with a satisfactory explanation of this epithet, if that is what it is.

If you have been a scoundrel in arrogance,   32
        and if you have schemed—put a hand on your mouth!
For squeezed milk produces butter,   33
        and a squeezed nose produces blood,
               and squeezed patience produces a quarrel.

---

33. *for squeezed milk*. This entire verse has the ring of a folk-saying. The term *myts*, "squeezed" (literally "squeezing [of]"), has been stretched in this saying to cover the churning of milk, though that is not its usual meaning.

patience. Some understand the Hebrew *'apayim* to mean "wrath." The singular form *'af* means precisely that, but the doublative *'apayim* (when it does not mean face) appears only in the idiom *'erekh 'apayim*, "patience" (literally, "long [or slow] in anger"). That idiom, in fact, occurs several times in Proverbs. If you push milk hard, it turns into something else, butter; if you push a nose hard, it spurts blood, something that does not usually come out of a nose; and if you push someone's patience hard, it turns into impatience, leading to a quarrel.

31

1   The words of Lemuel, king of Massa, with which his mother reproved
him:

2   No, my son. Oh, no, son of my womb,
    oh, no, son of my vows.

3   Do not give your vigor to women,
    nor your ways to destroyers of kings.

---

1. *Lemuel*. The name is unusual and nothing is known about him, not even
whether he is a historical figure or a literary invention. In any case, this is still
another unit of Wisdom exhortation, distinctive stylistically and rhetorically,
that the anthologist has culled from an unknown source and decided to include.
The advice here of a queen mother to her son has no precedent elsewhere in
the book.

 Massa. A kingdom in north Arabia.

 with which his mother reproved him. The mother rather than the father in the
role of the one who gives *musar*—reproof, admonitory moral exhortation—is
unusual, though in the preceding body of proverbs there are frequent pairings
of father and mother as the joint source of instruction. Her warning him not to
consort with loose women—or, perhaps better, with gold diggers—is especially
apt coming from a mother, as is the admonition to stay away from drink.

2. *son of my vows*. This locution suggests that she may have taken vows in a
prayer for pregnancy, like Hannah in 1 Samuel 1.

3. *vigor*. The Hebrew *ḥayil* is not an explicitly sexual term; it can also suggest
"wealth." In verse 10, it is used in a slightly different though related sense.

 destroyers. The translation, following a Hebrew fragment found in the Cairo
Geniza, reads *lemoḥot* instead of *lamḥot*, "to destroy."

Not for kings, Lemuel, not for kings,   4
      the drinking of wine, nor for rulers, hard drink.
Lest he drink and forget inscribed law,   5
      and reverse the judgment of all wretched men.
Give hard drink to the perishing man   6
      and wine to those deeply embittered.
Let him drink and forget his privation,   7
      and his misery let him no more recall.
Open your mouth for the dumb,   8
      for the judgment of all fleeting folk.
Open your mouth, judge righteously,   9
      grant justice to the poor and the wretched.

א   A worthy woman who can find?   10
      Her price is far beyond rubies.

---

4. *Not for kings.* A monarch has to exercise lucid judgment in determining state policy and administering justice, so he above all men should avoid drunkenness.

    hard drink. The Hebrew *sheikhar* (from a root indicating intoxication) is not beer, as some interpreters claim, but in all likelihood is grappa. Judges 13:14 makes clear that it is an alcoholic beverage other than wine that is extracted from grapes.

6. *Give hard drink to the perishing man.* While the monarch should avoid alcohol, for the poor man it can provide a way of temporarily forgetting his wretchedness.

7. *misery.* The Hebrew *'amal* means both "toil" (its usual sense in Qohelet) and "misery" or "wretchedness" (its usual sense in Job).

8. *Open your mouth for the dumb.* It is the obligation of a king to speak out on behalf of those lacking the power, capacity, or boldness to speak.

    all fleeting folk. The Hebrew *beney halof* ("those who are to pass away") might mean ephemeral or mortal human beings, as it does in modern Hebrew, or it might designate a specific disadvantaged segment of the population teetering on the brink of death, like "the perishing man" in verse 6.

10. *A worthy woman who can find?* This concluding unit of the Book of Proverbs is an alphabetical acrostic (the Hebrew letter for each line appears in the margin). Thus, "a worthy woman" is *'eshet hayil*, the first word beginning with *'alef*, the first

11   The heart of her husband trusts her,   ב
             and no prize does he lack.

12   She repays him good and not evil   ג
             all the days of her life.

13   She seeks out wool and flax   ד
             and performs with willing hands.

14   She is like merchant ships,   ה
             from afar she brings her bread.

15   She gets up while it is still night   ו
             and provides nourishment for her house
                   and a portion for her young women.

16   She sets her mind on a field and buys it,   ז
             from the fruit of her hands she plants a vineyard.

---

letter of the Hebrew alphabet. *Ḥayil* means vigor, strength, worth, substance. It is a martial term transferred to civic life. Some have proposed that the term invites us to see this exemplary wife as a heroic figure, a kind of domestic warrior. It is noteworthy that the editors chose to conclude the book, in which instruction by male mentors to young men predominates, with a portrait of the ideal wife.

11. *prize.* The usual meaning of the Hebrew *shalal* is "booty." The choice of this term might be an argument for an activation of the martial connotation of *ḥayil* in the previous line.

12. *She repays him good and not evil.* The editor may well have seen in this line a pointed antithesis to the sundry evocations of shrewish wives and adulterous wives in the body of the book.

13. *willing hands.* This apt phrase is borrowed from Fox. The literal sense of the whole Hebrew clause is "[she] performs with will / desire / delight with her palms."

15. *a portion for her young women.* These would be the female servants or slaves of the household, which is clearly a substantial one.

16. *She sets her mind on a field and buys it.* The exemplary wife is active not only domestically, acquiring wool and flax, weaving and sewing, but also as a businesswoman.
   from the fruit of her hands. As Fox notes, this means that she uses her earnings to buy property.

ח	She girds her loins in strength	17
	and gives power to her arms.	
ט	She understands that her wares are good,	18
	her lamp does not go out at night.	
י	Her hands she reaches out to the distaff,	19
	and her palms hold on to the spindle.	
כ	Her palm she opens to the poor,	20
	and her hands she extends to the wretched.	
ל	She does not fear for her household because of snow,	21
	for her whole household is clothed in scarlet.	
מ	Covers she makes for herself,	22
	linen and purple, her garments.	
נ	Her husband is famed in the gates	23
	when he sits with the land's elders.	
ס	Fine cloth she makes, and she sells it,	24
	a loincloth she gives to the trader.	
ע	Strength and grandeur are her garment,	25
	and she laughs at the day to come.	

---

20. *Her palm . . . her hands.* These terms form a neat chiasm with the preceding line: hands—palms—palm—hands.

21. *her whole household is clothed in scarlet.* This is a hyperbole: warm wool garments would suffice to keep everyone in the household comfortable through the winter, but the clothing she provides is regally sumptuous as well as warm.

23. *Her husband is famed in the gates.* Evidently, he is able to participate in the deliberations of justice while she is busy providing for the needs of their household. But the affluence that she has made possible also enables him to hold his head up among the elders.

24. *the trader.* The Hebrew says "Canaanite," a gentilic term that is also the designation of a profession because of the prominence of Canaanites—perhaps assimilated to Phoenicians—as traders.

25. *the day to come.* The literal sense of the Hebrew is "the latter day," which is to say, the future, something she need not fear because she has provided so well for her household.

26   She opens her mouth in wisdom,   פ
                teaching of kindness is on her tongue.
27   She looks after the ways of her house,   צ
                and does not eat the bread of idleness.
28   Her sons rise and call her happy,   ק
                her husband, he praises her:
29   "Many daughters have done worthy things,   ר
                but you—you surpass them all."
30   Grace is a lie and beauty mere breath—   ש
                a LORD-fearing woman, it is she who is praised.
31   Give her from the fruit of her hands,   ת
                and let her deeds praise her in the gates.

---

29. *Many daughters have done worthy things.* At this penultimate point in the poem, the thematic term ḥayil, "worthy," recurs. It is also strategically effective that the husband, who has benefited from the wife's prodigious efforts, and until now has been in the background of the poem, trusting his wife and sitting with the elders in the gates, steps forward to address her in superlative praise. The force of the direct address is underscored by the emphatic use of the second-person singular feminine pronoun 'at in the second verset: "but you— you surpass them all."

31. *Give her from the fruit of her hands.* Let her enjoy the benefits of the affluence she has amassed, and at the same time let her be praised for what she has achieved.

QOHELET
(Ecclesiastes)

INTRODUCTION

Qohelet is in some ways the most peculiar book of the Hebrew Bible. The peculiarity starts with its name. The long tradition of translation into many languages, beginning with the ancient Greek version, uses some form of "Ecclesiastes" for the title. The Septuagint translators chose that title because it means "the one who assembles," and the Hebrew root *q-h-l* does mean "to assemble." Some have claimed that what it refers to is the assembling of sayings, but this Hebrew verb always takes people, not words or things, as its object, so it may reflect the assembling of audiences or disciples for these discourses. The grammatical form of the word is also odd because one would expect *maqhil* (causative), not *qohelet*, and, in any case, *qohel* (masculine), not *qohelet* (ostensibly feminine). There are at least two instances in Late Biblical Hebrew of the *-et* ending to indicate—apparently—the term for a vocation, and that may be the use of the form here, though some doubt still remains. So, we are not entirely sure what Qohelet means, and whether it is a title (at one point in our text, it is preceded by the definite article) or perhaps a proper name. All this uncertainty, and possibly also the ponderousness of "Ecclesiastes," has led most modern scholars to use the untranslated Hebrew name, a practice I follow here.

In the opening verse, Qohelet is called "son of David," but that might mean only that he comes from the Davidic line. Jewish and Christian tradition famously identified him as Solomon because of this epithet, because of the repeated stress on his search for wisdom, and because of the autobiographical narrative in Chapter 2 in which he speaks of having built many houses and created elaborate gardens and amassed wealth and items of luxury. It is best to think of Qohelet as the literary persona of a radical philosopher articulating, in an evocative rhythmic prose that occasionally scans as poetry, a powerful dissent from the mainline Wisdom outlook that is the background of his thought. It has long been recognized that this is one of the later books of the Hebrew Bible. Some scholars have been tempted to see in it an influence of Greek philosophy, but C. L. Seow argues convincingly on linguistic grounds that the text was probably written a few decades before the conquest of Palestine by Alexander the Great in 333 BCE. There are two Persian loan-words and certain turns of language that belong to the late Persian period but no Greek loan-words. (In the Hellenistic period, a flood of Greek words would enter the Hebrew language.) In light of the fact that Aramaic had begun to take over as the vernacular as early as the later sixth and fifth centuries BCE, there are also, not surprisingly, turns of speech and terms that show an influence of Aramaic, and there are also some lexical and syntactic features that anticipate rabbinic Hebrew. As to any conceivable Greek background, we should keep in mind that even before Alexander's conquest, there were commercial and cultural connections between Greece and the Levant, so the possibility cannot be excluded that Qohelet indirectly picked up some motifs of Greek thought. On the whole, however, his unblinking, provocative reflections on the ephemerality of life, the flimsiness of human value, and the ineluctable fate of death read like the work of a stubborn and prickly original—one who in all likelihood wrote in the early or middle decades of the fourth century BCE. His frequent invocation of terms drawn from bookkeeping reflect the mercantile economy of the period. His class identity is uncertain, though his politics are conservative.

The way he wrote in some respects resembles traditional Wisdom literature but in others sharply departs from it. The stringing together of moral maxims in concise symmetrical or antithetical formulations, sometimes with rather tenuous connections between one maxim and the next, is clearly reminiscent of the Book of Proverbs. Often, though, Qohelet's maxims are subversive in content, or seem to be citations of traditional maxims that are challenged or undermined by the new context in which they are set. In a few passages, Qohelet offers entirely pragmatic counsel of a sort one might expect to find in Proverbs. For the most part, however, his observations are properly philosophic, inviting us to contemplate the cyclical nature of reality and of human experience, the fleeting duration of all that we cherish, the brevity of life, and the inexorability of death, which levels all things. Of the propositions he insists on most urgently, only the notions of life's brevity and of mortality accord with the consensus of biblical belief that had developed by the fourth century BCE. The central enigma, then, of the Book of Qohelet is how this text of radical dissent, in which time, history, politics, and human nature are seen in such a bleak light, became part of the canon. Perhaps the ostensible ascription to Solomon shoehorned the book into the canon, but that is hard to judge.

The peculiarity of Qohelet's philosophic stance is compounded by the peculiarity of his literary vehicle: he is a writer who works out philosophic thought through poetic prose. He has a finely developed sense of expressive rhythm; he makes central use of refrains and other devices of repetition, the stylistic repetition serving as a correlative for the cycle of repetition that in his view characterizes the underlying structure of reality. He often seems to think in metaphors, or, at least, metaphors are used where writers in a different tradition would use abstractions, and the range of overlapping meanings suggested by the concrete image is repeatedly brought into play. By and large, the various modern translations have not done much justice to Qohelet's literary style, which is inextricably linked with the force and conceptual subtlety of his thought. The King James Version is still the most adequate English rendering of Qohelet's style—in many respects, it is one of the best performances of the 1611 translators—though it does not always provide an apt equivalent for his verbal concision and rhythmic compactness, and it is not very reliable in the many places where the Hebrew wording is obscure or perhaps defective.

Qohelet's famous first words, which he will make a much repeated refrain and with which he will conclude the book proper, before the epilogue, are a prime instance of a metaphor serving the function of an abstraction. The King James Version rendered the initial words and all their recurrences as "vanity," "vanity of vanities." The seventeenth-century translators obviously had the Latin version in mind, with "vanity" suggesting a lack of value, not self-admiration. This choice has actually been preserved, a little surprisingly, in one recent scholarly translation, C. L. Seow's Anchor Bible Ecclesiastes. At least a couple of other modern translations have opted for "futility," and Michael V. Fox, in his admirable analysis accompanied by a translation of the text, insists on "absurdity." The problem is that all of these English equivalents are more or less right, and abstractions being what they are, each one has the effect of excluding the others and thus limiting the scope of the Hebrew metaphor. The Hebrew *hevel* probably indicates the flimsy vapor that is exhaled in breathing, invisible except on a cold winter day and in any case immediately dissipating in the air. It is the opposite of *ruaḥ*, "life-breath," which is the animating force in a living creature, because it is the waste product of breathing. If, then, one wanted to line up the abstractions implied by *hevel*, it would include not only futility, absurdity, and vanity but at least insubstantiality, ephemerality, and elusiveness as well. Because of these considerations, this translation has chosen to reproduce the concrete image of the Hebrew, rendering *hevel* as "mere breath" ("breath" alone doesn't quite work in English) and representing the Hebrew superlative form *havel havalim* as "merest breath." Altogether, Qohelet is preoccupied with entities that exhibit movement but can't be seen or grasped. *Ruaḥ* in its other sense of "wind" plays a prominent role in the opening lines of the book, and the metaphor for futility and pointless effort that is often paired with "mere breath" is "herding the wind," *re'ut ruaḥ*. (The King James Version seriously misrepresents this, introducing still another abstraction, as "vexation of spirit.") Even Qohelet's philosophic quest is repeatedly represented in the Hebrew in concrete, virtually physical terms: he turns around, turns back, like a man in restless pursuit of some maddeningly elusive quarry, trying to find true wisdom. Such wisdom would be the discovery of whether there is any point in human life. If there is not, as Qohelet seems inclined to conclude, he enjoins us to make the most of what we have while we have it—to enjoy in measured fashion good food and wine and a woman one loves, if only the unpredictable course of circumstances makes a person lucky enough to possess these things.

The rather slippery phrase I have just used, "seems inclined to conclude," is in fact in keeping with the to-and-fro movement of Qohelet's philosophic discourse. He is a serious thinker who is constantly in motion—another way in which the language of turning and turning back is appropriate to his enterprise. He has an interest in weighing antithetical propositions and moving dialectically among them. Absolute consistency is not his purpose, and so Michael Fox's title, *Qohelet and His Contradictions*, is perfectly apt. God appears with some frequency in his reflections on life, and though it is the same term, *'elohim*, used by the Elohist as well as by the Priestly writer at the beginning of Genesis (Qohelet never uses YHWH), this is clearly not the same deity as the one imagined in the dominant currents of biblical theology. The cosmic vista of the prose-poem with which the book begins (1:2–10) makes no mention of God. When the term *'elohim* is finally introduced in 1:13, the context is odd and unsettling: "all that is done under the sun—it is an evil business that God gave the sons of man to busy themselves with." This is surely a far cry from the God of Genesis 1 Who commands humankind, as the climactic product of the process of creation, to be fruitful and multiply and to hold sway over all things. The God of the earlier books of the Bible can sometimes be irascible or perhaps even capricious, but He means humanity to fulfill a grand destiny, and it is human dereliction that triggers His wrath and brings down His punishment. Qohelet, who does not altogether reject antecedent tradition, occasionally thinks that God will bring men to judgment, though it is unclear how or when. (Surely not in any afterlife, which is polemically excluded again and again by Qohelet.) Yet here God seems almost perverse in keeping the sons of man busy with an evil business—evil, as the larger context makes clear, not in a moral sense but because it is miserable and pointless, herding the wind. Qohelet has enough of a connection with tradition that he never absolutely denies the idea of a personal god, but his *'elohim* often seems to be a stand-in for the cosmic powers-that-be, for fate or the overarching dynamic of reality that is beyond human control. (It is worth noting that even in earlier texts *'elohim* sometimes has this sense, as in Abraham's words to Abimelech in Genesis 20:13, "when the gods [*'elohim*, here exceptionally treated grammatically as a plural] made me a wanderer," or when Joseph's brothers, scarcely inclined to pious locutions, discover the silver in their packs and say "What is this that God has done to us?" [Genesis 42:28].) On this issue as on others, Qohelet's position may fluctuate. He is not at all impelled to reject theism, but his sense of life is often readily translatable into post-theistic terms: the world is a theater of continuing frustration and illusion; that is the way that God / fate / the intrinsic constitution of reality has determined that it should be.

Do Qohelet's discourses have a formal structure? Much interpretive ingenuity has been exerted to show that they do. The more elaborate the proposed structure, the less plausible it appears. The movement of Qohelet's thought is freewheeling and associative. It includes segments of maxims and perceptions that clearly belong together thematically and sometimes in terms of literary formulation (such as the sequences of "better X than Y" sayings). Beyond that, it is hard to find architectonic design in the book; on the contrary, the relative looseness of form admirably suits the mobility of Qohelet's thought. There are, however, strongly articulated framing units at the beginning and the end. The book begins with the great prose-poem about the cyclical futility of all things. This unit is immediately followed by the quasi-narrative autobiographical section that runs through to the end of Chapter 2, in which Qohelet, in his persona as king of Jerusalem and hence a man endowed with the power and resources to explore all the possibilities of the human condition, steps forward and speaks about his quest from center stage. The autobiographical narrative establishes the context for much that follows since Qohelet the philosophic searcher and the explorer of experience makes repeated appearances in the pronouncements on life that he proposes. Then the book proper ends with the haunting poem on mortality that is a kind of matching end-piece to the prose-poem at the beginning. The vision of futility begins his book, and the vision of decay and death ends it. All along, Qohelet has thought much about the inescapability of death because it is the prime instance of how everything is mere breath: we dream and hope and lust and love, grasp for power and prestige, but the end that awaits everyone is the ineluctable condition of moldering in the grave. Thus the same words that initiated the prose-poem at the beginning aptly conclude the poem at the end: "Merest breath," said Qohelet. "All is mere breath."

How, then, did such a book come to be included in the canon? The process of inclusion, it should be said, was not long in coming, for fragments of Qohelet found at Qumran indicate that it was already part of the library of Scripture there only a century or two after its composition. Some interpreters attribute its embrace by the shapers of the canon to the pious tilt it is given in the epilogue (12:9–14). It has long been the scholarly consensus that the epilogue is the addition of an editor seeking to domesticate Qohelet's doctrinal wildness, though a couple of recent commentators have tried to argue—unpersuasively, in my view—that the epilogue is consistent with the body of the book and may be the work of the same writer. In any case, it is surely attributing far too much naivete to the ancient readers to imagine that a few dozen words of piety at the end would deflect them from seeing the subversive skepticism emphatically reiterated throughout the text. We are unlikely ever to have a confident explanation of why Qohelet—or, for that matter, Job or Esther or the Song of Songs—entered the canon, but its inclusion suggests that the canon may not have been determined solely on the grounds of ideological and theological conformity. In regard to its literary power and the uncompromising rigor of its observation of the human condition, this was clearly one of the most original texts produced in the biblical period, early or late. There must have been many Hebrew readers in the last two and a half centuries before the Common Era and on into the Common Era who were not willing to let go of Qohelet, who felt that it somehow belonged in the anthology of texts—not quite yet a canon—that constituted the literary legacy of the nation. They may well have felt this attachment to Qohelet despite the fact that it challenged long-cherished notions about human destiny and the nature of reality. It is even possible that they embraced the book precisely because of the challenges it posed, for there was not a great deal of doctrinal consistency in the whole body of incipiently canonical texts, and the so-called biblical world view, which is really a construct of later interpreters, was at this early moment far from a settled issue. The pious epilogue should probably be seen not as a way of transforming the audience's understanding of the text but rather as a no more than hopeful rhetorical gesture, an effort to conclude the book with a seal of official approval unlikely to fool anyone about its actual contents. What continues to engage the moral and philosophic imagination, as it surely must have done in Late Antiquity, is the writer who unblinkingly saw all human enterprise as herding the wind, who envisaged the same grim fate for rich and poor, for the righteous and the wicked, and who was led to question whether wisdom itself in the end had any advantage over foolishness.

1

The words of Qohelet son of David, king in Jerusalem.

1. *The words of Qohelet son of David.* This editorial superscription, together
with the account in the second half of the chapter of Qohelet's amassing wisdom, is the basis for the traditional ascribing of authorship to Solomon, though
Solomon's name is never mentioned in the book. Virtually all scholarly assess-
ments date the text nearly six centuries after Solomon.

Qohelet. There are two puzzles in this name. Though it appears to derive
from the Hebrew root *q-h-l*, which means "to assemble," one would expect it
to be in the *hiph'il* conjugation, which usually has a causative and transitive
sense, rather than in the *qal* conjugation (that is, *maqhil* rather than *qohel*).
Second, the name has a feminine verbal ending (*Qohelet* rather than *Qohel*),
although this is generally explained, on the basis of two such occurrences elsewhere in the biblical corpus, as a suffix indicating vocation. It could be a title
rather than a name, and in 7:27 it actually appears with a definite article. If one
follows the semantics of the Hebrew conjugations—where, for example,
shokhev in the *qal* conjugation means "he who lies down," whereas *mashkiv* in
the *hiph'il* means "he causes to lie down"—*qohelet* could even mean "he who
is part of the assembly" rather than "the assembler." In either case, the idea of
a group of people listening to philosophic discourse seems to be implied. Given
the uncertainty about the name, and whether it is a name or a title, it seems
wise to preserve the term in the Hebrew, as scholars generally now do.

2   Merest breath, said Qohelet, merest breath. All is mere breath.
3   What gain is there for man in all his toil that he toils under the sun.
4   A generation goes and a generation comes, but the earth endures forever.
5   The sun rises and the sun sets, and to its place it glides, there it rises.
6   It goes to the south and swings round to the north, round and round goes the wind, and on its rounds the wind returns.

---

2. *merest breath*. The form of the Hebrew, *havel havalim*, is a way of indicating a superlative or an extreme case. Rendering this phrase as an abstraction (King James Version, "vanity of vanities," or Michael Fox's more philosophically subtle "absurdity of absurdities") is inadvisable, for the writer uses concrete metaphors to indicate general concepts, constantly exploiting the emotional impact of the concrete image and its potential to suggest several related ideas. *Hevel*, "breath" or "vapor," is something utterly insubstantial and transient, and in this book suggests futility, ephemerality, and also, as Fox argues, the absurdity of existence.

All is mere breath. The constant use of repetition, from this initial verse onward, gives the rhythmic prose of Qohelet an incantatory power and at the same time registers one of its principal themes: that it is the very nature of reality for all things constantly to repeat themselves.

5. *The sun rises and the sun sets*. The cyclical movement of day and night is taken as prime evidence in nature of the repetitive cyclical character of reality. This notion is a radical challenge to the conception of time and sequence inscribed in Genesis and elsewhere in the Bible, where things are imagined to progress meaningfully (as in the seven days of creation) toward a fulfillment. The next two verses, invoking the cyclical motion of the wind and the rivers, continue this vision of pointless movement round and round.

glides. The Hebrew *sho'ef* usually means "pants," but this translation follows the Targum, Rashi, and many modern commentators in relating it to *shuf*, "to pass through," "to move," "to glide."

All the rivers go to the sea, and the sea is not full.   7
To the place that the rivers go, there they return to go.
All things are weary. A man cannot speak. The eye is not sated with   8
seeing, nor the ear filled with hearing.
That which was is that which will be, and that which was done is that   9
which will be done, and there is nothing new under the sun.
There is a thing of which one would say, "See this, it is new." It already   10
has been in the eons that were before us. There is no remembrance of   11
the first things nor of the last things that will be. They will have no
remembrance with those who will be in the latter time.

I, Qohelet, have been king over Israel in Jerusalem. And I set my heart   12,13
to inquire and seek through wisdom of all that is done under the sun—it
is an evil business that God gave to the sons of man to busy themselves
with.

---

7. *there they return to go.* The final "to go," which has been omitted in most
translations from 1611 onward, of course sounds a little odd (as does the
Hebrew), but it is part of the essential stylistic pattern of verbal repetition that
mirrors the concept of repetition in nature.

11. *There is no remembrance.* This is a radical and deeply disturbing idea for the
Hebrew imagination, which, on the evidence of many earlier texts, sets such
great store in leaving a remembrance, and envisages the wiping out of remembrance as an ultimate curse.

12. *I, Qohelet.* The Hebrew syntax equally allows one to construe this sentence
as: "I am Qohelet. I was king over Jerusalem." These words, after the thematic-
metaphoric prologue of verses 2–11, inaugurate a first-person account of Qohelet's frustrating quest for knowledge that continues until 2:20.

13. *I set my heart.* In biblical physiology, the heart is the organ of understanding, though sometimes it is also associated with feeling.

14 I have seen all the deeds that are done under the sun, and, look, all is
15 mere breath, and herding the wind. The crooked cannot turn straight
16 nor can the lack be made good. I spoke to my heart, saying: As for me,
look, I increased and added wisdom beyond all who were before me over
17 Jerusalem, and my heart has seen much wisdom and knowledge. And I
set my heart to know wisdom and to know revelry and folly, for this, too,
18 is herding the wind. For in much wisdom is much worry, and he who
adds wisdom adds pain.

---

14. *herding the wind.* The verbal root of the first Hebrew word here generally means to tend a flock (and in the Song of Songs, to graze), so the common modern translation, "pursuit of the wind," is an interpretive liberty. Herding the wind, which of course cannot be herded (it goes round and round), is an effective enough image of futile activity, coordinated with "mere breath."

15. *nor can the lack be made good.* The verb *lehimanot* appears to mean "be counted." Many emend it to *lehimalot*, "be filled." In any case, this verse adds to the concept of repetition the notion that events are irreversible and mishaps irreparable.

16. *all who were before me over Jerusalem.* It is not strictly necessary to make this, as some commentators have done, a reference to the pre-Israelite kings of Jerusalem because Qohelet is not explicitly identified as Solomon, and even the designation "son of David" could easily indicate a member of the Davidic line rather than David's actual son.

17. *to know wisdom and to know revelry and folly.* Qohelet's project is a comprehensive exploration of experience, which would include reflection on the sayings of the wise, observation of the broad variety of events, and also experimentation in the realm of the senses, with intoxicants and perhaps even orgies. The common rendering of *holelut* as "madness" (for which in biblical Hebrew, as in the modern language, the primary term would be *shiga'on*) confuses this idea; *holelut* suggests a wild and unruly indulgence of the senses in which lucidity is lost—hence "revelry."

18. *For in much wisdom is much worry.* Here this radical Wisdom text challenges the basic premise of Wisdom literature—that devotion to wisdom is the one true road to the good, fulfilled life.

2

I said in my heart, "Come, now, let me pour out wine in merriment and 1
enjoy good things." And, look, this, too, is mere breath. To mirth I said, 2
"Wild reveling," and to merriment, "What does it do?" I sought in my 3
heart to ply my body with wine, while my heart acted with wisdom, not
grasping folly, until I might see what is good for the sons of man that
they should do under the heavens in the number of the days of their
lives. I made me great works. I built myself houses, I planted for myself 4
vineyards. I made for myself gardens and orchards and planted in them 5
every kind of fruit tree. I made for myself pools of water from which to 6
water a wood growing trees. I bought male slaves and slave-girls, and 7

---

2. *To mirth I said.* The purely hedonistic probe of Qohelet's experiment with experience fails because the wildness of orgiastic release proves to be no more than a transient excitation, leading to nothing and providing no lasting satisfaction.

3. *not grasping folly.* The Masoretic text reads "grasping folly" (*le'ehoz besikhlut*), but this translation adopts a frequently proposed emendation, assuming that a scribe inadvertently dropped "not" (*lo'*) in copying because it had the same two letters, *lamed* and *'aleph*, that begin the next word, *le'ehoz*. The idea is that Qohelet gave himself over to drinking and revelry yet clung to his perspective of wisdom because his purpose in indulging the senses was to see if, indeed, that was part of "what is good for the sons of man that they should do under the heavens."

4. *I made me great works.* The fiction of Qohelet as king over Jerusalem is important for the philosophic argument because, as this passage makes clear, he is thus endowed with the means to explore everything that wealth can give a man—grand houses, splendid gardens, slaves, resident entertainers, a harem of lovely women. This fiction, of course, strongly invokes the story of Solomon.

had home-born slaves, too. Also many herds of cattle and sheep did I
8 have, more than all who were before me in Jerusalem. I gathered for
myself both silver and gold, and the treasure of kings and provinces. I
got myself men and women singers and the pleasures of humankind,
9 and many a concubine. And I grew great and added more than all who
10 were before me in Jerusalem. Still my wisdom stayed with me. And all
that my eyes sought I did not withhold from them, nor did I deny my
heart any merriment—for my heart was merry—from all my toil, and
11 this was my share from all my toil. And I turned about in all my deeds
that my hands had done and in the toil that I had toiled to do, and,
look, all was mere breath and herding the wind, and there was no gain
12 under the sun. And I turned to see wisdom and revelry and folly, for
what is the man who comes after the king, that which he has already
13 done? And I saw that wisdom surpasses folly as light surpasses dark-

---

9. *added.* The literal translation of this verb underscores the vocabulary of
accumulation and bookkeeping that Qohelet repeatedly employs—"add" (*hosif*)
and "gain" (*yitron*, the surplus that shows on the bottom line of the account).

   Still my wisdom stayed with me. This declaration is of a piece with "while my
heart acted with wisdom, not grasping folly" in verse 3.

11. *And I turned.* The repeated use of this verb points up Qohelet's project of
restless experimentation: he turns in one direction and then another, but of
course all proves to be mere breath and herding the wind.

12. *for what is the man who comes after the king, that which he has already done.*
This clause is somewhat obscure. The received text reads "they have already
done," but seventy different manuscript versions show the singular, which
makes more sense. The most likely meaning is: in the cyclical futility of the
generations (an idea spelled out in Chapter 1), the man who comes after me,
King Qohelet, can do no more than replicate what I have already done.

13. *wisdom surpasses folly as light surpasses darkness.* Qohelet's view of wisdom
is paradoxical, or dialectic. He recognizes that wisdom offers no way out of life's
futility and no escape from the inexorable fate of death that awaits the wise like
the fool, but wisdom nevertheless provides what one might describe as a privi-
lege of clarified consciousness: it is far better to live disabused of all illusion,
like Qohelet himself, than to live a deluded life, like the fool.

ness. The wise man has eyes in his head, and the fool goes in darkness. 14
Yet I, too, knew that a single fate befalls them all. And I said in my 15
heart, "Like the fate of the fool, it will befall me, too, and so why have I
become so wise?" And I said in my heart that this, too, is mere breath.
For there is no remembrance of the wise, as with the fool, forever. 16
Since in the days to come, all will be forgotten. Yes, the wise dies like
the fool! And I hated life, for all that was done under the sun was evil 17
to me, for all is mere breath and herding the wind. And I hated all 18
things got from my toil that I had toiled under the sun, that I should
leave it to the man who will come after me. And who knows whether 19
he will be wise or a fool, and he will have power over all that was got
from my toil for which I toiled and grew wise under the sun. This, too,
is mere breath. And I turned round to make my heart despair over all 20
the toil that I had toiled under the sun. For there is a man whose toil 21
is in wisdom and knowledge and skill, and to a man who did not toil for
it he will give away his share. This, too, is mere breath and a grievous evil.
For what does a man have from all his toil and from his heart's care that 22

---

14. *The wise man has eyes in his head, and the fool goes in darkness*. This statement is clearly cast in the form of a proverb, akin to what one finds in the Book
of Proverbs. It cuts two ways: on the one hand, it continues the idea expressed
in "wisdom surpasses folly . . ."; on the other hand, it may well be a traditional
proverb that, as Robert Gordis has argued, Qohelet means to subject to critique. What follows in the second half of this verse and in the next two verses
certainly looks like a challenge to this bit of proverbial wisdom.

16. *Since in the days to come, all will be forgotten*. A double-edged sword under-
cuts the efficacy of wisdom—the fact that the wise man will be swallowed up
by death like the most benighted fool, and that after he is gone, all remembrance of him will vanish.

18. *all things got from my toil*. Although the Hebrew says only "all my toil"
(*'amali*), the term *'amal* in this book alternately means the activity of toiling and
that which is gained through toil.

22. *his heart's care*. The term *ra'yon*, attached here to "heart," does not occur in
earlier biblical Hebrew. It is probably cognate with *re'ut*, the word used in
"herding the wind," and hence is rendered in this translation as "care" because

23 he toils under the sun? For all his days are pain, and worry is his business. At night, as well, his heart does not rest. This, too, is mere breath.

24 There is nothing better for a man than to eat and drink and sate himself with good things through his toil. This, too, have I seen, for it is

---

it may also derive from the activity in which a shepherd looks after or cares for
his flock. Extrapolating from the use in Qohelet, later Hebrew adopts the term
to mean "idea."

24. *There is nothing better for a man than to eat and drink and sate himself with
good things*. Though this affirmation may look like a contradiction (for example,
of verse 1), it is another expression of Qohelet's dialectic thinking. Immersion
in sensual pleasure, especially in its extreme forms, may bring no lasting good,
but in the futility of our ephemeral lives, the simple pleasures of the senses
here and now are all we have, and we might as well take advantage of them.

sate himself. At first blush, the Hebrew verb *her'ah* might seem to mean "to
show," deriving from the root *r-'-h*, which indicates sight, but in Qohelet it is
not infrequently a variant form of the root *r-w-h*, meaning "to slake" or "to sate
oneself." Similarly, the verb *re'eh* at the end of verse 1 probably does not mean
"see" but "sate oneself," or "enjoy."

for it is from God's hand. The introduction of God may be a little surprising,
but Qohelet, though a skeptical empiricist, is no atheist. God—always the
general term *'elohim* and never YHWH—is a given for him, but this God makes
decisions about whom to favor and whom to reject in inscrutable ways, and He
cannot be counted on to neatly reward the wise and the righteous, as other
biblical writers assume.

from God's hand. For who will eat and who will feel, save me? For to   25,26
the man who seems good before Him He has given wisdom and knowledge and merriment, but to the offender He has given the business of
amassing and taking in to give to him who seems good before God. This,
too, is mere breath and herding the wind.

---

25. *For who will eat and who will feel, save me?* This is the bedrock of Qohelet's
existential realism. All I know is the immediacy of my own bodily experience.
God has given this to me to enjoy, if I can; others, as the next verse makes clear,
may not be so lucky.

26. *the offender.* As elsewhere in biblical literature, *hote'* does not mean "sinner," as it is conventionally translated, but rather one who gives offense, who
misses the mark. How and why he offends is left unstated, and it may in fact
be a mystery to Qohelet.

    This, too, is mere breath and herding the wind. The appearance of this mel-
ancholy refrain at the end of this verse and of this whole sequence may be
dictated in context by the following logic: in this transient life, he who pleases
God may enjoy the worldly goods passed on to him from the unlucky man who
offends God, but under the aspect of eternity, even that difference amounts to
little, for in the end death serves as the great equalizer.

3

1 Everything has a season, and a time for every matter under the heavens.

2 A time to be born and a time to die.

A time to plant and a time to uproot what is planted.

3 A time to kill and a time to heal.

A time to rip down and a time to build.

4 A time to weep and a time to laugh.

A time to mourn and a time to dance.

5 A time to fling stones and a time to gather stones in.

A time to embrace and a time to pull back from embracing.

---

2. *A time to be born and a time to die.* The seven verses that begin here are the first instance of formal poetry in Qohelet. There are seven paired lines, with the number seven pointedly chosen because of its traditional association with the sacred. Each half-line is very short, containing only two accented syllables (with the exception of the end of verse 2, where *natua'*, "what is planted," is not strictly necessary and might be an explanatory gloss added by a scribe). Any English version would do well to emulate the King James Version in reproducing as much as feasible the compactness of the Hebrew. The parallelism between the half-lines is of course antithetical.

born . . . die . . . plant . . . uproot. There is a semantic pairing in each pair of lines: here, life and death for humans; planting and uprooting in the vegetable kingdom; then killing and healing, wrecking and building; weeping and laughing, mourning and dancing; and so forth.

5. *A time to fling stones.* In this instance, at least on the surface, there does not seem to be any semantic pairing between this first line and the second line, which speaks of embracing and avoiding embraces. This ostensible divergence

A time to seek and a time to lose. 6
       A time to keep and a time to fling away.
A time to tear and a time to sew. 7
       A time to keep silent and a time to speak.
A time to love and a time to hate. 8
       A time for war and a time for peace.

What gain is there for him who does in what he toils? 9
I have seen the business that God has given to the sons of man with 10
which to busy themselves. Everything He has done aptly in its time. 11
Eternity, too, He has put in their heart, without man's grasping at all

---

from the overall pattern gives some credence to the proposal by Gordis that the flinging and gathering of stones are a metaphor for ejaculation and refraining from ejaculation. Gordis cites the Midrash Qohelet Rabba on this verse, which reads it in this sexual sense.

6. *to lose.* The context suggests that the sense of the verb here, as an antithesis to "seek," is "to give up for lost."

7. *to tear . . . to sew.* These may refer to acts of mourning and emergence from mourning, which would then be matched by the silence and speech of the next line.

9. *What gain is there.* This verse, taken together with what follows, may spell out the philosophic point of the catalogue of times. The contradictory events of human life, both good and bad, are beyond man's control. At one moment he will be called upon to laugh, at another, to weep, but he can scarcely hope to derive any gain from this alternating pattern not determined by him.

11. *Eternity, too, He has put in their heart.* The Hebrew *'olam* means "eternity" in the biblical language, though some interpreters argue that here it has the sense of "world" that it carries in rabbinic Hebrew—that is, God has planted in the human heart the love of the world. It seems more likely that the intended meaning is: man is conscious of the idea of eternity (Qohelet as philosopher surely is), but that is the source of further frustration, for he is incapable of grasping "what it is God has done from beginning to end." Other interpreters reverse the second and third consonants of *'olam* to yield *'amal,* "toil."

12 what it is God has done from beginning to end. I know that there is
nothing good in it but to be merry and to partake of good things in his
13 life. And also every man who eats and drinks and enjoys good things in
14 all his toil—this is a gift from God. I know that whatever God does will
be forever. One cannot add to it and one cannot take away from it. And
15 God has acted also that they should fear Him. That which was already
has been, and what is to be already has been, and God seeks out the
16 pursued. And further did I see under the sun: The place of judgment—
17 wickedness there, and the place of justice—the wicked there. I said in
my heart: The just man and the wicked God will judge, for there is a
18 time for every matter, and every deed He assesses. I said in my heart
in regard to the sons of man, God has sifted them out to show them they

---

12. *in it*. The Hebrew says "in them." The unclear antecedent might be "life"
(which is a plural in Hebrew).

13. *this is a gift from God*. Qohelet repeatedly urges us to enjoy the pleasures of
life here and now, but he is perfectly aware that it is a matter of luck, or God's
unfathomable determination, whether we are given the time and means to
enjoy the good things of life, or whether we are condemned to die, to uproot,
to rip down, to mourn.

14. *that they should fear Him*. The absolute determination of events, beyond all
human control, is understood as a reason for man to fear the deity that controls
all things.

15. *God seeks out the pursued*. This is what the Hebrew literally says, but no one
has been able to make good sense of it. If "the pursued" is equivalent in meaning to "him who is sought," the meaning of the clause might be coordinate with
"what is to be already has been," but the verse remains doubtful.

17. *and every deed He assesses*. The translation understands *sham* not as the
adverb "there" but as a verb (infinitive *shum*), common in rabbinic Hebrew.

18. *God has sifted them out to show them*. This string of words is not intelligible
in the Hebrew and continues the patch of scribal scrambling that spreads over
four verses here. The translation derives "to show" (*lar'ot*) by revocalizing the
Masoretic *liro't* ("to see"), but the meaning of the clause is still uncertain.

are but beasts. For the fate of the sons of man and the fate of the beast 19
is a single fate. As one dies so dies the other, and all have a single spirit,
and man's advantage over the beast is naught, for everything is mere
breath. Everything goes to a single place. Everything was from the dust, 20
and everything goes back to the dust. Who knows whether man's spirit 21
goes upward and the beast's spirit goes down to the earth? And I saw 22
that nothing is better than that man should rejoice in his works, for that
is his share, for who can bring him to see what will be after him?

---

19. *man's advantage over the beast is naught.* This is another instance in which
Qohelet's unblinking view rejects a fundamental premise of the biblical consensus. In the Creation story, the human creature is brought into the world
after the beasts and is enjoined to hold sway over all other living creatures.
Here, man and beast are seen to share the same fate of mortality, and there is
no qualitative difference between them.

21. *Who knows whether man's spirit goes upward.* Qohelet may be referring to a
new doctrine that was beginning to circulate in the Late Biblical period that
imagines the ascent of the soul after death. If so, he is entirely skeptical about
the idea, suspecting that the spirit of man and beast alike descends into the
earth (the Hebrew can also mean "underworld").

22. *for who can bring him to see what will be after him?* The "after" of the question, following the logic of the previous verse, could refer to the fate of the
departed spirit after death. Perhaps more simply, and in keeping with such
previous reflections as the one in 1:11, the reference could be to the course of
events after one's death—that is, one can never know what will happen after
one is gone, so the only sensible thing to do is to take advantage of the pleasures
that present themselves in life while one possesses it.

4

¹ And I went back and saw all the oppression that is done under the
sun: the tears of the oppressed who have none to console them, and
from the hand of their violent oppressors there is none to console them.
² And I praised the dead, who have already died, more than the living,
³ who are still alive. And better than both is he who has not yet been, who
⁴ has not seen the evil deeds that are done under the sun. And I saw all
the toil and all the skilled deeds—that it is a man's envy of his fellow.

---

1. *oppression*. The Hebrew noun is plural, probably meaning "acts of oppression," but English usage prefers "oppression" as a collective term.

the tears of the oppressed who have none to console them. It is notable that
Qohelet registers the suffering of the oppressed as a given fact without the
slightest indication, as in Psalms or elsewhere, that God will rescue them from
their suffering, and without any exhortation, as in the Prophets, that we must
act to rescue them.

2. *the dead, who have already died . . . the living, who are still alive*. The seeming
redundancy of this wording is of a piece with Qohelet's pointed stylistic use of
emphatic repetition.

3. *And better than both is he who has not yet been*. Though there is a point of
similarity to Job's wish in Job 3 never to have been born, that refusal of existence is an expression of Job's own unbearable suffering, whereas Qohelet puts
forth the idea as a general philosophic reflection on the human condition.

deeds. The Hebrew *ma'aseh* is singular but stands as a collective noun. The
same is true for "deeds" in the next verse.

This, too, is mere breath and herding the wind. The fool hugs his hands 5
and eats his own flesh. Better a palmful of ease than two handfuls of 6
toil and herding the wind. And I went back and saw mere breath under 7
the sun. There is one without a second, neither son nor brother he has. 8
And there is no end to his toil, nor is his eye sated with wealth: "And for
whom do I toil and deprive myself of good things?" This, too, is mere
breath and an evil business. Two are better than one, for they get good 9
reward for their toil. For if one should fall, the other will lift up his 10
friend. But if the one alone should fall, there is no other to lift him up.
If two lie together, they are warm, but as for one, how will he be warm? 11

---

5. *The fool hugs his hands and eats his own flesh.* This is a traditional-sounding
proverb, of the sort that one finds in the Book of Proverbs, enjoining against
indolence. The eating of one's own flesh is, of course, a metaphor for causing
devastating harm to oneself.

6. *Better a palmful of ease than two handfuls of toil.* This declaration, cast in the
formula of a traditional proverb ("better than . . .") at least partly contradicts the
previous proverb. Gordis's proposal that Qohelet first quotes a conventional
saying and then offers a critique of it is plausible, though it has not been
embraced by all scholars.

8. *And for whom do I toil.* These words are evidently a quotation of the single,
childless man. It is at least possible that Qohelet identifies with him and is
speaking autobiographically as well.

9. *for they get good reward for their toil.* Throughout these lines, the argument
for friendship is pragmatic, invoking neither companionship nor love.

10. *if one should fall.* The Hebrew uses a plural, but the sense is partitive.
  the other. Literally, "the one."
  the one alone. "Alone" is added in the translation for clarification.

11. *If two lie together.* It is not necessary to conclude that either marriage or sex
is implied, especially since what has been envisaged to this point is the advantage gained through a man's having a companion. The warmth of a shared bed
could easily be that of two companions, without sexual intent (like Ishmael and
Queequeg at the beginning of *Moby-Dick*).

12 And if one should attack him, the two will stand against him. And the
13 triple cord will not quickly be snapped. Better a poor but wise boy than
14 an old and foolish king who no longer knows how to be wary. For from
the prison-house he came out to be king, for in his kingship, too, the
15 impoverished man was born. I have seen all the living who go about
16 under the sun alongside the next boy who will stand in his place. There
is no end to all the people, to all before whom he stood, nor would the

---

12. *And the triple cord will not quickly be snapped.* The whole sequence on the
advantages of having a friend takes the proverb form of a succession of numbers (one-two-three). The triple cord, as many scholars have observed, is a
citation from the *Gilgamesh* epic, or of a saying in general circulation that is
quoted in *Gilgamesh*. In the epic, Gilgamesh, urging his friend Enkiddu to stick
with him in the endeavor to slay the monster Hombaba, declares, as evidence
of the advantage of joining forces, that a towed ship will not sink because "no
man can snap the triple cord" by which it is fastened.

13. *Better a poor but wise boy than an old and foolish king.* Many futile attempts
have been made to anchor this exemplary tale in the succession of two or more
particular historical monarchs, but it seems more sensible to understand it as
another illustrative instance of the pattern of futility from one generation to the
next—in this case, in regard to the exercise of power. Some of the details
remain obscure, but the following narrative outline is likely: A clever boy (a
young man) is preferable to a doddering old king, perhaps senile, and not able
to look out for his own interests. The boy, once imprisoned (perhaps for debt)
and powerless, somehow manages to get out and assume the throne. He in turn
is succeeded by a third figure like himself. In this chain of succession, no one
gets lasting benefit from the exercise of power.

14. *for in his kingship, too, the impoverished man was born.* This is obscure but
might refer to still another "poor boy" who will be poised to seize power. This
would be "the next boy" of the following verse.

16. *before whom he stood.* The Hebrew says literally "before whom he was." The
translation follows Fox in understanding this as a reference to the second boy's
leadership of the people.
    nor would the ones who come later be happy with him. In the succession of
generations, the leader's power is always precarious because those led are
fickle. ("him" refers to the third of the three kings.) All this constitutes an
application to the political realm of Qohelet's idea that it is pointless to amass
wealth through toil because there is no way of knowing who will inherit it.

ones who came later be happy with him. For this, too, is mere breath and herding the wind.

Watch your step when you go to the house of God, for understanding is 17 more favored than the offering of sacrifice by fools, for they do not know even how to do evil.

---

17. *understanding is more favored than the offering of sacrifice by fools*. Some interpreters construe *lishmoaʿ* to mean "obedience" because that is the sense it has in 1 Samuel 15:22, where it is also contrasted with "sacrifice." The antithesis with "fools," however, argues for the other meaning, "understanding."

for they do not know even how to do evil. The Hebrew sounds enigmatic, and "even" has been added interpretively. The sense would then be that they are so stupid that they don't even have the consciousness of doing evil, let alone the mental clarity to do good.

5

B̲e not rash with your mouth, and let your heart not hurry to utter a
word before God. For God is in the heavens and you are on earth.
2 Therefore let your words be few. For a dream comes with much busi-
3 ness and the fool's voice with much talk. When you make a vow to God,
do not delay to fulfill it, for there is no pleasure in fools. What you vow,
4 fulfill. Better that you do not vow than that you vow and do not fulfill.
5 Do not let your mouth make your body offend, nor say before God that
it was a mistake. Why should God rage over your voice and ruin your

---

1. *Be not rash with your mouth*. As the next five verses make clear, the reference
is to the pronouncement of vows. Thus "God is in the heavens and you are on
earth" is a reminder of man's exposure, as a mere terrestrial creature, to the
all-seeing scrutiny of God on high. Verses 1–6 here, to which the last verse of
Chapter 4 must be attached, are a somewhat surprising, and conventional,
stress by Qohelet on appropriate behavior in the sanctuary and an injunction
to act in a way that will deter divine punishment. The second-person-singular
imperatives are also stylistically different from what precedes. Either this section was editorially patched into the text from a different source, or one must
assume that Qohelet, for all his radical views, does not doubt the presence of
an omniscient God who punishes man for vows left unfulfilled.

2. *much business*. In this context the phrase seems to refer to the confusion of
ideas and images characteristic of dreams, which are said to resemble a fool's
chatter. The "talk" of the fool would include rash vows that the fool has no
intention to fulfill.

3. *for there is no pleasure in fools*. Only a fool would make a vow and not fulfill
it, and such behavior will give no pleasure to God.

5. *Do not let your mouth make your body offend*. This reference is still to vows.

handiwork? For in many dreams are mere breath and much talk. Instead, 6
fear God. If you see the oppression of the poor and the perversion of 7
justice and right in the province, be not amazed at the matter, for he
who is high has a higher one watching him, and still higher ones over
them. And the gain of the land is in everything—a king is subject to the 8
field. He who loves money will not be sated with money, and he who 9
loves wealth will have no crop. This, too, is mere breath. As bounty 10
multiplies, those who consume it multiply, and what is the benefit for
its owner except what his eyes see? Sweet is the worker's sleep, whether 11
he eats little or much. And the rich man's surfeit does not let him sleep.

---

6. *For in many dreams are mere breath and much talk.* The Hebrew of this
clause looks defective, at least in its prepositions. As the Hebrew text stands,
the literal sense is "For in many dreams and mere breath and much talk." This
translation deletes the "and" before "mere breath" (*havalim*) and thus construes
the relation between "dreams" and "mere breath" as subject and predicate.

7. *for he who is high has a higher one watching him.* This whole clause is
obscurely worded in the Hebrew, as it is in this translation, but the preceding
clause about the perversion of justice suggests a reference to bureaucratic hierarchy—not an exclusively modern phenomenon—in which rights are easily
made wrong. Others interpret the Hebrew to mean "arrogant" rather than "high."

8. *a king is subject to the field.* The Hebrew is ambiguous, and some construe
it as "a king belongs to the tilled field." The evident sense of the whole verse is
that both the economy and political power depend on agriculture.

9. *This, too, is mere breath.* The invocation of this refrain of futility after a
proverb with which Qohelet might well agree may express a general skepticism
on his part about all such formulations of wisdom: we don't really know how to
control consequences in our lives.

10. *what is the benefit.* The noun *kishron* elsewhere means skill, but, as ibn Ezra
and sundry modern commentators have argued, the meaning in context is
something like "benefit."
   what his eyes see. The one benefit he can absolutely count on is beholding
his possessions. Given the uncertain fluctuations of human circumstances, he
may not be given the opportunity to enjoy them.

11. *the worker's sleep . . . the rich man's surfeit.* The worker's hard labor, however

12 There is a blighting evil I have seen under the sun: wealth kept for its
13 owner for his harm. And that wealth is lost in a bad business, and he
14 begets a son with nothing in his hand. As he came out from his
mother's womb, naked will he return to go as he came, and nothing
15 will he bear off from his toil that he brings in his hand. And this, too,
is a blighting evil: as he came, so he goes, and what gain does he have
16 that he should toil for the wind? All his days, too, he goes in darkness,
17 with much worry and illness and rage. Look, I have seen what is
good: it is fit to eat and to drink and enjoy good things in all his toil
that he toils under the sun in the number of the days of his life that
18 God gave him, for that is his share. Also the man whom God has
given wealth and possessions and whom He has empowered to enjoy
it and bear off his share and delight in his toil—this is God's gift.

---

little he may get by it, gives him the gift of sound sleep, but the rich man's full
belly—or his worries about his possessions—keeps him awake.

12. *a blighting evil*. The literal sense of the Hebrew is "a sick evil."

13. *that wealth is lost in a bad business*. The rich man has "kept" his wealth, then
invests it foolishly, leaving both himself and his heir without resource. As elsewhere, Qohelet reflects the preoccupations of a mercantile society.

14. *As he came out from his mother's womb*. As many interpreters have recognized, these words are close to the ones Job pronounces (Job 1:21) when he has
been stripped by disaster of all that he has.

16. *illness*. The Hebrew has a possessive suffix ("his illness"), which scrambles
the syntax, but the Septuagint plausibly reads here simply "illness."

18. *this is God's gift*. The exhortation of the preceding verse to enjoy life's pleasures, which Qohelet has pronounced before, here undergoes a dialectic correction: we should enjoy the good things given us—if, that is, we are fortunate
enough to have the opportunity to enjoy them, if economic vicissitude or illness
or political disaster does not intervene. Thus, the opportunity to follow a course
of simple hedonism is a gift of God—or perhaps fate, for the two exhibit some
interchangeability in Qohelet.

For not much will he recall the days of his life, for God makes him busy 19
with his heart's delight.

---

19. *not much will he recall the days of his life*. Fox suggests that this means he
will not be very conscious of life's brevity. It could also mean that he will pay
little attention to the uncertainty and the sheer potential for misery of a human
life.

God makes him busy. The received text shows merely "makes busy" (*ma'aneh*),
but the Septuagint and the Syriac have "makes him busy" (*ma'anehu*, an addition of a single letter as accusative suffix).

1 There is an evil that I have seen under the sun, and it is heavy on
2 humankind: a man whom God gives wealth and possessions and honor,
and he lacks nothing for himself of all he desires, and God does not
grant him to enjoy it, for a stranger will enjoy it. This is mere breath and
3 an evil sickness. If a man begot a hundred children and lived many
years, and many were the days of his life, he might yet not be sated with
good things, and even a burial he might not have. I said: better than he
4 is the stillborn. For in mere breath did it come, and into darkness it
5 goes, and in darkness its name is covered. The very sun it did not see

---

1. *heavy*. The literal sense of the adjective is "great." Derivatives of that word—
rav, rabbah, rabot, harbeh—punctuate this entire section.

2. *enjoy*. The Hebrew is literally "eat" (and so the King James Version). The
usage is an anticipation of a common idiom in rabbinic Hebrew, in which
the verb "eat" (*'akhal*) means to enjoy the fruits of something.

3. *he might yet not be sated with good things*. The logical connection with the
two preceding clauses is not entirely clear, and "yet" has been added
interpretively.
  and even a burial he might not have. Some interpreters prefer to attach this
clause to the stillborn at the end of the verse and in the two following verses,
but the Hebrew text clearly ties it in with the man who lives many years. The
idea expressed jibes with Qohelet's general pessimism about life: a man may
beget many children and live a very long time, but this does not mean he won't
come to a bad end, not having enjoyed his own material benefits and finally
being subjected to the ignominy of lying unburied.

or know—more ease for it than for him. And were he to live a thousand 6
years twice over, yet good things he did not enjoy—does not everything
go to a single place? All a man's toil is for his own mouth, yet his appe- 7
tite will not be filled. For what advantage has the wise over the fool? 8
What good is it for the poor man to know how to get round among the
living? Better what the eyes see than desire going round. This, too, is 9
mere breath and herding the wind. What was has already been called 10
by name and is known, as he is man and cannot deal with one more
powerful than he. For there are many words that increase mere breath; 11

---

6. *yet good things he did not enjoy*. Again, "yet" is added in the translation for
clarity. In fact, the whole verse would make better sense if it read "and good
things enjoyed"—that is, even if a man had an unbelievably long life filled with
enjoyment, in the end everything is swallowed up by death.

8. *to get round among the living*. The Hebrew *lahalokh neged haḥayim* is not
altogether clear—the preposition *neged* could mean "before" or "against," and
haḥayim could be either "the living" or "life." The translation follows a consensus of interpreters that the phrase indicates an ability to manage with people.
If that is the intended meaning, Qohelet suggests that the poor man's compe-
tence in dealing with others does him no more good than wisdom does the wise
man.

9. *Better what the eyes see than desire going round*. The evident sense is that one
is better off simply enjoying what one sees—let us say, a beautiful woman—
than embarking on the dangerous and potentially frustrating path of trying to
fulfill desire. Although the King James Version's "the wandering of the desire"
has a nice ring and has been adopted by many modern translators, the Hebrew
halokh means "to go" or "to go about," not really "to wander," and it is surely
intended to echo the *halokh* in the phrase "get [or go] around among the living."
Because Qohelet also uses "to go" as a euphemism for dying, and because *nefesh* means "life-breath" as well as "appetite" or desire, Seow construes this
phrase to mean "the passing of life."

10. *What was has already been called by name*. To call something by name in
biblical Hebrew and other ancient Near Eastern languages is to designate its
nature and define its being, so the entire clause expresses Qohelet's sense of
determinism.

he is man and cannot deal with one more powerful than he. Because of the
context of determinism, many see "one" as a reference to God, though it could

12 what is the advantage for man? For who knows what is good for man in life, in his days of mere breath, for he spends them like a shadow? Who can tell man what will be after him under the sun?

---

just as well refer to a human being who exercises power, given Qohelet's sense of political hierarchies and the social limitations of freedom.

12. *For who knows what is good for man*. This question follows on "there are many words that increase mere breath." Qohelet is a Wisdom writer who constantly questions the value of wisdom. He knows that a human life is likely to be bleak, that it is intrinsically unpredictable, may end badly, and will surely be blotted out by death. His "wisdom" is to register this perception, but, apart from his occasional exhortations to enjoy, he does not presume to know what is good for man, unlike the purveyors of mainline Wisdom.

7

Better a good name than good oil, and the day of death than the day ₁
one is born. Better to go to the house of mourning than to go to the ₂
house of carousing. For that is the end of all men—let the living take it
to heart. Better worry than merriment, for by a scowl the heart is glad- ₃
dened. The wise men's heart is in the house of mourning, and the heart ₄

---

1. *Better a good name.* This verse inaugurates a sequence of maxims cast in the
traditional proverb form of "better than" (*tov*). The "good" before "name" is
merely implied in the Hebrew.

and the day of death than the day one is born. Many commentators understand this to mean that one can never be sure of one's good name till the end
of life, but this makes Qohelet blander than he actually is. He begins with a
rather anodyne proverbial saying, that a good name (*shem*) is better than precious oil (*shemen*), but then he goes on to say that departing life is better than
entering it, for life itself, whatever one's reputation, is a miserable affair from
one end to the other.

2. *carousing.* The Hebrew *mishteh* literally means "drinking," and feasting is
also implied.

For that is the end of all men. This sentence essentially explains the preceding one: since our common fate is mortality, it is better to confront this bleak
existential fact by going to the house of mourning rather than to try to evade it
through revelry.

3. *by a scowl the heart is gladdened.* Some understand the expression *yitav lev*
to mean "the heart is improved," but *tuv* (as a verb) linked with *lev*, "heart,"
means in biblical idiom to be in a happy mood. The paradox of gladness through
grimness would have appealed to Qohelet's sensibility.

5 of fools in the house of mirth. Better to hear the rebuke of the wise than
6 a man hearing the song of fools. For like the sound of thorns beneath
7 the pot, so is the laughter of the fool. And this, too, is mere breath. For
oppression's profit drives the wise man wild, and a bribe destroys the
8 mind. Better a thing's end than its beginning; better patience than
9 haughtiness. Do not be rash in your mood to be angry, for anger rests
10 in the lap of fools. Say not: What has happened, that the days gone by
11 were better than these? For you asked not about this in wisdom. Better
12 wisdom with a legacy, it is an advantage to those who see the sun. For
in wisdom's shade is money's shade, and the gain of wisdom's knowl-

---

5. *than a man hearing*. An emendation eliminates the slightly odd "a man."

6. *the sound of thorns*. Most translations since the King James Version read
"crackle," which is more vivid but unfortunately is translation through embel-
lishment. The Hebrew *qol* means simply "sound." The idea is that the laughter
of fools is grating, like the noisy sound of a quick-burning fire of thorns. The
Hebrew uses a pun, *sirim*, "thorns," and *sir*, "pot."

7. *oppression's profit*. Though the Hebrew merely says "oppression," what is
implied is the consequences of oppression, as "toil" may be either the activity
or what is gained from it.
    a bribe. Though *matanah* usually means "gift," in context it is an illicit gift.

10. *Say not*. This verse appears to record, as Seow has suggested, an exchange
between Qohelet and his students. He would of course view this as a foolish
(and nostalgic) question because in his philosophy things were never better—
the same cycle of futility has always occurred.

11. *Better wisdom with a legacy*. Most interpreters construe this—again,
blandly—to mean "better wisdom than a legacy," but the Hebrew *'im* clearly
means "with" and is not a term of comparison. The saying is another expression
of Qohelet's hardheaded practicality: wisdom is nice to have, but still better is
wisdom with a good annual income.

12. *For in wisdom's shade is money's shade*. This follows from the previous verse.
"Shade" probably means "shelter," as it often does in biblical Hebrew: the security provided by wisdom will help one attain (or help one manage) the security
provided by wealth.

edge keeps its possessors alive. See God's work, for who can straighten 13
what He has made crooked? On the day of good luck, enjoy the good, 14
and on the day of evil, see: one against the other God has set, so that
man find nothing after him. Everything have I seen in my days of mere 15
breath: the righteous perishing in his righteousness, and the wicked living a long life in his evil. Do not be over-righteous and do not be over- 16
wise. Why should you be dumbfounded? Don't be over-wicked and 17
don't be a fool. Why should you die before your time? It is good that you 18
seize this, and from the other as well do not take back your hand, for he
who fears God will get out of them all. Wisdom is stronger for the wise 19
than ten rulers who are in the town. For there is no man righteous on 20
earth who does good and will not offend. To all the words, too, that they 21
speak, do not pay heed, that you hear not your servant reviling you.

---

14. *one against the other.* Life is an imponderable mixture of good fortune and
misfortune, making it impossible for man to discern any pattern of meaning or
purpose in it.

15. *the righteous perishing.* This declaration, of course, deliberately denies a
fundamental assumption of Psalms, Proverbs, and other biblical books.

16. *do not be over-righteous.* Any kind of excess, whether in righteousness or in
evil, is a provocation of men and fate.
   dumbfounded. The Hebrew *tishomem* could also mean something stronger,
"devastated."

18. *this . . . the other.* This cryptic formulation appears to refer to foolishness
(though perhaps not to wickedness) and righteousness. This would be in keeping with Qohelet's declaration that he has explored all realms of experience,
foolishness and revelry as well as sober wisdom.
   will get out of them all. This phrase is obscure. The attempt of many interpreters to align it with the rabbinic idiom that means to fulfill an obligation
(*yatsa' yedey*) is unpersuasive because the component *yedey* is absent here. Perhaps the meaning is that the God-fearer will manage to escape the dire consequences of being either too righteous or too foolish.

19. *is stronger.* The Qumran fragment of Qohelet reads "will help," a difference
of one additional consonant in the Hebrew.

22 For many times, too, your heart has known, that you, too, have reviled
23 others. All this I tried out through wisdom. I said, Let me grow wise, and
24 it was far away from me. Far away that which was and deep, deep—who
25 can find it? I turned round in my heart to know and to inquire and seek
wisdom and reckoning and to know foolish wickedness and mad folly.
26 And I find woman more bitter than death. For she is all snares, and nets
her heart, and fetters her arms. He who is good before God will escape
27 her, and an offender will be trapped by her. See, this have I found, said
28 Qohelet: one by one to find a reckoning. Further I sought and did not
find—one man in a thousand I found, and a woman among all these I
29 did not find. Except, see this I found: that God made men upright, but
they sought many reckonings.

---

22. *you, too, have reviled others.* By introspection, we all recognize the ubiqui-
tous impulse to be malicious, hence one is well-advised not to eavesdrop on
one's servant's conversation, for one is all too likely to hear distressing things.

23. *it was far away from me.* The reference is to wisdom.

25. *reckoning.* As several commentators have observed, this, like other elements in Qohelet's lexicon, is a bookkeeping term.

26. *I find woman more bitter than death.* This misogynistic declaration is notori-
ous, but the language of the rest of this verse and the next one makes clear that
the kind of woman Qohelet has in mind is the seductress or "stranger-woman"
who often appears in Wisdom literature (as, memorably, in Proverbs 5 and 7).
   He who is good before God. That is, who finds favor before God.

27. *one by one to find a reckoning.* The formulation here makes clear the bookkeeping aspect of the idiom: Qohelet has sifted through experience, counted
the sums of all the numbers, and this is what he has found.

28. *and a woman among all these I did not find.* Perhaps extrapolating from the
case of the seductress, Qohelet extends the scope of misogyny: if only one honest man in a thousand can be found, there is no honest woman at all.

29. *God made men upright, but they sought many reckonings.* Human nature
begins with the potential for honesty ("upright" is literally "straight"), but people pervert this potential by devising devious calculations, like wily accountants
juggling figures in their books.

8

Who is like the wise man, and who knows a word's solution? A man's 1
wisdom lights up his face, and the impudence of his face transforms it.
Keep a king's utterance as though it concerned a vow to God. Do not be 2,3
hasty. From his presence you should go. Do not persist in a bad business. For whatever he desires, he may do, since a king's word is power, 4
and who can say to him, "What are you doing?" He who keeps a com- 5
mand will know no evil thing, and the time of judgment a wise heart

---

1. *a word's solution*. "Word," *davar*, could also mean "thing." *Pesher*, "solution,"
occurs only here in the Bible, though it is common in later Hebrew. It is cognate with *patar*, the verb used for Joseph's solving the enigma of dreams, and
would seem to suggest laying open a hidden meaning.

2. *Keep a king's utterance*. This verse begins a series of purely pragmatic admonitions involving the dangers lurking in the corridors of power. The literal meaning
of "king's utterance" is "king's mouth." The Hebrew here is prefaced by the word
"I," which has no plausible syntactic linkage with anything that follows or precedes it. Since the two final letters of the last word of the previous verse are *nun*
and *'aleph*, and the first two letters of *'ani*, "I," are *'aleph* and *nun*, this looks
suspiciously like dittography and hence the word is omitted from the translation.

4. *since a king's word is power*. The abstract noun *shilton*, recurrent in Qohelet,
is linked to *shalit* of earlier biblical Hebrew, which means "ruler." In Qohelet,
it suggests the exercise of authority or power (the claim of some scholars that
it means "proprietorship" dilutes its actual force).

5. *command*. The likely meaning in this passage is a royal command, not a
divine commandment.
   the time of judgment. The Hebrew is literally "time and judgment," but
some manuscripts delete the "and," and even if one leaves it in the text, the

6 knows. For every happening has a time of judgment, for man's evil is
7 heavy upon him. For one knows not what will be, for what will be—who
8 can tell of it? No man has power over the wind, to shut in the wind, and
there is no power over the day of death, and there is no sending away
9 from war, and wickedness will not make those who do it escape. All this
have I seen and set my heart to all that is done under the sun, a time
10 when man holds power over man to his harm. And so have I seen the
wicked brought to the grave, and from a holy place they went forth,
while those who did right were forgotten in the town. This, too, is mere
11 breath. The sentence for an evil act is not carried out swiftly. Therefore

---

expression could simply be a hendiadys. What is less certain is whether the
time of judgment refers to the king's judgment or to God's. The context of this
verse argues for the former—if you are so imprudent as to get yourself in trouble, the king's judgment will catch up with you. The phrase in the next sentence might point to divine judgment, but it is perhaps best to construe both
verses as addressing royal judicial power.

8. *No man has power over the wind.* Fox, Seow, and others construe *ruaḥ* in its
other sense as "life-breath," chiefly because of the reference to death in the
next clause. That construction is unlikely because of the verb "to shut in" (or
"imprison"), which is far more appropriate to the wind. The idea is that just as
a man has no power to shut in the wind—which, as we recall, goes round per-
petually to the four corners of the earth—no one has power over death.

sending away. The Hebrew *mishlaḥat* elsewhere means "delegation." It may
refer to sending a substitute or delegate (*shaliaḥ*) for military service or, alternately, being released (one meaning of this verbal root) from service.

10. *so have I seen the wicked brought to the grave.* The received text reads, enig-
matically, "I have seen the wicked buried and they came" (*qevurim uva'u*). This
translation follows the Septuagint, which appears to have had a Hebrew text
that read *qevarim muv'aim*, a difference of two consonants in the second word.

holy place. At this late moment in the biblical era, the reference is probably
to a synagogue, where the funeral was held.

This, too, is mere breath. In this particular instance, Fox's contention that the
idiom refers to absurdity in its existential sense is persuasive. The wicked are
given a proper burial while the righteous are forgotten—nothing stands to reason in this world.

the heart of the sons of men brims over within them to do evil. For the   12
offender does evil a hundredfold and lives a long life, though I know,
too, that it will be well with those who fear God, who fear His presence.
And it will not be well with the wicked, and like a shadow, he will not   13
live long, as he does not fear God's presence. There is a thing of mere   14
breath that is done on the earth—there are righteous to whom it befalls
as though they did wickedly, and there are wicked to whom it befalls as
though they did righteously. I said that this, too, is mere breath. And I   15
praised merriment, for there is nothing better for man under the sun
than to eat and to drink and to make merry, and that will attend him in

---

11. *The sentence for an evil act is not carried out swiftly.* This is another of Qohelet's arguments with the moral calculus of Psalms. In many psalms, the speaker,
confronted with the worldly success of the wicked, says that they flourish only
for a moment and will soon suffer judgment. The empirical Qohelet, observing
social and political realities, sees that the wicked often endure long in their
success and in this way they actually encourage others to emulate their evil
acts.

    brims over. Literally, "is filled." The idiom suggests presumptuous eagerness
to do something.

12. *a hundredfold.* The form of the Hebrew *me'at* is anomalous. This translation
follows a long tradition in deriving the term from *me'ah,* "a hundred," but others
variously emend the word.

    though I know, too, that it will be well with those who fear God. This seeming
contradiction is perhaps best understood as a swing of feeling in an ambivalent
Qohelet. He knows as a matter of observation that the wicked flourish with no
sign of retribution, but he wants, desperately, to cling to the idea that there is
nevertheless a divine moral order in which the righteous are rewarded and the
wicked punished.

14. *there are righteous to whom it befalls as though they did wickedly.* Now Qohelet swings back to the other pole of his ambivalence—one might say, from
moral hopefulness to unblinking observation.

15. *I praised merriment.* This particular affirmation of the pleasures of the
senses is probably a response to the articulation of life's moral absurdity in the
preceding verses: because in this insubstantial fleeting existence of mere
breath, we cannot make head or tail of any system of reward and punishment,
now or later, we can do nothing better than to enjoy what is given to us.

all his toil in the days of his life that God gives him under the sun.
16 When I set my heart to know wisdom and to see the business that is
17 done on earth, day and night my eyes saw no sleep. And I have seen
every deed of God, that man cannot grasp the deed which is done under
the sun, in as much as man toils to seek and cannot grasp it. And even
if the wise means to know, he will not be able to grasp it.

---

16. *day and night my eyes saw no sleep.* The Hebrew says, incongruously, "his
eyes saw no sleep" (literally, "with his eyes he saw no sleep"). This translation
follows the proposal of several interpreters to emend the suffix of the Hebrew
words for "eyes" and for "no" from the third person to the first person. The idea
of sleepless pursuit of wisdom is surely appropriate to Qohelet's repeated affirmation of his dedication to philosophical investigation.

17. *grasp.* The Hebrew verb means literally "to find."

9

For on all this I set my heart to sort out all this—that the righteous and ₁
the wise and their acts are in God's hand. Neither hatred nor love does
man know. All before them is mere breath. As all have a single fate, the ₂
righteous and the wicked, the good and the bad, and the clean and
the unclean, and he who offers sacrifice and he who does not sacrifice,
the good and the offender, he who vows and he who fears the vow. This ₃
is the evil in all that is done under the sun, for all have a single fate, and

---

1. *are in God's hand.* Though the formulation may sound unexceptionally pious,
what is expressed is a sense of fatalism: even the wise and the righteous do not
control their own destinies.

Neither hatred nor love does man know. The key term here is "know," with
the emphasis on understanding rather than on experiencing. Every person is of
course acquainted with hatred and love but is not able to fathom the meaning
or the sources of these powerful emotions.

1–2. *All before them . . . is mere breath.* The Masoretic text reads "All before
them," followed by a full stop, and then begins the next verse with "all." Neither
"all before them" standing alone nor the second "all" makes much sense. This
translation follows the Septuagint and two other ancient versions in reading
instead of the second "all," *hakol,* "mere breath," *hevel,* a difference of one
consonant. The sentence then is coherent.

the bad. This word is absent in the Masoretic text but appears in two ancient
versions, and all the other positive terms in this verse have a matching negative
term.

he who fears the vow. He is afraid to make a vow lest he be unable to fulfill
it and suffer dire consequences. In this whole catalogue, Qohelet again stands
in opposition to the biblical majority view: it makes no difference what a person
does morally or ritually—the same fate of death awaits all. That idea is then
vividly stressed in the next three verses.

also the heart of the sons of man is full of evil, and mad revelry in their
4 heart while they live, and afterward—off to the dead. For he who is
joined to the living knows one sure thing: that a live dog is better than a
5 dead lion. For the living know that they will die, and the dead know
nothing, and they no longer have recompense, for their memory is for-
6 gotten. Their love and their hatred as well, their jealousy, too, are
already lost, and they no longer have any share forever in all that is done
7 under the sun. Go, eat your bread with rejoicing and drink your wine
8 with a merry heart, for God has already been pleased by your deeds. At
every season let your garments be white, and let oil on your head not be
9 lacking. Enjoy life with a woman whom you love all your days of mere
breath that have been given to you under the sun, all your days of mere
breath, for that is your share in life and in your toil that you toil under
10 the sun. All that your hand manages to do with your strength, do, for
there is no doing nor reckoning nor knowledge nor wisdom in Sheol
11 where you are going. I returned to see under the sun that not to the

---

4. *joined*. The translation follows the marginal *qeri*, which reads *yeḥubar*,
instead of the text proper, which has *yebuḥar*, "chosen."

   knows. Literally, "has."

   a live dog. Dogs in ancient Israel were scavengers, not pets, and hence were
despised.

7. *Go, eat your bread with rejoicing*. This exhortation to enjoy follows logically
from the somber meditation on death's inexorability that has preceded. If the
same grim fate awaits us all, we are well advised to take advantage of the pleasures of this life while we have them.

   God has already been pleased by your deeds. If you have been granted the good
things of this life to enjoy—a loaf of bread, a jug of wine, white garments, a
head of hair moistened with oil—that in itself is a sign that you have found
favor in God's eyes.

9. *all your days of mere breath*. Though some scholars regard the second occurrence of this phrase as an inadvertent scribal duplication, Qohelet throughout
exhibits a stylistic fondness for this kind of incantatory repetition.

10. *for there is no doing nor reckoning . . . in Sheol where you are going*. It is
possible that Qohelet's uncompromising insistence on death as a realm of utter

swift is the race and not to the mighty, the battle, nor to the wise, bread, nor to the discerning, wealth, nor to those who know, favor, for a time of mishap will befall them all. Nor does man know his time, like fish 12 caught in an evil net and like birds held in a trap, like them the sons of man are ensnared by an evil time when it suddenly falls upon them. Wisdom, too, have I seen under the sun, and it is great in my eyes. 13 There was a little town, and few people within it, and a great king came 14 against it and went round it and built against it great siegeworks. And there was found within it a poor wise man, and that person saved 15 the town through his wisdom, but no one recalled that poor man.

---

extinction is a polemic response to the new doctrine of an afterlife that was beginning to emerge toward the end of the biblical period.

11. *for a time of mishap.* The Hebrew *'et upega'*, literally "time and mishap," is in all likelihood a hendiadys, hence the translation. The phrase is probably an oblique reference to death. Qohelet is not saying that the fastest runner will lose the race or the mighty warrior will be defeated in battle but rather that all human triumphs are temporary and therefore illusory, for death obliterates everything.

12. *Nor does man know his time.* In consonance with the use of "time" in the previous verse, this means the time of death, as "evil time" later in the verse makes clear. The imagery that follows of trapped fish and birds then concretizes the sense of humankind caught in the grip of its fate of mortality.

13. *great in my eyes.* The literal sense of the Hebrew is "great to me."

14. *There was a little town.* The features of this miniature narrative suggest that it is a hypothetical case rather than a historical anecdote. The whole story is a dialectic challenge to the celebration of wisdom in the preceding verse because it illustrates that if wisdom does not come from a prestigious source, it is liable to be ignored or forgotten.

15. *there was found within it.* The Hebrew appears to say "he found within it," but as often is the case in biblical Hebrew, the third-person masculine singular is used in place of a passive verb.
   and that person saved the town. Some interpreters understand the verb as a conditional, "that person might have saved the town," linking this clause with "the poor man's wisdom is scorned" in the next verse. However, the end of this

16 I said: Better wisdom than might, but the poor man's wisdom is scorned
17 and his words are unheard. The words of the wise gently said are heard
18 more than the shout of the ruler among fools. Better wisdom than weapons, yet a single offender destroys much good.

---

sentence, "but no one recalled that poor man," suggests that in fact he saved the town, but afterward his act was forgotten by the townspeople, who preferred not to think that their welfare had depended on the wisdom of a man of lowly status.

16. *Better wisdom than might, but the poor man's wisdom is scorned.* Qohelet takes us through still another dialectic turn. Wisdom is a supreme value, but given society's concern with status, if wisdom is not accompanied by prestige, it will have no audience.

18. *yet a single offender destroys much good.* This is another observation about the precariousness of the efficacy of wisdom. Wisdom may be more powerful than even the best of weapons, but a single reckless or irresponsible person can do great damage over which the calculations of wisdom have no control.

10

A dead fly makes the perfumer's oil chalice stink. Heavier than weighty 1
wisdom is a bit of folly. A wise man's mind is at his right, and the fool's 2
mind at his left. Even when the fool walks on the road, his mind is 3
absent, and it says to all, he is a fool. If the ruler's mood goes against 4
you, do not leave your place, for calmness puts great offenses to rest.
There is an evil I have seen under the sun, a true error that comes forth 5
from the person in power. Folly is set on great heights, and the rich 6

---

1. *A dead fly*. The Hebrew, *zevuvey mawet*, seems to say "flies of death," but if
one moves the final *yod* at the end of the first word to the beginning of the
second word, the consonantal text reads *zevuv yamut* (literally, "a fly that
dies")—the single fly that spoils the ointment.

   chalice. With many analysts, this translation reads *gavi'a*, "chalice," for the
puzzling *yabi'a* ("bubbles"? or "ferments"?). A dead fly would not make oil
ferment.

   weighty. The form of the Hebrew *mikavod* is peculiar and syntactically awry,
but the context argues for the sense of "weight," one of the meanings of this root.

2. *mind*. The Hebrew is literally "heart," thought to be the seat of understanding, but the context puts an emphasis on cognition, not feeling, and one must
avoid the comic error of Molière's physician despite himself, who places the
heart on the right side.

4. *mood*. The basic meaning of the Hebrew *ruaḥ* is "spirit."

5. *a true error*. "True" is added because the particle *kaf* before the noun is an
indication of emphasis, not, as it is more commonly, of comparison.

6. *Folly . . . the rich*. This opposition, especially because of the second term,
reflects Qohelet's social conservatism. He accepts established hierarchies and
thinks something is out of joint if the foolish (or the lowly) are on top and the

7 dwell down below. I have seen slaves on horses and noblemen walking
8 like slaves on the ground. He who digs a pit will fall in it, and he who
9 breaches a wall, a snake will bite him. He who moves stones will be hurt
10 by them, and he who splits wood is endangered by it. If the iron is dull
and he has not honed its edge, he will exert great effort. And the advan-
11 tage of skill is wisdom. If a snake bites with no snake-charm, there
12 is no advantage for the expert of incantations. The words of a wise
man's mouth bring favor, and the lips of a fool bring him ruin. The first
13 of the words of his mouth are folly, and the last of them evil revelry.
14 And the fool speaks many words. Man knows not what will be, and
15 what will be after him, who can tell him? The toil of a fool wears him
16 out, so that he knows not how to go to town. Woe to you, land, whose

---

wise (or the rich) on the bottom. A similar sentiment is expressed in the next
verse in his dismay over slaves mounted on horseback.

8. *He who digs a pit . . . he who breaches a wall.* This maxim is purely prudential,
much like what one finds in the Book of Proverbs: you have to be careful of the
consequences of your actions. The walls were built of piled-up stones without
mortar, so it was easy to make a small breach in which a snake could hide.

10. *If the iron is dull.* This is again prudential advice: if you don't prepare your
tools properly for the task to be performed, you will have a harder job.
   the advantage of skill is wisdom. The Hebrew is equally cryptic. Some scholars revocalize *hakhsher,* "skill," to yield *hakasher,* "the skilled man," which miti-
gates the difficulty but does not remove it.

11. *If the snake bites.* This is a little obscure. The likely meaning is that if the
snake charmer does not bother to practice his art before the snake bites, what
good is his skill?

14. *Man knows not what will be.* The relevance in context of this reiterated idea
is that since no one knows what will be, the chattering of the fool is all the more
pointless.

15. *so that he knows not how to go to town.* The fool is so exhausted by his wit-
less efforts that he ends up having no idea where he is headed. Fox cites an
Egyptian saying, "does not reach the city," that has the sense of "does not know
where he is going," and the expression here sounds like such a proverbial idiom.

king is a lackey, and your princes dine in the morning. Happy are you, 17
land, whose king is a noble, and your princes dine in fit time, in manli-
ness, not in drunkenness. Through sloth the roof-beam sags, and 18
through slack hands the house leaks. For food is set out for merriment 19
and wine that gladdens the living. And money keeps everyone busy.
Even on your couch revile not a king, and in your sleeping chambers 20
revile not a rich man, for the fowl of the heavens will carry the sound
and the wingèd thing will tell the word.

---

16. *lackey.* The Hebrew *na'ar* means "lad" or "youth" but also by extension a
servant or anyone in a subordinate position. The opposition to "a noble" in the
next verse suggests that the sense of an underling is intended. Once again,
Qohelet's attachment to established social hierarchies is evident.

dine in the morning. They give themselves over to a life of irresponsible
carousing at all times, again in contrast to the princes in the next verse. The
implication is that a country ruled by a lackey will lose all sense of appropriate
restraint and fall into a round of hedonistic merrymaking.

18. *Through sloth.* This is more prudential counsel in the spirit of the Book of
Proverbs.

19. *money keeps everyone busy.* The verb here, *ya'aneh*, most commonly means
"answer" in biblical Hebrew, but as several recent commentators have argued,
this verbal stem in Qohelet's distinctive vocabulary is associated with business,
as in the reiterated noun *'inyan*, which means "business." The evident idea here
is that people may fling themselves into feasting and drinking, but their over-
riding preoccupation is money—which, among other uses, pays the bills for the
carousing.

20. *Even on your couch.* The Hebrew noun *mada'* generally means "knowledge"
(in modern Hebrew it is the term for "science"). Many modern interpreters
construe it as "thought" or "mind"—an understanding already registered in the
King James Version. But if a person is merely thinking nasty thoughts about
the king without speaking them, how could the fowl of the heavens carry the
sound? The parallelism between the two clauses here invites the emendation
of *mada'akha*, "your thought," to *matsa'akha*, "your couch." Perhaps an emendation is not even necessary: Seow proposes that the "knowing" reflected in the
root of the word is knowing in the sexual sense, which could make this an
otherwise unattested term for the place where sexual intimacy is consummated.

11

¹ Send out your bread upon the waters, for in the long course of time
² you will find it. Give a share to seven and even to eight, for you know
³ not what evil will be on earth. If the clouds fill, they will empty out rain
  on the earth. And if a tree falls in the south or the north, the place
⁴ where the tree falls, there it will be. He who watches the wind will not
⁵ plant, and who gazes on clouds will not harvest. As you know not the

---

1. *Send out your bread upon the waters.* These words initiate a series of prudential maxims on how to conduct one's life in the face of the unpredictability of
events and their deterministic character that is beyond human control. The
sending out of bread on the waters is surely not advice about overseas investments, as some commentators have imagined, but rather a didactic metaphor.
The proposal of Rashi, ibn Ezra, and other medieval commentators that the
reference is to acts of charity is perfectly plausible: perform acts of benefi-
cence, for you never know when you yourself may benefit from having done
them. The idea is then continued in the next verse: be generous to any number
of people, for in the course of events you yourself may end up in need and enjoy
a reciprocation of support from one of those you have helped.

3. *If the clouds fill.* The sense of this entire verse is that there is a system of
strict causation in the structure of things, though the second sentence puts this
in terms that verge on tautology.
     if a tree falls. This image conveys a sense of events occurring with an inevi-
tability that, like trees in the forest, is not controlled by man.

4. *He who watches the wind . . . who gazes on clouds.* The good agriculturalist
does not waste his time looking for signs of changing weather before he acts
but plants at the fixed season ("a time to plant") in the expectation of an even-
tual harvest.

path of the life-breath into the limbs within the full womb, so you know
not the deeds of God, Who does everything. In the morning plant your 6
seed and at evening let your hand not rest, for you know not which will
be fit, this one or that, or whether both be equally good. And light is 7
sweet, and it is good for the eyes to see the sun. Should man live many 8
years, let him rejoice in all of them, and let him recall the days of darkness, for they will be many. Whatever comes is mere breath. Rejoice, 9
young man, in your youth, and let your heart be merry in the days
of your prime, and go about in the ways of your heart and what your
eyes see. But know that for all these God will bring you to judgment.

---

5. *into the limbs within the full womb.* The "limbs," *'atsamim,* are the body of
the fetus. The Masoretic text reads "like the limbs," *ka'atsamim,* but many
Hebrew manuscripts as well as the Targum have, more plausibly, *ba'atsamim,*
"into the limbs." The received text also reads "the womb of the full one [that is,
the pregnant woman]," which could be correct, but a change of the initial vowel
from *bᵉ* to *ba* yields "the full womb" and enables the translation to reproduce
the play on "full" in verse 3. This may be the more likely reading because there
are no other biblical instances of "the full one" as a synonym for a pregnant
woman.

6. *for you know not which will be fit.* This is more prudential advice. Qohelet
recommends that, given the uncertainty of future events, one would do well to
diversify one's investments, figuratively and perhaps literally.

7–8. *light is sweet . . . recall the days of darkness.* These moving words are
another exhortation by Qohelet to enjoy the good things of this fleeting life
while we still have it. As Nabokov movingly puts it in the opening sentence of
Speak, Memory, "common sense tells us that our existence is but a crack
between two eternities of darkness."
     Whatever comes is mere breath. It is unlikely that this refers to death, as some
have claimed, because in Qohelet it is darkness that is associated with death,
whereas "mere breath" is rather the futile substance of worldly experience.
Whatever happens, then, in our lives is mere breath—fleeting, insubstantial,
without meaning—and all we can do is to take pleasure in what seems
pleasurable.

9. *for all these God will bring you to judgment.* It is tempting to follow the suggestion of many commentators who see this whole sentence as an editorial
intrusion, perhaps from the same hand that was responsible for the epilogue of

10 And remove worry from your heart, and take evil away from your flesh,
for youth and the time of vigor are mere breath.

---

the book. It must be said, though, that Qohelet does sometimes entertain the
idea of a God who judges every human creature, even if at other points "God"
in his usage is close to "fate."

10. *take evil away from your flesh*. "Evil" here does not carry a moral sense but
means something like "harm," "unpleasantness."

the time of vigor. As a long exegetical condition assumes, the term *shaharut*
probably derives from *shahor*, "black"—that is, the time of life when the hair is
still black. (Others connect the word with *shahar*, "dawn," though the dawn of
life would be infancy, not youth.) This moment is evanescent, mere breath, for
the gray hair and its attendant infirmities will soon come.

12

And recall your Creator in the days of your prime, until the days of evil 1
come, and the years arrive, when you will say, "I have no delight in
them." Until the sun goes dark, and the light and the moon and the 2
stars, and the clouds come back after the rain.

On the day that the guards of the house will quake 3
and the stalwart men be twisted,

---

1. *in the days of your prime*. The stress on the evanescence of the years of vigor
before decrepitude and death continues the theme of the last four verses of the
previous chapter.
   the days of evil. Again, the sense of "evil" is not moral but physical—when
the body begins to fall apart.

2. *the clouds come back after the rain*. This seeming reversal of the order of
nature is an indication of the personal catastrophe of aging: everything goes
dark, and in this ultimate storm, the clouds continue to blanket the sky even
after the rain—perhaps because (verse 3) the sense of sight is dimmed. As
many commentators have noted, there is an affinity between the imagery here
and some of the apocalyptic imagery of the Prophets.

3. *On the day that the guards of the house will quake*. The book of Qohelet
proper aptly concludes with this haunting—and also mystifying—poem on the
waning of human life and on impending death. The poem abounds in textual
difficulties, and some of the references are ambiguous or simply unclear. A
tradition of interpretation that goes back to Late Antiquity reads the poem as
an allegory of the deterioration of the body, but as Fox and others have argued,
the allegory, plausible for some of the images, breaks down elsewhere. The
literal picture of a house, or an estate, in decay is eloquent in itself, and rituals
of mourning are clearly enacted outside the house. At best, one may say that

and the maids who grind grow idle, for they are now few,
      and those who look from the casements go dark.
4   And the double doors close in the market
        as the sound of the mill sinks down,
and the sound of the bird arises,
      and all the songstresses are bowed.
5   Of the very height they are afraid,
      and terror is in the road.
And the almond blossoms,
      and the locust tree is laden,
        and the caper-fruit falls apart.

---

certain lines, but not others, also invite comparisons with parts of the aging body.

the maids who grind grow idle. Grinding grain with a hand-mill would have been the work of female servants in an affluent ancient Near Eastern household. But the Hebrew feminine plural *tohanot* could also suggest teeth (mostly fallen out here), and in later Hebrew it is in fact the word for molars.

those who look from the casements. The corresponding body part would be the eyes, feminine plural in Hebrew like this verb.

4. *the sound of the bird arises.* The Hebrew phrasing is obscure and has generated highly divergent interpretations. One possible understanding is that in the silence that falls as the maids cease their labor of grinding, the sound of a solitary bird—no cheerful songbird—stands out, and the songstresses on their part fall silent and are bowed low. The literal sense of "songstresses" is "daughters of song," which has led some to construe the phrase as a reference to birds, but that would create a contradiction with the singular "sound of the bird."

5. *Of the very height they are afraid.* The meaning of the Hebrew has been much debated. It is unclear whether "they" refers to old people or to the songstresses, but the idea seems to be that they are afraid in all directions, above and below.

almond . . . locust . . . caper-fruit. The allegorizers have exercised strenuous ingenuity on these lines (the almond blossom corresponding to white hair, the sagging locust to an impotent penis, and so forth). It is less strained to read these lines simply as images of the cycle of growth and decay in nature as man is about to depart from that cycle. The most puzzling reference is to the laden

For man is going to his everlasting house,
>and the mourners turn round in the market.

Until the silver cord is snapped,   6
>and the golden bowl is smashed,

and the pitcher is broken against the well,
>and the jug smashed at the pit.

And dust returns to the earth as it was,   7
>and the life-breath returns to God Who gave it.

Merest breath, said Qohelet. All is mere breath.   8

---

locust. Some see this as indicating a plant, not an insect (in fact a meaning carried by the English word as well); others detect a reference to the female locust heavy with eggs, after laying which she dies. Perhaps the least strained construction is a locust tree heavy with ripe fruit.

the mourners turn round. Here at the end of the book, Qohelet invokes the same verb he used repeatedly at the beginning for the futile cycle of the natural world and then for his own turning about in quest of wisdom.

6. *the silver cord . . . the golden bowl.* Again, without allegory, precious things fall apart, like human life.

the pitcher is broken . . . the jug smashed. Seow points to archaeological evidence that pottery was actually broken at burial sites as a sign of mourning. *Galgal,* "jug," elsewhere usually means "wheel," but here it is evidently related to *gulah,* the word used for "bowl." The sense of "wheel" remains a possibility.

pit. The Hebrew *bor* is a pit, sometimes a well, but also a term for the grave or the underworld.

8. *Merest breath, said Qohelet.* In a gesture of tight closure, Qohelet repeats precisely the refrain with which he began the book.

9 And more than being wise, Qohelet further taught knowledge to the
10 people and weighed and searched out and framed many maxims. Qohe-
11 let sought to find apt words and wrote honestly words of truth. The
words of the wise are like goads and like nails driven in—from the com-

---

9. *And more than being wise.* The strong consensus of scholarship is that the
verses from here to the end of the text are an epilogue added by an editor, with
the aim of bringing Qohelet's radical vision in line with more conventional
piety. Many interpreters construe the initial word *yoter* as "furthermore," but
that strains Hebrew usage, which clearly attaches *yoter* to *shehayah Qohelet,*
literally, "than Qohelet was." The stated idea as it is understood in this translation is plausible: Qohelet was not merely a sage but, one might say, a lecturing
and publishing sage, one who gave public instruction and edited and formulated maxims.

    further. Others construe this as "constantly."

    weighed. This verb derives from the word for "ear," *'ozen,* but only here does
it appear in the *pi'el* conjugation. Many understand it as "listen," but listening
seems too passive for the other activities of compiling and formulating listed
here. The verb could easily be connected with the word for "scales," *m'oznayim,*
as it is in later Hebrew, where it means "balance" or "weigh."

    11. *goads . . . nails.* The images suggest that the words of the wise may sting or
hurt, which seems especially apt for Qohelet.

    from the composers of collections. The meaning of the Hebrew is uncertain,
but a reference to anthologists or collectors of sayings is plausible in context.
Syntactically, there is an ellipsis here, the sense being "[the words of the wise]
from the composers of collections."

    given from a certain shepherd. Traditionally, this highly obscure phrase is
understood as a reference to God ("from one Shepherd"). Fox and Seow both
argue convincingly that the simile of the goad leads to a reference to an actual
goad-wielding shepherd, and that *'ehad,* "one," is used here as it is sometimes
used elsewhere as what amounts to an indefinite article. Nevertheless, this
phrase is oddly detached in the syntax from the goads and nails.

posers of collections, given from a certain shepherd. And more than   12
these, my son, beware: of making many books there is no end, and much
chatter is a weariness of the flesh. The last word, all being heard: fear   13
God and keep His commands, for that is all humankind. Since every   14
deed will God bring to judgment, for every hidden act, be it good or evil.

---

12. *chatter*. The Hebrew *lahag* refers either to speech or to study, and the parallelism with making many books has encouraged many interpreters to opt for
study. But the author of the epilogue, at once praising Qohelet and interposing
a certain distance from him, wants to warn readers that all this writing, including Qohelet's, may simply exhaust one and perhaps distract one from the simple duties of piety, so the sense of "chatter" has some plausibility. This is the
regular meaning of *lahag* in later Hebrew.

13. *The last word*. The author of the epilogue is at pains to have the last word,
which will neutralize the many subversive words Qohelet has uttered.
     for that is all humankind. Though the King James Version's interpretive "this
is the whole duty of man" may catch the intention of the original, that rendering
makes the clause sound more strictly didactic than it is, and it seems better to
preserve the slightly ambiguous inclusiveness of the Hebrew.

14. *every deed will God bring to judgment*. Qohelet, too, at a couple of points
expresses the idea that we are subject to God's judgment, but this monitory
flourish at the very end is an affirmation of the staunch piety with which the
epilogist seeks to contain the more disruptive ideas of Qohelet.

FOR FURTHER READING

Alter, Robert. *The Art of Biblical Narrative.* New York: Basic Books, 1985.
    Includes chapters on Job and Proverbs that attempt to define the distinctive poetic form of each and to describe its role in articulating a particular vision of the world.
Alter, Robert, and Frank Kermode. *The Literary Guide to the Bible.* Cambridge, Mass.: Harvard University Press, 1987.
    Includes an instructive essay on Job by Moshe Greenberg and a lucid account of Proverbs and Qohelet by James G. Williams that sets both books in the larger context of biblical Wisdom writing.
Crenshaw, James L. *Old Testament Wisdom: An Introduction.* Atlanta: John Knox Press, 1981.
    An historically informed scholarly investigation of the Wisdom books of the Bible and of what can be reconstructed of Wisdom activity in ancient Israel.
Fox, Michael V. *Proverbs 1-9.* Garden City, N.Y.: Doubleday, 2000. *Proverbs 10-31.* New Haven, Conn.: Yale University Press, 2009.
    These two volumes are among the best in the Anchor Bible Series, keen in philological analysis and copious in their treatment of the meanings of the text and of its ancient Near Eastern backgrounds.
———. *Qohelet and His Contradictions.* Sheffield, England: Almond Press, 1989.
    A study rich in reflections on Qohelet's philosophy and acute in the philological treatment of the Hebrew text, including its many cruces.
Gordis, Robert. *Qohelet: The Man and His World.* New York: The Jewish Theological Seminary of America, 1951.
    A translation and commentary that contain valuable philological work, though some of the views expressed are now dated.
Murphy, Roland E. *The Tree of Life: An Exploration of Biblical Wisdom Literature.* New York: Doubleday, 1990.
    A succinct, clear, and helpful survey of the Wisdom books of the Bible and the Apocrypha and of their later legacy.

Pope, Marvin. *Job*. Garden City, N.Y.: Doubleday, 1965.

A scholarly translation and relatively brief commentary incorporating some useful illumination of the language of the text and its historical contexts, though much of the philology follows scholarly fashions of the day that are no longer viable.

Rad, Gerhard von. *Wisdom in Israel*. Nashville: Abingdon Press, 1978.

A thoughtful series of reflections on the Wisdom books, their background, and the outlooks they express by one of the leading German Bible scholars of the mid-twentieth century.

Williams, James G. *Those Who Ponder Proverbs*. Sheffield, England: Almond Press, 1981.

An intelligent consideration of the Wisdom books that devotes special attention to the proverb as a literary form.

THE
WISDOM BOOKS

JOB, PROVERBS, AND ECCLESIASTES

ALSO BY ROBERT ALTER

PEN OF IRON: AMERICAN PROSE AND THE KING JAMES BIBLE

THE BOOK OF PSALMS: A TRANSLATION WITH COMMENTARY

IMAGINED CITIES: URBAN EXPERIENCE AND THE LANGUAGE OF THE NOVEL

THE FIVE BOOKS OF MOSES: A TRANSLATION WITH COMMENTARY

CANON AND CREATIVITY:
MODERN WRITING AND THE AUTHORITY OF SCRIPTURE

THE DAVID STORY: A TRANSLATION WITH COMMENTARY

GENESIS: A TRANSLATION WITH COMMENTARY

HEBREW AND MODERNITY

THE WORLD OF BIBLICAL LITERATURE

NECESSARY ANGELS: TRADITION AND MODERNITY
IN KAFKA, BENJAMIN, AND SCHOLEM

THE PLEASURES OF READING IN AN IDEOLOGICAL AGE

THE LITERARY GUIDE TO THE BIBLE
(*coeditor with Frank Kermode*)

THE INVENTION OF HEBREW PROSE

THE ART OF BIBLICAL POETRY

MOTIVES FOR FICTION

THE ART OF BIBLICAL NARRATIVE

A LION FOR LOVE: A CRITICAL BIOGRAPHY OF STENDHAL

DEFENSES OF THE IMAGINATION

PARTIAL MAGIC: THE NOVEL AS SELF-CONSCIOUS GENRE

MODERN HEBREW LITERATURE

AFTER THE TRADITION

FIELDING AND THE NATURE OF THE NOVEL

ROGUE'S PROGRESS: STUDIES IN THE PICARESQUE NOVEL